Nark!

Nark!
by Joe Eszterhas

Acknowledgments

To Jann Wenner, the only editor in America willing to commit himself
to a lengthy and costly investigation of narcotics enforcement;
to Paul Scanlon, for his advice, encouragement, and patience.

Portions of this book, in slightly different form, have appeared
in *Rolling Stone* magazine.

Library of Congress Catalog Card Number: 72-88839
ISBN: 0-87932-051-6

First printing

Straight Arrow Books
625 Third Street, San Francisco, CA 94107

Distributed by Simon and Schuster

Order number: 102051

Production by Planned Production
Printed in the United States of America

For Michael Murphy

"**nark,**
n. Its ori-
gin is probably
the Fr. *narquois,*
sly, slyly cunning, hence: **1.** as a disagreeable or un-
charitable person; **2.** a person who obtains information under seal of confidence and afterwards
breaks faith; **3.** applied to the lowest class
of informers; **4.** among professional
beggars, a nark is one who, not a
true beggar, does odd jobs or even has
a small income, yet avails himself of the
common lodging houses and persists in doing
so, to the inevitable detriment of the genuine beggars."—Eric Par-
tridge, *A Dic-*
tionary of the
Under-
world

Contents

Introduction

This isn't an anti-cop book.

For the better part of two years I worked in a midwestern town as a police reporter and spent most of my time in the company of policemen. I rode their squad cars down nightmare alleys where snipers sometimes waited. I crouched behind an ambulance once for two hours, caught in a cross fire, and watched a patrolman a few hundred feet from me bleed to death.

I drank with cops and went to their parties and tried to understand the often desperate psychic fabric of their lives: The money wasn't good, the wife was forever worried, the kids never saw them, and ... around every corner and down every dead-end street was the threat of sudden madness, of senseless doom: the flash of a switchblade, the roaring sound of a shotgun, flecks of tissue to be hosed from the asphalt.

I liked most of the policemen I met. They were doing a job for money, yes, but most of them were doing it bravely, and many were trying to do it honorably.

But when, a few years later, I began looking into narcotics enforcement, I found myself in an Orwellian netherworld. My research is done now, and I know that most narcotics agents aren't cops. They are deputized gangsters, hoods legitimized by the shields they've been given, their shields a symbol of corruption. They act from a sense of profound cynicism. Marijuana isn't going to lead anyone to the grave or the smack needle, and they know it. But a hundred marijuana arrests will garner a hundred headlines—ninety-nine more headlines than working anonymously all year to bust a single kingpin heroin dealer. They work busily for their hundred headlines because the headlines pay off in raises, promotions, prestige, and power.

The victims they choose are mostly powerless. Smack kings might have influential friends, but long-haired kids whose very life style is an

xiii

affront to the all-American codex are legally and politically impotent. A kid who's been busted for possession of a lid doesn't have the clout to spark public outrage. So the kid claims he was pistol-whipped during his arrest ... so he claims his girl was propositioned by arresting officers. So what? He's just trying to stir something up; the girl is probably a slut. Nobody listens. The nark doesn't have to worry about losing his job.

The three cases in this book are, sadly, not unique. They received little national attention—even though, in one case, a man was shot in the back and, in another, a man's career was nearly destroyed. The cases are but symptoms of a malaise rampant in the land in the late Sixties and early Seventies, a time when our taxes were payment for a kind of sleazy societal crusade. We financed goon squads that, acting solemnly on behalf of the Law, made a burlesque of it. Thousands of young people across the country were victimized. Many of them are still in jail.

No Senate committee lamented their fate on prime-time television; the newspapers assigned no Pulitzer Prize task forces to investigate the circumstances of their arrests. Indeed, it took a full-scale vigilante assault on perfectly middle-class citizens in an Illinois town to focus any national attention at all on the tactics of narcotics enforcement. Yet even in that case the victims were forced to move to another town because their middle-class neighbors began harassing *them*—for stirring things up and causing the agents problems.

I wrote this book for my policemen friends and for the victims of narcotics enforcement. I wrote it with the hope that in a non-Orwellian future fewer shields will be tarnished, fewer persons legally brutalized.

Joe Eszterhas
San Francisco
January 1974

I. Nark–
A Tale of Terror

"So, like the third or fourth deal that I set up for them, they gave me $75—$25 from Marin and $50 from Van Raam. Van Raam said, 'You're on the road to recovery; straighten out! Move out of that place with all those people. You're a good kid. We could use you.' Make me into a superstar, you know, this and that: meaning a good nark. I said, 'Right on, boys, yeah! Keep up the work!' I ran home after they gave me the money to the place where we were crashing. I said, 'Hey, guys! You want to shoot up tonight? I've got $75 here.' So we went out that night and copped on the narks' money. Everybody got loaded on junk."

—Sandy White, twenty-four years old, police informer. Title: Law enforcement operator. Experience: Responsible for the arrest of more than 350 persons. Employer: Gerritt Van Raam, field supervisor, Bureau of Narcotics Enforcement, state of California, Northern Division. Operator White's code name: Bonnie Parker. "I picked it out myself," she says. And giggles.

The years have been kind. He doesn't look cruel or vicious or very tough. The street cop's scruffiness has been soft-soaped by a toothy middle-class élan: he wears a mask of cunning cordiality. He is fleshy and soft in the belly, a victim of martinis and crisco, and his eyes are webbed by a thousand tiny wrinkles. His hair is swept back and graying. He has a weak chin and a limp handshake. Gerritt Van Raam doesn't look like a face off the *Wanted!* posters anymore; he looks like a used-car salesman.

The reporter is sitting across a desk from him, playing eye-contact chess, lighting Gerry Van Raam's filter-tip cigarettes. The field supervisor of the Bureau of Narcotics Enforcement, one of the most feared policemen in Northern California, is sitting there, with his voice un-

1

steady, his hands trembling, saying, "We don't like to be the bad guys." The field supervisor's office is small and relatively bare, a few hundred feet through the doors of the rocklike state of California Office Building on San Francisco's McAllister Street. A few plaques spot the walls; one of them identifies Gerritt Van Raam as a member in good standing of a national narcotics enforcers association. There is a framed color photograph of a barreling locomotive. On top of a corner cabinet are some boxes of shell casings.

Gerry Van Raam is sitting there in a dark suit and worn striped shirt, his tie loosened, smiling, being the nice guy, just your average Joe, talking about never being able to keep his desk in order, tugging at the cigarette with dancing fingers, a picture of openness and jittery candor. "We don't have anything to hide," he says.

The reporter, taking advantage of the openness, ticks off a series of allegations. Allegations hurled at narcotics agents in general and, sometimes, at Gerry Van Raam in particular.

Like dealing dope on the side; busting people and pocketing an amount of the stuff and using it to supplement the police income. "How about you?" the reporter asks. "Have you ever sold dope?" "Nope," he says. . . . Like planting evidence; busting someone for a personal motive, a vendetta motive, and making the case with the oldest police trick, the frame. "We hear that, too," Gerry Van Raam says. "If we were planting people, I wouldn't have to work so hard or so long. . . ." Like taking personal advantage of certain suspects, especially women; going in and getting laid and then busting them anyway. "I have never had any sexual relations," Gerry Van Raam says, "with anybody I've ever arrested. . . ."

"Have you ever smoked any dope?" the reporter asks.

"Nope. Never had the inclination. Ever."

"Ever curious?"

"No."

At the age of fifty-one, Gerritt Van Raam looks like the hero of a star-spangled success story. He has four children. He is a churchgoing Roman Catholic. He is highly respected by his back-slapping office colleagues and, in Sandy White's words, "is a helluva father figure. One of his kids just started smoking. I asked him if he thought the kid would smoke dope, and he said, 'No way!' " He is a man consumed by his job, working, by his own estimate, an average eighty-hour week. "It's not the type of thing," he says, "where you can turn it over at the end of a shift to another person because you'd probably be explaining everything that happened, the intricacies of the investigation, for four hours.

"It's a very challenging job. It takes an awful lot of your time. You have to be smarter than the dope peddler. Some of them are very intelligent people—and very successful. I happen to believe that the use of narcotics, including marijuana, is a crime. It says so in the book. I've seen marijuana mess up a lot of people's lives. I think it's a lousy thing because it doesn't help people at all. I've seen a lot of people go downhill. It certainly does lead to personality changes. A kid starts smoking grass; suddenly he's not doing so hot in school. He changes his square friends to hip friends. He changes appearance, goes for the long hair. I don't say straight-looking kids don't use grass because I know they do. We heard about how great the Haight-Ashbury was, and anybody who was out there had to see the human degradation that was taking place. It was bad."

He is paternalistic toward his narcotics agents, the "boys" on his "team," and encourages their involvement in the world of civic affairs: many of them are Kiwanians and/or members of the Knights of Columbus. No matter how busy, he's always willing to listen to their problems. They are cop problems, and Gerry Van Raam knows about those. He has been a cop most of his adult life. His career's most dramatic hurdle—except for the recent *fuss*, the *allegations*, the lie-detector *conspiracy*—was a cop problem that exploded in his face in 1959, when he was a San Francisco patrolman.

Gerry Van Raam had been on the police force nine years, working as a Central Station patrolman assigned to the tourist-plagued Fisherman's Wharf district. He was sandbagged by too many debts and was forced to work an off-duty job. He did not bother to tell his department superiors about his new job, though it was a stringent requirement of police regulations. He was a vending-machine collector. He went around town emptying nickels and dimes from stamp machines. On the afternoon of July 8, 1959, he was working on Church Street, near the heart of the city's Mexican community. He went into the Mercury Drug Store, a neighborhood landmark at Twenty-fourth and Church, and, after bagging the coins from the machines, stepped to the counter. A group of hoo-hawing Mexican kids entered the store and saw the coins. According to a witness, twelve-year-old Joseph Mondregon started picking at the change. According to another witness, Gerritt Van Raam,

off-duty cop, looked hard at Joseph Mondregon and said, "Take your
fingers off those coins, kid, or you'll get them burned." The kids were
ordered out of the place, and minutes later Van Raam went to his car.

But Joseph Mondregon and his buddies were still playing outside. As
Van Raam got into his car, a witness said, the boy called the vending-
machine cop a "fucker." According to the witness, Van Raam, then a
squat thirty-nine-year-old, allegedly grabbed the boy, tore at his shirt,
and slapped him across the face. Van Raam said at the time that the boy
spat at him twice. He didn't mean to hit the boy, he said; the blow was
"an accident". . . . Sitting in his office, Van Raam gives the reporter a
more elaborate account: "The boy stole out all the coins. Which I got
back from him and scuffled to get it. He claimed that I slapped him.
What I did was grab him". . . . Van Raam was ordered to face a police
department hearing. He faced three charges: unofficerlike conduct;
working an outside job without permission; failing to submit a written
report of an incident in which he was involved. "Holding the outside
job was a violation of the rules," Van Raam says. "It was quite generally
done. Other policemen had outside jobs. Firemen. All kinds of outside
jobs because of the hours. And I was sort of in a dilemma. If I arrested
him [Mondregon] like I should have done, I would have been saying
I'm working an outside job, which I know is a no-no. So that's why the
report wasn't made out." Van Raam pleaded guilty to two of the
charges and was reprimanded. He resigned from the department.

The reporter asks him whether the resignation was connected with
the incident or the hearing. "No," Van Raam says. The reporter asks
how long after the hearing he remained on the San Francisco police
force. Van Raam says, "I can't give you the exact date, but I think it's a
couple years." Yet his answer is a strange misstatement of fact. The
hearing took place in September of 1959. He resigned on January 7,
1960—less than four months after the hearing. He insists the resignation
had nothing to do with the incident or the investigation. "Certainly the
BNE wouldn't hire a person that was under investigation," he says. He
joined the state's Bureau of Narcotics Enforcement on January 9, 1960.
"I had one evening off," he says. He became an agent and worked his
way up the cop career ladder.

Today he is one of the top narcotics agents in the state of California.
He does not face "unofficerlike conduct" charges these days. He doesn't
empty vending machines. He's no longer in debt. He sails, takes pic-

tures, and hunts. He took great pleasure, for a while, in a gleaming, pearl-handled .45. He kept the gun tucked into his belt. "I thought he'd shoot his balls off with the damned thing," Sandy White says. He doesn't wear the ornate gun anymore; he goes out of his way to show the reporter a dull, small-caliber revolver he wears on his hip. For a long time his desk was decorated by a music box that played a German march. The carved figure straddling its lid was Baron Wolfram von Richtofen, the Red Baron.

He has become particularly known in police circles for his use of informers. "A lot of the people we deal with [informers]," he says, "are certainly not the most upstanding people in the community. Some of them are the lowest order of society. But who am I to judge whether that person is a worse person than someone else? How do you weigh morality against the type of thing that you're trying to do?"

But as the record of his busts spiraled and policemen praised him in chorus, his victims were describing him in increasingly ugly terms, talking about brutality and psychic violence. He became the most feared and well-known nark in Northern California.

Sitting in that bare little office a desktop away from this strangely friendly and nervous man, the reporter says: "Narcotics agents in general, you in particular, are accused of psychological and physical terror at the scene of an arrest, to try to get the arrested person to turn out, give you other names. Things like guns being put up against the temple." Gerritt Van Raam says: "Certainly that does occur, where you have to put guns against the temple. As you're aware, we've had agents killed. As much as we'd like to believe narcotics defendants are not violent, we know better. They are."

"But if you scared them shitless, wouldn't they cooperate?"

"I'm sure many people are scared when they're arrested. Maybe a lot of people do become informers out of fear. I'm sure most of them don't do it because they're upstanding citizens."

"Listen," the reporter says, "lawyers, young people, they look at Gerry Van Raam, and they kind of see him as the King of Paranoia, a man who freaks everybody out—"

"Gee," he interrupts, smiling, "I hope I'm not that bad."

"Knocking down doors," the reporter says, "and there's this general frightening image—"

The smile widens into a blushing grin.

"I really was quite surprised," he says angelically, "that all of a sudden this is me."

The field supervisor laughs. "Little old me," he says.

Once, a long time ago, before he started using the word "Kafkaesque," Michael Metzger saw himself as a famous prosecutor, perhaps, even, a judge. But that was before Michael Metzger met Gerritt Van Raam and called him a liar; before Van Raam's men handcuffed him and took him to jail; before Michael Metzger started coming to his law office in his blue jeans.

Michael Metzger, attorney, booked and fingerprinted; the same man who, in 1965, was named "German American of the Year" by the New York police department's Steuben Association; who was given an honorary citation in 1968 by the Mount Vernon Police Association.

In 1970, his cathartic thirty-third year, Michael Metzger became a liberal *cause célèbre* in the Bay Area; the same man who, working as an assistant New York district attorney, sent seventeen anti-war protesters to jail for cluttering up a sidewalk; who once asked that a Congress of Racial Equality official be sent to jail for his "arrogant attitude" with respect to the law.

The man who would become a liberal cause, the victim of the law, was such a starched, buckram-stiff D.A. that, when an underworld figure refused to talk for fear he'd face Cosa Nostra execution, Metzger flippantly said, "When he's finished serving his jail sentence this time, we will again bring him before a grand jury, and, if he refuses, we will again ask for contempt charges, and we will continually ask for contempt charges until he stops his illegal refusal to answer questions."

Today Michael Metzger replays the frozen stills of his nightmare, laments that it was not at all unique, and thinks about the narks and nark laws he must wrestle with. "I'm surrounded by shit," he says. He stands at his desk, leafing through an ornate book of news clips from his D.A. days—days spent on the other side—and says, "Wasn't I an asshole back then?" On the first page of one of those neatly assorted clip books—as lovingly compiled as a Baby Grows Up collection—there is a picture of Frank Hogan, celebrated New York district attorney, standing, cigar in hand, on the cover of a national magazine. In Hogan's handwriting there is a note to Metzger: "With much appreciation and kind regards."

Michael Metzger, son of an industrial magnate, elected to forsake the career possibilities of his father's business. He came from a wealthy and socially prominent background, and many of the people who surrounded him in adolescence and shaped his milieu were judges, policemen, and district attorneys. He grew up with an idealized love and a boyish respect for the Law. He got his bachelor's degree from New York University in 1960 and his law degree from the University of Michigan in 1963. Out of school, he went to work for Hogan, the venerable deity, as an assistant district attorney. He was proud of his niche in Hogan's world. He got married; he lived a routine, suburban existence; he took his vows to the Law.

He found that being a D.A. for Hogan was an almost religious calling. The monastic little man, famed for his prosecution of the powerfully corrupt, Lived the Law. Metzger found Hogan's atmosphere "almost incestuously insular." But he prospered. True to the rigors of Frank Hogan's discipline, he didn't go out to lunch, he didn't go to see Broadway shows. He lived the law, eating bologna sandwiches and drinking syrupy milk shakes at his desk, turning into a twenty-four-hour windup doll prosecutor.

Ambitious and tough, he soon found himself prosecuting fast-drawing men, tough, brass-knuckled mobsters. Metzger battled the Mafia and its gunslingers: Sonny Franzese, Rosario Nostasa, Sunshine Sonnenschein. Statutes in hand, he fought pitched battles against labor racketeering and municipal corruption: a paint scandal involving a city official; a labor leader trying to fix a judge. He gained a reputation not only as unflinchingly honest but as a cagey courtroom technician, a first-rate textbook mind. His name was inching into headlines.

Something clawed, though, at Metzger's soul. He was discovering that he was human, incapable of being that twenty-four-hour human legal machine. He started questioning the sinister delight he took in making powerful men cringe, nonchalantly cowing them with the latent power of his subpoenas. He began to feel himself too elated by "finding sinners." And he began deeply to resent the twisted, robotized stamp Frank Hogan had put on his forehead. He was tiring of sandwiches and milk shakes. It came to a head one morning on his way to work. Metzger suffered an attack of acute identity crisis in a Manhattan traffic jam. He was late, mired in traffic, hemmed in by chrome. The seat next to him was a mountain of affidavits; a bus ahead of him drenched his horn-rimmed face in black smoke; his eyes were tearing; a cab driver behind him kept leaning on the horn, orchestrating the horror. His ears were numb. He was sweating, but he couldn't even wipe the sweat. The seat belt was too tight: He felt himself physically and psychologically paralyzed. A thought whacked at his brain:

What are you doing here?

Michael Metzger still wasn't using the word "Kafkaesque," but he was learning about the surreal. He quit his job and was bound for San Francisco as an assistant U.S. district attorney. His going-away party in New York was one of the august legal happenings of the year. Dozens of FBI men, judges, prosecutors, wiretappers. Even the Presence Himself, Frank Hogan, was there. Metzger thought he'd be happy as an assistant U.S. district attorney in California. He hoped he could specialize once again in busting organized crime, civic corruption, the shadow world of the Cosa Nostra. He didn't expect to be crippled by any more traffic jams. But he didn't know then that he'd soon be rubbing shoulders with narks. Working, first, not against them. With them: prosecuting a skinflinty, hapless man named Frank Werber, formerly the manager of the Kingston Trio.

Told then that the road from New York to San Francisco would dead-end one night in jail, that he would become an accused felon, Metzger would have laughed. He laughed easily in those days.

Less than three years after he got to San Francisco a federal narcotics agent pushed the former U.S. D.A. against the kitchen cabinet of his own home. The former D.A. was under arrest, being searched. He protested. The narcotics agent pulled his jacket back to show the ex-D.A. what it was hiding.

It was hiding a gun. Metzger wasn't laughing.

He was thinking. About the love and respect he had nurtured for the Law. About the Cosa Nostra figures he had jailed. About Frank Hogan. About the gun staring him in the face. About Gerritt Van Raam.

He shook his head and said . . . "Far out."

Dialogue. Sandy White, ace nark informer, and her boy friend, Ted Donnelly. Subject: trust.

Sandy: *Listen to your friends, I'm a very dangerous woman.*
Ted: *Huh? Um, what do you mean?*
Sandy: *I mean, don't ever trust me, not even in bed.*

Unlike Michael Metzger, agent Van Raam would never look through his newspaper clippings, his reviews—a record of busts and legal scalpings—and call himself an asshole. Okay, Metzger might look into the mirror of his past public accomplishments and call himself that, but why would Gerry Van Raam do so? His salary comes out of our taxes; we pay him for his zealousness and his methods. A look into his mirror plainly shows what the agent considers himself to be: a public servant.

Much of it, naturally, comes down to the quality of the mirror—one man's reflection being another man's fun-house grotesque—and to semantics. Metzger may use phrases like "getting myself together" and "straightening out my trip," but Gerry Van Raam's words are the Groupthink of the public servant, a strange approximation of Winston Smith's Officialese, of the rectangular mind-set that fireman Guy Montag fled through the fruit of his forbidden reading. Gerry Van Raam is not, in his own mind, a "nark" but an "agent"; his informers are "operators"; the drugs he expropriates "contraband"; the booty he recovers always a "cache."

Sometimes, though, Gerry the public servant, the ex-vending-machine collector, has trouble meshing with the style and verbal posture of Officialese—under oath, Sandy White would quote him using the words "riffed by those motherfuckers"—and when the need arises for a public statement designed for gullible mass consumption, then Gerry Van Raam goes hunting with a favored rare blunderbuss. The Official-Think is left to Matthew O'Connor, top nark linguist.

Matthew O'Connor is Gerry Van Raam's boss, the head of the Bureau of Narcotics Enforcement, a daguerreotype of the bureaucrat, pink-cheeked and twinkly-eyed, suitably gray-haired, mild in manner, and disposed to lip-pursing. A man like Matthew O'Connor looks perfectly harmless, speaks perfectly harmlessly, attends banquets at the Saint Francis and the Mark Hopkins, acts as consultant to several of the unified school districts, is a member of the California Council of Criminal Justice. He laughs like a pleasant little man, a college prof perhaps, and when it comes to the final local responsibility for the doings of Gerritt Van Raam, then Santy Claus cherub Matt O'Connor is the man.

The Officialese he babbles for reporters, television cameras, PTA groups, and conventions puts everything "into its proper perspective" and always manages to look "at the Big Picture." In 1972 Matthew O'Connor received the ultimate accolade of his narking colleagues across America. He became president of the International Narcotics Enforcement Officers Association, which is to narks what the Knights of the Altar is to altar boys.

Matthew O'Connor explains "The Problem" in crisp Officialese through the tortured contortions of Official-Think. To begin with, there is no "drug problem" in America; there is only a "drug promiscuity problem." Dig: "drug promiscuity," a stab that goes directly to the jugular of suburbia, a phrase that, to the martini-sipping middle class, manages to conjure images of hopped-up hippies in primitive animalistic tit-flopping orgy, a very highfaluting bureaucratic phrase that turns the Haight-Ashbury into Sodom and Gomorrah; a phrase, finally, of cold-stone politico-etymological brilliance. This plague of "drug promiscuity" is defined as "an attitude change by society and in particular young people, having to do with the concept—Is drug use really that bad? A lot of our young people in 1966–1968 were listening to persons sometimes well-intentioned and well-credentialed to comment favorably on drug usage, and they didn't feel that sufficient research was that stable, I guess. A certain ambiguity was created in our young people.

"So we became concerned," the Stengelese drones on, "about that large number we regarded in the drug-promiscuity field using some of the initial drugs, including marijuana, and thinking even a small percentage of that number would be a future problem with a strong residual effect." Matthew O'Connor admits that, fearing this "strong residual effect" and confronted by "drug promiscuity" apocalypse, his agents faced "a terrific challenge." And how did his harried agents react to that "challenge"? By abuse? By lies? By brutality? By vendetta? Of course not. His agents, Matthew O'Connor explains with a bright smile, reacted by *education*. Yes, education! The solution for every modern malaise. His agents became teachers, pot-bellied gurus to the young.

"School children actually got an awful lot out of the presentation by narcotics enforcement agents in their classrooms. There were teacher groups and persons representing other disciplines saying, with very loud voice, that they had to have agents as guests in their classrooms in order to present the material correctly, depending very heavily on the presentation by law enforcement." His agents may collect tommy guns and pearl-handled .45s, but to believe Matthew O'Connor, the nark's chief contribution to the cleansing of "drug promiscuity" is not in the back alley but in the classroom, not with finger on trigger but with fingers chalk-stained on grade school blackboards. And, when they get into the classrooms, what do these nark-gurus teach? "We try to paint a realistic picture," Matthew O'Connor says. "We don't have the tendency to dwell on the bizarre." The bizarre? "Our files are filled with individuals who, taking a drug for the first time, encountered a bizarre experience. We try to place that in its proper perspective without undue emphasis."

The Official-Think reaches thin-air heights: "There was even a claim that you get high with one marijuana cigarette or with one puff. Well, that's not exactly untrue. There are people who have had unusual experiences in the use of marijuana. This is not to say that everybody who smokes a marijuana cigarette or takes a puff *will jump off the Golden Gate Bridge*. We know that and the doctors know it, and we want to say this very honestly. At the same time *we should not be so dishonest as to say it never happens."*

So, when Gerry Van Raam, Matthew O'Connor's paid hand, goes into a classroom with his pearl-handled revolver at his side, lecturing, he can be excused for any messianic tendencies. He is actually stopping someone in that room from lighting a joint and diving off the Golden Gate Bridge. More than that, an elevated profundity: The public servant who once emptied coins from vending machines is now paid overtime for blocking the depth-bound nosedive of an entire generation. With this kind of motivation fueling him, naturally, a public servant will work very hard, and, judging by Van Raam's mirror, his front-page headlines, he has worked above and beyond the call of duty. Whenever the BNE makes a bust, Gerry Van Raam can be relied on to make a single, all-encompassing statement: "This is one of the largest busts in the city's history."

Those who deal dope on the streets, or those who study the word-of-mouth Dow Jones index of the latest shipment of grass, also rely on him to do one other thing. The value the narks will put on the captured "contraband cache" will be higher than the street experts could ever fantasize. (Coincidentally, the higher the police estimates, the bolder the newspaper headlines will be that day.)

In their above-and-beyond-the-call-of-duty pursuit of contraband, Van Raam and his agent-colleagues have led or been involved in some hair-raising, media-prone busts; the kind of busts that combine Hitchcock and the Keystone Kops—Popeye Doyle the cinematic nark and Popeye the cartoon sailor man.

There was, for example, a huge contraband recovery that has become memorialized in local police circles as the Clothesline Caper. A group of agents, acting on "confidential reliable information" (i.e., an informer like Sandy White), showed up at an apartment, looking for a marijuana cache. The cache was discovered "in plain view," a favorite nark term suited for judges' sensitive ears. But this time the grass really was in plain view—about twenty-five kilos. A clothesline running from the apartment was filled with it. The bags in the long johns and jockey shorts were labeled Neeta Weeda.

A few months earlier an airborne nark assault team decided to zero in on two suspected grass dealers. The dealers lived within two blocks of each other, and both their homes had steep banks behind them. This posed an awkward tactical enforcement problem: How to stop the dealers from scooting over the bank and through the woods to freedom? The solution was a stroke of nark genius. At a certain appointed time of night (some people would describe it as the witching hour) two helicopters showed up above the dealers' houses. The helicopters shined super-watted lights on the banks, earth-shining an entire two-block area. The dealers, finding the night suddenly ablaze, threw up their hands and volunteered for handcuffs.

A much-publicized bust at San Francisco International Airport attests to nark ingenuity. Agents received information—"info" in nark talk—that a man from Tucson was coming in with twenty-six kilos of grass. They had no description. Yet they still managed to get their man. How did they know him? "It was easy," an agent said. "The fact that he sported a full beard, shoulder-length blond hair, and was carrying a red suitcase made him pretty easy to spot."

In all of these arrests and countless others the standard statement issued afterwards stressed the close cooperation of state / local / federal officers, a well-timed nark jig. Interestingly, members of all three busy bureaus seemed to show up for the more dramatic (and more publicized) busts.

Michael Metzger, who was just beginning his job as a federal district attorney, a few years from the night state / local / fed agents came to his door, would marvel at the way these agencies interlocked. He had battled the Cosa Nostra, the mythical family of crime. But he would find that narks—state, local, and fed—are a fraternity unto themselves. "You fuck with one, you fuck with all." It is a kind of Hell's Angels law enforcement concept. A family that drinks together busts together, and always seems to see chains of events exactly the same way.

Dialogue. Sandy White, ace nark informer, and her boy friend, Ted Donnelly. Subject: ethics.

Sandy: *I'll shit on anybody.*

Ted: *Yeah?*

Sandy: *I busted my old man. I can bust anyone.*

Ted: *Yeah. Your ex-old man, right?*

Sandy: *My old boy friend. I lived with him.*

Ted: *What did you bust him for?*

Sandy: *He screwed another chick in my bed one night.*

Ted: *Oh, yeah? What did you get him for?*

Sandy: *Everything. Got him busted. In fact, I busted every fucking person in that house. Plus a few other friends of mine.*

Ted: *Yeah?*

Sandy: *So, you know, I have no heart when it comes to that. I can fuck anyone.*

Ted: *On anything.*

Sandy: *On anything. Not you. I have no reason to. Because you know too much about me. Right?*

Ted: *Right.*

Sandy: *So. Well, you're cool.*

There already was an assistant U.S. district attorney tracking organized Bay Area crime when Michael Metzger arrived. The method of racket-busting used here was not like Frank Hogan's. The D.A. would clip news stories about the underworld and neatly file them in manila folders. In that way U.S. District Attorney Cecil Poole's office could claim to be containing the rackets. In a single file cabinet.

Michael Metzger, the traffic-jam victim, was soon flapping in a puddle of office quicksand. The man who once hectored Frank Costello in the courtroom was now prosecuting draft dodgers. The high-IQ textbook mind was just another clerk assigned his cases in unbending alphabetical order. It was his fortune that the letter of the alphabet he guarded was the W. And so it happened that fate dealt Michael Metzger three Ws, people named Whitehorn, Wentworth, and Werber, who would change his life.

His clerkish duties suffocating him, he still did his job. He was still admired by FBI men and fellow prosecutors. A graduate of the Hogan Ministry of Law, he got things done! The trapped man who fled New York was, paradoxically, a razzle-dazzle red-tape expert. The government will be eternally grateful for a typical Metzger red-tape breakthrough: A soldier in Saigon was badly needed in San Francisco as a government witness. Unless he got back within a few days, the government would lose its case. But how to reach him? Reaching a serviceman by telephone in Vietnam could itself take weeks. Metzger got things done! He called the military brass at the Presidio of San Francisco and told them of the government's fix. The brass at Presidio, alerted to the peril awaiting the government, reached the soldier in one day. The next day the soldier was in San Francisco. The government was saved! Metzger had done it!

He threw himself, with equal resolve, into making sure that eighteen-year-old Erik Whitehorn got his chance to serve in Uncle Sam's Army. Erik claimed he didn't register for the draft because his mother, a spry real-estate woman, forbade him. Mrs. Whitehorn asked that she be substituted for her son as defendant. Erik smiled angelically. Mrs. Whitehorn, who did not know that the D.A. was a red-tape expert and a traffic-jam victim, said she was "appalled at a legal system that puts you through a computer-like operation, as everyone fits nicely in their place." But Michael Metzger, who was once buried under a colossus of affidavits, wouldn't hear any of that. "The mother," he said, "is a red herring. It is simply a publicity issue . . . a naked appeal to the jury to ignore the law, to violate your oath to follow the law." He was equally hardnosed (the style, after all, had put Cosa Nostra gunsels in jail) when he spotted a woman juror with a bouquet of flowers. He wasn't going to tolerate any flower children, albeit aging ones, on this jury. "Where did you get the lilacs?" the D.A. sternly demanded. The woman gave the bouquet a sniff. "From some girls in the lobby," she said. The D.A. did his job well. The jury took two hours to reach a guilty verdict. (Joan Baez and David Harris were in the courtroom to see Michael Metzger at his moment of triumph. They could not have imagined that in a few years this man, ready to browbeat at the sniff of a lilac, would be walking around in blue jeans.)

The triumph, though, was a bit hollow. Metzger relished busting corrupt civic officials and underworld moguls, but he found throwing the book at eighteen-year-old draft dodgers a bit pale by comparison. He had aged since the day he sent those seventeen New York war protesters to jail. He always liked to think that his zeal in behalf of the law was for the public's benefit. But forcing eighteen-year-olds to war—was that in the public's benefit? Was prosecution of the war the public benefit?

The next W fate dealt him was a booby trap, after which he would conclude: *Fuck, you won't last long around here.* Walworth R. Wentworth, twenty-four, was a conscientious objector. His draft board turned him down, claiming there was information of "military bent" in the boy's background. He refused to report for induction, holding firm to his C.O. claim, and was prosecuted. Metzger the D.A. reviewed the case on the eve of the trial and couldn't figure out why Wentworth was not granted his C.O. request. The background seemed perfectly good to him. He checked with the Selective Service liaison officer and pin-pointingly asked what the information of "military bent" amounted to. The liaison officer explained that, when he was sixteen and a ham radio nut, Wentworth had belonged to the Military Affiliate Radio Service. At the time, in those hyped-up Civil Defense heydays, the Army had deduced a way to keep America communicating when mushroom clouds smeared its horizon. Ham radio operators would keep us together and alive. Any boy, any ham, who joined the Military Affiliate Radio Service (MARS) could get free equipment. Wentworth, eager for his free equipment, had joined. Joining MARS was more fun than getting a Captain Midnight badge. But MARS was the evidence of his military bent. Metzger, pining for cases where "people were fucking the public," couldn't stomach the MARS rationale. He was himself a ham operator, had himself been a member of MARS, and didn't consider himself to have a "military bent." He had joined MARS for free equipment, as had thousands of Americans. On the day of the trial he went to the judge and told him that he wouldn't prosecute this case. "The draft board acted improperly," the D.A. said. The Selective Service was furious.

So, it turned out, was U.S. District Attorney Cecil Poole, Metzger's boss, measuring up to Frank Hogan "the way a polecat stands up to a tiger." Poole didn't like having the Selective Service placed in that kind of a position. Metzger's action, he said, "would give the impression we have perpetrated a great injustice on this young man." Metzger was quarantined from the case, and the case was sent back to trial. But it was too late. The D.A.'s un-D.A.-like action saved Wentworth. He was found not guilty.

The assistant U.S. district attorney entrusted with Ws and Joe Blow cases was getting a horrible taste in his mouth. The taste became so rancid the first time he steeped himself in the drug-law area that it almost made him gag. The W responsible was Frank Werber, a middle-aged hippie, a man with a considerable repute in the budding and bothersome counterculture.

Werber was charged with conspiracy to smuggle into the country a large quantity of marijuana. His attorneys offered to plead him guilty, accepting a two-to-ten-year prison term. But Metzger's superior, Cecil Poole, rejected the offer. The bulldozer was being oiled for Frank Werber. "The narcotics agents talked in a most vindictive way about Werber," Metzger said. "They said things like: 'We want to give the guy twenty years; let's get him life.' They were calling him names." Other agents argued with Metzger to shift the case to Texas, where they might be more certain of a conviction and a stiffer sentence. "We're not going to go shopping around for another forum," Metzger told them.

He began to look very closely at these narcotics agents. The nark was an odd and serpentine police animal. "I never liked the narks. Most of the ones I dealt with were feds. They were very devious. You always had the feeling they weren't telling you everything, that they were holding back things, which they thought would hurt their case. They just weren't candid. They seemed to have a personal animosity, a personal stake, which most policemen investigating other crimes didn't have toward the violator. I got the same impression about their personal involvement—you know, when some cop sees the horribly mutilated body of a little girl who was raped. Well, the narks showed this same kind of reaction—against people who were smoking joints. Strangely, I never saw the same animosity in narks working heroin cases. It was just grass and LSD. You got the feeling that it wasn't the drugs that got them riled but the kind of people using them. Heroin was a ghetto drug, and ordinary criminals dealt in heroin. But grass and LSD seemed to threaten them in their own minds. They wanted to stamp it out. It seemed to represent something far beyond the drug in question. I finally reached the conclusion that these guys were fighting a class struggle rather than a drug struggle. Grass seemed to sum up all their political vexations: Vietnam, the environment, the long hair, the drive against racism."

Of all the many federal narks he worked with, the agent who left the worst taste was Kenny Krusco, the top federal nark in the Bay Area. "He was the one I distrusted the most. He never gave a straight answer. He never looked you in the eye. Things always happened very fortuitously to him in the performance of his duty. Of all the feds, he was the most vindictive, the most aggressive. He got the biggest thrill out of the cops-and-robbers thing." Some of the other D.A.s, Metzger remembers, compared Krusco to a drinking buddy of his, a state agent Metzger hadn't yet dealt with, Gerritt Van Raam.

Metzger pursued the Werber case, convinced that he gave Frank Werber more of a fair shake than any other D.A. would have. When the jury came back, though, and found Werber not guilty, Metzger was incredulous. He couldn't understand this verdict. He thought the case looked open and shut. He started talking to jury members. One juryman after another told him the verdict was the result of a pervasive belief that the narcotics agents, the principal prosecution witnesses, were lying on the stand. Michael Metzger, man of Hogan ethics, didn't want to work with these people. "That was it for me. I hadn't spent all that time with Hogan, all my time in school, so I could railroad people with agents juries believed to be liars."

The red-tape expert who grew up with a love for the Law was trapped in an even more profound and spine-chilling traffic jam. He had come to an agonizing personal realization that, if he continued the business of prosecution for the United States of America, he would be off his "white horse, on a mangier one, heading in a dubious direction." So Michael Metzger, man of boyish ideals, quit working for the United States of America.

If American justice is that mangy horse "heading in a dubious direction," then Sandy White, professional narcotics informer, is a scabrous Lady Godiva. Sandy White, who has sent more than 350 persons to jail, excelling at the chameleonlike art of duplicity, sometimes fingering her closest friends, is not the complete moral monster. She is the mother of a four-year-old girl and the daughter of a college professor who keeps copies of *The New Republic* around the house. She considers herself, perversely, "a person of the Left," and she declares, "I'm for Angela Davis."

She is, however, a physical and mental dreg, a former heroin addict who went through thirteen electric-shock treatments and a methadone program. Say this for Gerry Van Raam: He didn't let thirteen shock treatments stop him. He visited the wrecked woman in the hospital, spewing paternalism, a solicitous, friendly buzzard hovering over vulnerable prey, making sure Sandy White got well enough to do her job. She left the hospital and then, against her parents' wishes, went back to Gerry Van Raam and the BNE. Today she lives in a tastefully plastic suburban house with her parents. The house looks onto the Bay: a peaceful, lilting ambience of sea gulls, blue sky, and variations of tides. She says she is trying to get herself together again, to salvage some order and accord and future out of the past two years of her life.

She is an overwhelmingly unattractive woman. She is homely and overweight; her complexion is pasty-faced and pimpled; she is utterly without charm, crude, neurotic. She has brown hair matching dim brown eyes and in an upstairs bedroom a dozen wigs that the BNE bought her. She is the kind of discolored woman you have seen countless times hanging around small-town dime stores: bulging at the seams, big-boned, hair in curlers, make-up overlaid. She is incredibly petty, a storehouse of gossip. For almost two years the BNE referred to her hundreds of times in court as "confidential and reliable." Her version of the truth, the minutiae of detail she noted before the BNE got its search warrants, sent countless persons to jail.

"Sandy White" is not her real name. The pseudonym is not used to protect her from the BNE or Gerritt Van Raam. They know, because of certain affidavits she swore to, certain things she said in court, that she has switched sides once again: informing, this time, on them. But they haven't given up hope they will use her again. Sandy White was a multi-talented informer. She could con with ease. She had quick and alert eyes. Most of her cases stood up in court. The pseudonym is used (after a night the reporter tiptoed to the edge of his compassion) to protect her livelihood. Informers are not ticker-tape celebrities. Sandy White is trying to survive as a teacher. Her students, understandably, would never understand. "What could I do if I couldn't teach?" she asks. "Go back to Van Raam?"

Why? After the charges the BNE held over her head had been dropped, after she realized the shock treatments had scarred her mind—why then did she continue being an informer? "I was so ashamed of myself," she says, "for all the shit I had done. My friends rejected me. They said, 'Fuck you. We want no part of you. You're going to bust us.' I really fucked things up. So I figured I might as well continue to be a nark because they're my only friends now."

To begin to understand Sandy White, you have to dwell on how critically wrecked ... devastatingly wasted ... she really is and to ponder the crippling inferiority she has been victim of since childhood. "I've always had an inferiority complex about being—well, look, I'm about five-ten, you know. I've been big, you know. I have been thinner, and I've been fatter. People have told me—guys have told me—you have beautiful eyes. I'd believe them. Then again I wouldn't. I'd always think that guys were after me for one reason or another—sometimes it was the money I had, sometimes it was what I could do for them. Like write a paper for them at school. But I've always felt inferior. It comes from being an overweight child, I guess, and being teased tremendously by a lot of people, and, like, since my friends rejected me—I mean, what the hell? It was exciting. There were a lot of men around all the time, and I was the center of attention."

The road that led Sandy White to Gerry Van Raam started, metaphorically, as she was sitting next to Jerry Rubin. She met her husband, Ben, that way. It was an affair that ended in beatings and a divorce. The court awarded the child, Debbie, to Sandy's care. "Well, I was dealing grass back then," she says, "and the way I met Ben, I was sitting at the Forum in Berkeley one day talking to Jerry Rubin before Jerry Rubin became, you know. I knew all these guys before they became. Jerry Rubin and I were tight. So he and I were sitting there drinking cappuccino, trying to act revolutionary, and here comes my cousin Phil from Chicago, and he says, 'There's my cousin; she's a dealer,' real loud. 'Let's see if we can smoke some pot with her.' Jerry says to me, 'Oh, my God, will you tell him to stop it.' Ben overheard the whole thing and laughed, and that's how I met him."

19

But the marriage folded: "He fucked up. Like, ah, the responsibility, the baby, made him so conservative. I was going so far to the left and he was going so far to the right at that time. And he was beating me, and, like, I have no respect for a man that hits you. I think that we can negotiate and talk things out, you know, if we have a relationship, rather than hit each other. Like, that's my philosophy. So, like, I have no respect for a man that hits a woman. That's the last thing, you know. So, like, I said, 'Fuck you. I can do better. Get out.' Even though he came from a very la-di-da family."

When she got into the informer business, she found herself getting off behind it, luxuriating in her new role, venting her frustrations, getting even with the world. "There's part of me," she says, "that loves everybody, but if someone turns on me or shits on me, I'll use everything I can, every power I own, to destroy that person. If you shit on me, I'm not guaranteeing it, but I'll make a doll of you and stick pins in it. I'll go that far. But I mean, you know, there's something in my personality that I don't like. I have to work on the vindictiveness and revengefulness. Perhaps I was encouraged in that by Van Raam and everybody in that office."

She found, too, a missing fulfillment in her job, a courage that perversely flooded her with self-respect. She imagined herself, finally, a realized woman, a spy lady power-tripping around the Bay. "There was a girl friend of mine, Judy Simmons, who found out what I was doing and tried to be an operator, too. She failed—tried to be Sandy White and just blew it. She didn't have the aggressiveness that I have, or the stamina, or the intelligence that I do to con people, to make them trust me. Or the experience of being a dealer. That helped in getting into people's houses. Or the balls to knock on any door, you know. It takes a lot of balls and a lot of guts, because you don't know what's behind the door, a gun or a friendly handshake. And I always said a prayer before I knocked on the door. In my head I always said a prayer because I didn't know if it was going to be the Last Door or not."

Working inside the BNE, she found that at first even the agents themselves looked down on her for being an informer, but she always retained a childlike, faraway belief in the power and benevolence of Gerritt Van Raam. "Those guys looked down on me for a long time, until I proved that I could be as sharp as they wanted me to be. Until I was going out for lunch with Matthew O'Connor. Just him and me.

Then the agents realized I was, you know, okay. They tried to talk me into being a policewoman. Said that would give me more money than an operator and we could go out on dates. "I really dug Van Raam even though one agent blew it a bit. I had an affair with an agent for a few weeks, and he broke down and told me, 'You know, Van Raam thinks he's just a big, you know, guy because he's got a beautiful pearl-handled .45 and he thinks he's got power. He's got all these men at his side. He's on a power trip.' The agent couldn't take it and got out of the bureau."

The "good vibes" between Sandy White and Van Raam continued even after, in rare pique, she had refused an assignment because of her "political principles." "I was quite a political radical at Cal. I knew Mario [Savio] and all those guys. SDS was about as radical as I went, but I still support the Weathermen to a certain extent. The BNE wanted me to become a political informer and send me up for a weekend, all expenses paid, to Seattle, Washington, to sit in on the Weathermen or SDS or something. I said 'No' and walked out of the office. But at the time I had built up a charisma of being such a notorious dope informer that they didn't give a shit what my political views were. I said I couldn't sell out that way. *I wasn't going to be that weird."*

Underneath her "good vibes" for Van Raam, the shock treatments, the betrayals, the loyalty oaths to Angela Davis, there are two visceral reasons why Sandy White became an informer and continued being one for two years. An insecure woman's fear and a homely woman's headlong vulnerability to "love." Fear of what would happen to her if she didn't play the nark game; "love at first sight," after the ruin of her marriage, with three men: Mike Jackson, a junkie, who betrayed her for another girl; Bob Elsberg, one of Gerry Van Raam's BNE agents, who arrested her and then, by his own admission, used her to set up most of his busts; and Ted Donnelly, a grease monkey, who, suddenly and with brutal haste, left her.

"If someone shits on me," Sandy White said, *"I'll use everything I can . . . to destroy that person."*

She got even with Mike Jackson by having him busted. In a sense she finally got even with Bob Elsberg, who spurned her attentions, by informing on the BNE. She couldn't get even with Ted Donnelly. By the time she figured out what he'd done, the grease monkey—taking no chances—had scampered to anonymity somewhere in the middle of America.

Love Story: A/K/A Bonnie Parker + the Junkie + a Nice Jewish Nark

"I was living on Brooklyn Avenue, you know. It was a commune, it was a dealing commune. I was the biggest dealer in the commune. I was the only girl in the commune except for one other girl who was a junkie and who lived in the basement. So I was a dealer. Like, I was really doing good, you know. But I was making so much I started getting into coke and heroin. Heroin really blew my mind. I loved it. I love coke like a lot of other people do. And like, oh, heroin, I really dig the high. I used to shoot up and get into Mick Jagger and his musical smack trip.

"I had long hair, you wouldn't recognize me, and I was maybe twenty pounds thinner. And, oh, I was really living with a guy who was good-looking. His name was Mike Jackson. One night I caught him sleeping in my bed with another girl, and I took a good look in the mirror and I looked just terrible. You know, the laughter that I once had. If you ask one of my friends, I used to be very extroverted, always laughing, the life of the party. I always was bringing around a $50 sampler of coke with me. I used to dig everybody and used to be very happy. I was accepted, man, you know, and drugs put me up there. But then everybody heard that I started shooting smack, and they were freaked out 'cause my money was running out. I started going to my friends for money. I didn't have a $50-a-day habit, but I'd buy a $20 bag for myself and split it up, like half of it went to Mike, my old man. I was supporting his habit.

"And to see him in bed with another girl actually going through it, the sexual thing, the trip, to me, just destroyed me. The sexual thing with a guy is a very intimate thing to me. I'm a romantic. I'm not old-fashioned, but I'm a romantic. But you're giving of yourself no matter who you're screwing. At one point, there's a point there, maybe a point before orgasm, that you're really close, like you're really one. I saw it. They were at that point, and he was giving himself to someone else. And that just blew my mind. Plus the fact the heroin distorted everything. And I got so enraged that, after a few days of moping around the house and coming off of heroin and not having enough money to cop a bag at that particular time, I made an anonymous call to the BNE and I said, 'Do you want to bust a houseful of dope?' and I

22

gave them the names, everything, and said there'd be more info to come.

"I waited a week, and nothing happened. I stayed away from the place. And I said, 'What the hell? I thought these narks were efficient!' So I called again because by now Mike had moved out of my bedroom down into the basement with the girl. And life then was really getting unbearable. I was still shooting heroin, but I was miserable because I thought I loved this guy. I'm supporting his habit, right? He betrayed me, and, like, my friends didn't like what I was turning into. I was losing my personality, and I was becoming manic-depressive. You know, just a very ugly person. I figured I needed straightening out. There's a little old alarm in my head that said, 'Your limit! You're going to get busted eventually, you're hot now as it is.' I was hot. The narks did know about me. It was only a matter of time before they got me if I hadn't gotten myself.

"So I called again. I said, 'You fuckers, what are you waiting for? There's one person in that house that can blow the whole Bay Area drug scene. All you have to do is bust the house.' And that stirred up the pot a little bit. And the next day I was sitting there waiting for a piece of smack to come in. I gave my car to some friends, and they were going to the City to cop a piece of smack for me. I prefer the brown Mexican stuff to the China white. And so I'm sitting around, rolling a joint, playing bridge with some friends of mine from Berkeley. I was in my last quarter at Cal in political science. And, oh, a knock at the door. And here's this beautiful nice little Jewish boy and another guy.

"Later I find out that the other guy was just one of Elsberg's operators, who just came along to hold Elsberg's hand, right? Because Elsberg never knocks on doors. So this nice Jewish boy, Elsberg, he smiles at me. And I was really stoned. He smiled at me, and I looked at him, and he looked familiar. I thought I recognized him from my bas mitzvah or temple or something. He was that kind of guy. He was the kind of guy that my mother wants me to marry. So I smile. I go, 'Hi, what's happening?' He goes, 'Ah, is Mike here?' I said, 'No, Mike's not around.' And so he says, 'Well, can I come in?' And I said, 'Yeah, come on in.' He says, 'I'd like to buy a little; I mean I'd like to buy a lid.' Meanwhile I was giving the other guy a look. I said, 'Are you a nark?' Just, really, gave it to him, third-degree.

"But this nice Jewish guy, I left him alone. I looked at him and said, 'What are you doing later tonight?' He said, 'Nothing.' I said, 'Why don't you come back, and, ah, I'll get some coke.' You know, in so many words, I was asking him to ball me. You know, I was playing that game.

"I said, 'What do you want, a lid? Or would you like a key? Or what? What do you want? It's a matter of time. If you want a lid, I'll give it to you, you know. If you want a key, wait twenty minutes. I'll have to make one phone call.' You know, that trick. So he's amazed. He's looking around the house all the time. There's a lot of syringes in a corner. The place was a doper's paradise. There was grass all over the place. We had a big mantel full of opium pipes, roach clips, syringes, everything, and a big hookah. Anyway, he's looking at all this para-phernalia, and all these weird people around are waiting for my friends to come back with the piece of smack, right? He says, 'What's going on here?' I said, 'Oh, nothing much.' He didn't know what to think of me. He said, 'Well, can I have that lid?' When he pulls out some crisp bills and gives them to me, I said, 'No, I don't want your money. Come back a little later and we'll blow a little weed and we'll talk about the temple or something. I'll give it to you on the house. You look like a nice Jewish boy. Are you?' He says, 'Yes, I'm Jewish.' I said, 'Good, I'm Jewish, too.' So let's keep it in the family, right? Here's a groovy lid, you know. He looks at it, smiles, and looks at the lid again. He says, 'Okay, I'll see you. I'll be back as soon as I can.' I smiled at him, and they leave.

"And I go back to put the Stones on, and my friends are ready to come back any minute with the junk. And at that point there's another knock at the door. And this time they didn't wait for us to answer the door, they just rushed right in. And everybody said, 'All right, put your hands up!' with, you know, guns pointed. And I said, 'Oh, my God, I finally blew it. They finally did it.' And I figured, 'Fuck, you don't want to go to jail. So what if you fuck your friends?' And I really dug Elsberg. So I said, 'Okay, you got yourself a rat.' And Elsberg, he smiled and said, 'That's great.' So he drove me home, and about an hour later I got that piece of smack I'd been expecting for two days and I shot up."

When Sandy White became a rat, Joseph Barann, twenty-nine, a graduate biology student at Berkeley, was the king of the rat pack. He still is. He is responsible for more than 1,000 arrests, a gung-ho wizard of betrayal and stealth. Joseph Barann is a scholar. He is a snake specialist. He spends most of his time on a slimy little amphibian with a whiplash tail, the salamander. Very few people, even few agents, know his real name. They know him by his code name, Joe Salamander. The operator lives a perfect Jekyll-Hyde existence. He is Barann by day, lecturing three times a week on the sleazy little creatures he knows so much about. He is Joe Salamander by night, the master of a different, if equally slippery, discipline. Those who know Joe Salamander say he has an all-American motive: money. In four years he has made more than $10,000 on grass busts, another $5,000 on acid busts. He made enough money to go off last year on a field trip to Yugoslavia, an around-the-globe search for a rare species of salamander.

When lawyers began looking into the use of BNE informers, they kept running across the snake expert's tracks. They were astounded. More than 1,000 setups! Salamander is bookishly proud of his job, keeping a neat record of persons arrested and moneys accrued. He is Gerritt Van Raam's star recruit, prestigious enough now to free-lance in his off-lizard time for agencies around the state. For a while, he was on a regular retainer from the Berkeley police department.

"Sometimes," Sandy White says, "especially in the beginning, he and I would talk shop, and I'd say, 'What do you do when someone passes you a joint?' He says, 'Well, I go like this.' He shows me a cigarette. He says, 'Always have a cigarette available to blow smoke out so they'll think you're smoking dope.' Salamander," she says, "was expert at the art of the Duke-In." The way it works cuts directly to the crux of the narcotics informer's basic function. When Gerry Van Raam or one of his agents suspects someone is using dope or dealing it, a little hasty detective work establishes the identity of the suspect's friends and associates.

The friends' names are given to the informer. The informer, sometimes wearing a Fargo, a hidden tape microphone, is driven to the suspect's home by an agent. The informer must get inside the suspect's home so that a search warrant can be obtained. The informer must either see what looks like "contraband"—"in plain view"—or smell the "pungent odor" of the contraband, or observe the suspect "imbibing" the contraband. (Some attorneys maintain that the informer will get in, see nothing, and then lie so that agents can get their search warrant anyway.) At the very least, the informer must be able to describe the suspect's home with a modicum of detail—though some informers have described second floors of houses without second floors.

The catch is getting into a wary suspect's home. This is where the Duke-In names of friends and associates become passwords to the living room. Salamander, or Sandy White, talking to a suspect at the door, would casually recite a litany of petty details, dropping names, trying to conjure closeness to one of the suspect's friends.

Sandy White says, "The details can get you by. Take this one case. I knew from Van Raam who the guy's friends were and what kinds of things they did together. Mentioning a few names made him more secure about me. And who would suspect a girl coming into the house? You think a girl wouldn't do it. It's really a brilliant ploy."

The Duke-In is also successfully used to set up dope buys. This is Salamander's specialty. Sandy White says, "His main gift is a beautiful voice on the telephone. Like, he's got a string of Duke-In names for you, right? And you're a medium heavy dealer. He'll call you up and he'll say, 'Hey, man, I'm Joe Smith's brother, and Joe says he really copped some good shit from you the other day. You got an extra lid?' Then he starts rattling off all kinds of personal details about Joe Smith and, pretty soon you're taken in. The Duke-In has worked, and Salamander's supposed to go over there and pick up the lid. Except Salamander has got this really refined, and he's very busy with his lizards and all. So he's got an arrangement where he doesn't even have to pick the stuff up. He'll call Van Raam and tell him what happened, and Van Raam will call Kenny Krusco of the feds and ask him for one of his long-haired agents. And some freaky-looking nark will go over there and pick the stuff up and bust the dealer. And Salamander has stayed home, made one phone call, and picked up his bread."

The classic Bay Area rat pack story that BNE agents still laugh about involves a commune that Van Raam suspected of being a dope house. He lined up an informer, Ron Jenkins, who had been busted in another drug raid. The deal with Jenkins was the same as the initial deal with Sandy White: Help us set them up, or go to jail. Jenkins didn't want to go to jail.

He lived in the commune for three months. He became one of its grooviest members. He shacked up with a chick, who became his old lady. He got so close to the chick that he told her he wanted to marry her. The commune scheduled a festival, a down-home wedding ceremony, for the next day. The groom was a bit late. He got there ten minutes after the festival, misting in clouds of grass, had begun. The bride wore a garland of flowers. The groom came in with a team of narks. Even the bride was busted. Charges against the groom were dropped. He had done a good job.

The use of informers also helps narcotics squads in an even more devious way. If, for instance, a police officer is used to set up a bust, the policeman can be subpoenaed to court and cross-examined. Not so with an informer. Narks tell judges that exposing their informers publicly would mean exposing them to danger. Some judges let them get away with it. The picture narks paint in the courtroom is that they are ever vigilant to protect their informers from the forces of vendetta. "They told me," Sandy White says, "that they'd keep me covered and protect me. Bullshit. They just left me on my own."

If a tough attorney does succeed, after tromping through a mine field of legal hassles, in subpoenaing an informer into court, the answers he gets will be less than honest. Perjury? "No, not that," says Sandy White. "But it's like this. The BNE taught me that, if some attorney starts asking questions about a part of the events that would hurt the case, I should just say, 'I don't recall.' You should see how many times agents use that phrase, too."

Isn't that still a lie under oath? Still perjury? she is asked.

"No," she says, "it's just a little white lie."

Gerry Van Raam denies any standing order of that sort.

"No," he says, "there is no standing order to forget."

He says agents will go out of their way to reveal facts *that may help the defense.*

"A very good prosecution tactic is: Even though the fact may be damaging to the prosecution, say it. We don't have anything to hide."

On a recent sunny morning in his office on McAllister Street the affable Matthew O'Connor, top nark linguist, is losing his commissar's grasp of Officialese. His smile has been knocked crooked. The elfin little cheeks are glowing crimson.

The reporter is jabbing him in a tender, underexposed area, asking him about the use of the professional informer.

Matthew O'Connor, scanning the pictures on his wall, is thinking that this is one interview he should not have granted.

How do you recruit your professional informers? he is asked. What qualities do you look for?

"Well," he says, "you look for a variety, and this depends on the ingenuity of the official agent. I won't go into it any more than that. We've had an incredible public response saying, 'Why in the world would you expose your techniques in dealing with these people?' We don't say that we have secrets. The people who are required to know, the congressional groups, they know."

"What," the reporter asks, "about an informer like Sandy White, who works with your office. Sandy White—"

O'Connor interrupts him. He sits up very straight in his chair. "Wait a minute. Wait a minute," he says. "We're not going to go through and identify any particular informer who works with this office, or even a hypothetical case."

"Okay," the reporter spars, "I won't use her name then. Take an informer who became an informer when she was busted—"

Again O'Connor interrupts. The wrinkles around his eyes harden. "Now I'd rather not go into that area," he says. His voice is accusing. "You surfaced something. You are obviously interested in something. You have pursued this informer. Her background."

Matthew O'Connor doesn't want to carry this interview any further, and he reaches into his bureaucratic grab bag, trying to dead-end the interview. "I'm afraid we're pushing our time," he says. "I have some appointments."

"You mean you don't want to go into Sandy White," the reporter says, "or Salamander or anyone who is used as an informer?"

"When you came here," Matthew O'Connor says, one finger jabbing the air, his Officialese quaking, "you said you wanted to review the attitudes of law enforcement and the Big Picture."

"I think the use of informers applies directly to that," the reporter says.

"Well, I don't," Matthew O'Connor says and escorts the reporter out of the nark-squad lair, staying close behind him, covering him, until he and his evil tape recorder are gone from the place where Big Pictures are unveiled . . . where a snake expert and an electrode casualty fade into the Law's thin air.

Filled with guns and security guards, the ornate byzantine building on McAllister Street supposedly is the place where Gerry Van Raam hangs his hat. But if you read some of the recent court cases the hunter has starred in, there is room for doubt; case after case refers to a place where Van Raam met an informer or another agent, a place where deals are made and people are betrayed, where nark posses foregather when raiding parties are being assembled.

It is a bar called LaRocca's, on Columbus Avenue in North Beach. It is hard and raunchy, filled on most nights with stumblebums, hookers, barflies, and narks. In the late Fifties and early Sixties LaRocca's gained repute as a rackets bar where silk-suited *mafiosi* sat edgily on their barstools downing martinis, their shoulder holsters bulging. Guns still bulge at LaRocca's these days, although most of the *mafiosi* are gone. These are the respected guns of the Law. LaRocca's is part of Gerry Van Raam's narkdom. He is here four or five times a week. He sweeps around the bar, drink in hand, Runyonesque, paternally friendly to the stray hooker or two who obviously know that the man with the ski nose and the cobwebbed wrinkles is a cop to be reckoned with. The bartender is a stiff, balding guy who struts with a military posture, goose-stepping back and forth to the jukebox, playing Frank or Vaughn Monroe. He treats Gerry Van Raam with wide-eyed deference, smiling, splay-toothed, bringing him a free drink after every three or four. It is clear that Gerry Van Raam has been good for this man's business.

On a night before or after a big bust, in anticipation or celebration, the interlocking nark agencies—state / local / fed—meet here, around this bad-vibes bar with the picture of Vic Damone above it, and whisper secrets about trucks packed with hashish, clotheslines stuffed with grass. In attendance on a night like this will be Van Raam and his pearl-handled gun, top federal agent Kenny Krusco of the shifty eyes, BNE agents Bob Elsberg (the Nice Jewish Nark), Dick Violet, Lenny Bacarlo, and San Francisco nark agent Billy Morrow, a black man with a squeaky laugh who Stepin-Fetchits around Gerry's aura.

Always hovering around Gerry, wherever he moves, will be another, younger man in his late twenties, a man with long, out-of-place jet-black hair, Al Teixeira, nark-in-charge of the Marin County sheriff's office. Al Teixeira, who has a dear, doting, infantile quality about him, likes to tell his friends, "You know, Gerry is really my *father* in the narcotics business."

Over the course of two years Sandy White spent quite a few nights at LaRocca's with these men, getting to know all of them, falling in love with one of them, furthering all of their professional careers. She had a chance, too, to turn her informer's wiles on them, gaining entrance to the narks' private lives. Gerry Van Raam and his gang never dreamed that their shock-casualty informer one day would inform on them, that they had created (Frankenstein's handiwork was an electrode creature) a monster.

Give Sandy White credit. She got to know her narks well: "We were all sitting around in a bar one time, getting loaded on wine. Van Raam, Kenny Krusco, Elsberg, Teixeira, Violet. Krusco turns to me, and, since I'm the only chick, he says, 'Hey, Sandy, how do you feel about being the only girl in this crowd of lecherous old men?' I said, 'Fairly safe.' It jarred Krusco because Krusco fancies himself a real stud anyway. Every time he sees me he goes, 'He-ey, Sandy, how are ya?' You know. And all I see in him is a thirty-seven-year-old man who really made it to the top. You know, he's in the top of the fed office. He's among the top three team leaders. He and Van Raam are very close."

Her favorite agent, of course, is Bob Elsberg, her partner on almost every bust, a typical young nark careerist who parlayed Sandy White into a $15,000-a-year personal success, who arrested her and then turned her out.

What kind of man is Bob Elsberg? Sandy White says, "One time I was in his house. I heard he was dying. Someone called me up and said he was really sick, you know. I thought I'd better go over there and see him before he dies. So I brought him four dozen roses. I come over to the house and there's his mother at the door. He's always being protected by his lovely mother. Well, there's Bob in bed. There are pictures of him all over the house, hundreds of them, hundreds of pictures of Bob all over this tiny house. His mother keeps asking me, 'Are you a narcotics secretary?' I say, 'Oh, I'm a teacher, and I know him from a Jewish group.' Elsberg sees me, he looks at me and the flowers, and he says, 'What are you doing here?' I say, 'I thought you were dying.' He says, 'Well, I'm not. So long.'

"Of course, he'd been using me all along. He knew how I felt about him. He knew it from the very minute I opened that door and gave him that lid. He knew it, and he used me. But he'd tease me, right? He always tried to make me feel inferior. He says, 'Lose weight. You have a beautiful face, but you should lose weight. Guys won't like you unless you lose weight.' And then I was always with him, trying to bust people. He spent more time with me than with his mother. Once in the car, driving me across the Bay Bridge, he said, 'Ah, if an agent knows that a female operator likes him, he is instructed to play her along for the law."

She also got to know Lenny Bacarlo, Elsberg's partner. "Lenny is one of those guys who is always playing with his gun, you know, fondling it and stuff. He'd let his handcuffs hang from his belt, and when he walked on the street people could see it dangling away. And, you know, he's very gross. One time we're in a restaurant and he's sweating, and he takes his jacket off. Well, there's his shoulder holster and his gun out for everybody to see. Wow! I got embarrassed, and I said, 'Leonard, put your coat back on, God damn it. You're so fucking uncouth.' "

Gerry Van Raam's Number One Son, Al Teixeira, the Marin County nark, always treated her kindly. "Al's really all right, except that Gerry totally monopolizes him. Van Raam says, 'Fart,' and Teixeira says, 'How loud?' Sometimes it's pretty funny because—like when Al let his hair grow. Al had made so many busts in Marin that he was getting burned out, becoming a nark superstar, becoming a celebrity, losing his effectiveness. So they told him he had to grow his hair really freaky-long so people wouldn't recognize him. That's pretty funny because all of Van Raam's men have instructions to keep their hair short. So Gerry would make fun of Al's hair, right? After Al has just grown it so he can bust more people, right? After he can't keep it short anymore because he was so good of a nark. And Gerry looks at the long hair, and he's calling him a percy and flicking his wrists at him.

"Al used to be an operator just like me. He was, essentially, just an average guy out to score a career, and there was a guy in Van Raam's office named Hector Lopez that Al got really chummy with. So Hector lines him up as an operator, and Al starts working for Gerry. He did all right, and then the Marin job opened up, and Gerry recommended him for it. Al's big dream is to make it in the BNE. He wants to become a BNE agent. Gerry keeps telling him, 'We've got an eye on you. We'll see what we can do.' "

Billy Morrow, the black nark, is a San Francisco police department agent known as "the cat with nine lives." A junkie once put a gun into his face and pulled the trigger. Morrow survived. The gun jammed. "It's weird," Sandy White says. "I once asked Elsberg, 'How come there's not a whole lot of blacks in nark work?' You know what he said? He said, 'We can't trust them. They usually end up using dope or selling it. Just like we can't trust Orientals either.' "

Dick Violet is one of the BNE's youngest agents, a man who reads *The French Connection* around the office, a man Sandy White says "is the only person capable of smoking grass in the whole place. He told me once he really didn't want to be a nark and he'd get out of it eventually and go back to graduate school. I said, 'You're going to loosen up then, huh?' He goes, 'Maybe.'

"But I don't understand why young guys, twenty-three-year-old good-looking young guys, get involved as narks. Maybe it's just a power trip. Like I talked to a lot of them, and, you know, it takes a doper to know a doper. I could tell some of them looked like they had turned on, but they wouldn't admit it to me—me of all people because I'm an informer, right? I give information to police officers. I'm a trained spy. So I'm the last person to confide in, even though they trained me."

She is also convinced that, while Gerry Van Raam may be power-trucking with each new flashy arrest, scaling new headlined career heights, he also views himself as an angel of righteousness leading his nark forces against the armies of evil dope.

"Van Raam thinks grass is evil because, the way he sees it, it's the first step to heroin. You know, he's been a cop all his life. So how could you expect him to see it any different? Most of the guys feel that way. Maybe it's just a self-justification mechanism, I don't know. Like one time when I was doing busts with them Elsberg finds out that I'm still doing dope, and he says, 'How could you still be doing it?' I said to him, 'Grass is nothing.' He says, 'Grass is nothing? You know how it is, Sandy,' and he shakes his head and says, 'Come off it. I tried to rehabilitate you for almost two years, and you're smoking marijuana again.' I said, 'Well, I'm sorry.' But I didn't tell him I was horning coke, too."

The scene inside LaRocca's one particular night seemed pleasant enough. Gerry Van Raam, playing king to his nark court, ambling between his agents and their ladies, a bit high, his footsteps shambling, Vic Damone warbling away in the background. Except for the bulges around the belts of the men at the bar, the hardness of some of the ladies' eyes, the browbeating scrutiny aimed at wayward long-haired intruders, the ambience was about as mellow as it ever becomes.

Sandy White, who used to sit at that bar kibitzing with winos and narks, doesn't go back there anymore. The operator saw too much in the line of duty, witnessed too many of the occult after-dark exercises of these grinning men at the bar. Hell hath no fury, she learned, like a law-upholding nark.

A narcotics bust is not a peacetime pursuit, an exchange of papers, the ritualistic donning of handcuffs. It is guerrilla assault, a psychic search-and-destroy mission meant to turn its victim inside out, to make him beg for compassion, to betray his friends in return for personal immunity.

If you've been busted, then you know the scenario all too painfully. To begin with, the bust will come in numbers, because, if you are into intimidation and psychic violence, there is strength in numbers, the fulfillment of primal instinct. A team of narks will knock at your door, announce its warrant, and order you to open up. If you hesitate for a moment, if your instincts aren't keeping pace, they will kick your door down, claiming your hesitation was intent to dispose of the contraband. Their guns will be drawn. If they find their contraband or claim they've found it, you will be handcuffed and searched. The handcuffs will impair your circulation; the search will jab your privates. If you are a nobody, an average longhair with little money and no Main Street connections, there may be a slap or two, a cold gun butt in the face, or the netherworld feel of a gun barrel placed against your temple.

Lawyers who specialize in narcotics cases know the pattern, perfected by the BNE, all too well. Attorney Tony Serra, a fiery, long-haired man who almost got a personal whiff of those methods, says, "The terror they inspire in a recent 'arrestee' is the primary damage. They try to bring out the Judas instinct in a man. A nark who has busted you tries to scare the fucking shit out of you. He tries to torture you physically or psychologically into betraying your fellowman. He hopes to remake you into a moral leper."

Attorneys are very familiar with a litany of psychical and psychological torture tactics. "I've heard so many cases of physical abuse, guns against the temple, and a punch or two, that I more or less take those things for granted," Serra says. "The psychological weapons, in my mind, are the more deadly, the more damaging. They'll threaten to turn you into a punk in jail, tell you they'll put you in the most violent sadomasochistic block. They'll threaten to bust your old lady if you don't help them, take your kids away and institutionalize them, take it out on your parents. Everything and anything."

The case of Eddie, a seventeen-year-old boy who sold a few lids to his teen-aged friends—a fragile, delicate kid who believed in the Desiderata and preached love for his fellowman, giving lids away as often as selling them—is a cruel portrait of a nark-bust victim. Eddie wound up in a psychiatric clinic. "They came and busted him, really leaning on him psychologically at the time of the bust," Serra says, "and then they took him down to jail, where they really grilled him again. You have to understand that we are talking about a seventeen-year-old kid who was a very minor league dealer—shit, a Little League dealer. They wanted him to tell them the names of all the other kids he sold to, all the other kids he smoked grass with. Well, they kept leaning on him, and the kid still wouldn't crack. So then they leaned on his father. They went to his father and told him they were going to make sure the boy got five years at California Youth Authority. They told the father the boy would probably be raped and abused in jail, told the father that his boss would probably find out about the whole thing. They essentially threatened the father's existence. Well, the father cracked. He went to see the kid and told the kid all the things that would happen to the family, that it would cost him his job and so forth. Well, the kid finally cracked. Remember that they went this far, to all these vicious lengths, to get the names of a bunch of kids who were smoking a few joints. We're not talking about any international dealers, you know. So the kid cracked and gave them the names of his friends. But now this wasn't enough. They knew they had the kid. They knew they had his father squirming. So now they started crying about how they were going to make their busts. So they turned this kid, who wouldn't even crack at first, into an operator. The kid was forced to go into his friends' houses and sell each of his friends a few joints of grass. The narks were waiting outside. When each kid had bought a few joints, all the kids were arrested. They got eight or nine teen-agers this way. I decided to put the kid on the stand. The whole episode is so horrendous to me that I felt by putting him on the stand I'd expose a much more horrible evil. Those were Gestapo tactics they used on the kid, the brainwashing terror tactics of the KGB. I made the kid go into each detail of betraying his friends. He broke down and sobbed. He turned into a complete whimpering baby, and he suffered a nervous breakdown. The boy had been forced to betray every ounce of his self-respect, to wipe out and negate all of the things he believed in."

Sandy White says narcotics agents reserve special wrath for people like her—for operators who are on the payroll and then become either "unreliable" or double-dealing. The easiest way for a nark to even the score with an operator is to set him or her up—i.e., send him to jail.

"Do you know for a fact they've set operators up?" she is asked.

"It's common knowledge," she says.

She tells the story of Eddie Turner, known as "Turk," an operator who incurred the wrath of the BNE. "What Turk was doing was this: He was working on our payroll. He got busted for a cocaine bust, a heavy bust, right across the border. There were some other friends in the car and they were caught in the L.A. area. He came up here and started setting people up on Telegraph. Well, anyway, he did the BNE a few good people, and just recently he did a good piece of heroin for the feds. He was on the BNE payroll, getting $80 every two weeks. Then he started going back to heroin. He was a junkie before. And the narks found out that he was tipping certain people off that they were hot, and they busted him again. They knew that he was a junkie while informing, that he was doing dope all along while working with them, but, when he pissed them off, they popped him again."

She tells the story of Pat, another junkie informer whose heroin habit was consciously fed by the BNE and who was busted when he stopped being useful. "Pat was a junkie, but someone had OD'd his old lady, and, you know, she died. And he wanted to get back on all heroin dealers because they were no good. And he was trying to get off junk, but he didn't want to go on the methadone program yet. They gave him to Joe Salamander to work with because the guy knew all these big-time coke and heroin dealers. They had a pile of money for this case: Oakland money, BNE money. And the feds gave Salamander money to spend, to cop a bag at each house maybe to get the warrant or maybe a setup of a piece-buy. Well, Joe would buy one for the warrant, the record, and get one for Pat's personal use.

"I asked Salamander about it, and I said, 'How could you let this happen? How could you let him keep a bag?' I mean it's not correct procedure, it's not right, you know.

"And he says, 'Well, I know, the cops know. There's nothing we can do about it. He's got good information. That's the only way we can do it, and he won't go on the methadone program."

"When they got all the info they needed out of the guy, they busted him for heroin and sent him away."

Van Raam denies it. "We don't allow people to violate the law or use drugs," he says. "Period."

Sandy White was present when Gerry Van Raam and federal agent

Kenny Krusco arrested John Eric Anderson, an operator who had missed a key court appearance. Van Raam and Krusco "roughed him up a bit."

"They were really pissed off," she says, "that he was fooling around again, and he skipped an important court appearance. Krusco said he was an operator and 'that motherfucker, when I get my hands on him'—any operators, it's common knowledge that, if you blow it, that, if you're caught dealing or if you double-cross them in any way, well. . . . They both grabbed him by the shoulders and by the arms and shook him like and threw him against the wall. They felt that Anderson had really betrayed them because he had helped them a great deal."

Van Raam denies it. "I'm denying the allegation and telling you why it wasn't true," he says. "Because she wasn't there, and it didn't happen."

The urbane and charming Matthew O'Connor, asked what happens when one of his men is charged with brutality, said, "It's investigated, fairly investigated."

Asked whether narcotics agents purposely intimidate victims to gather further information, O'Connor said curtly, "That's not true. Many people who are arrested *want to talk to agents*."

"In other words," he is asked, "suspects are not shoved up against the wall or pistol-whipped?"

"I know," he said. "I've heard that people use reports, they've been investigated by law enforcement teams. Don't forget that we're very cognizant of our image, our integrity."

O'Connor administers the coup de grace to brutality charges: "I certainly don't want to sit here, nor does any other person in this office wish to be around people who would conduct themselves like that. And if we had anyone around here who abused people, *the other agents would come right in, report them,* make a complaint of it."

Sandy White, told that her former lunch partner Matthew O'Connor says agents would tattletale on each other's brutalities, giggled. "Sure," she says, "right on!"

Months ago, before the BNE discovered its pet informer had betrayed it, she was talking about writing a book of her experiences.

"You and I can write a fucking book about this," she said, "if we live that long. They might kill us both." She giggled. "If they do that, I ought to make a will out."

She giggled again. "Uh, I don't think they would kill us. That was a joke. I'm still laughing about that."

How would the BNE react?

"They're going to be, when they find out—I hope it's not soon. Uh, they'll be—first of all they'll be terribly shocked that I could turn like that because I'm still their number one groovy child. I'm in the family and all the good vibes and stuff—uh, they'll be shocked. Elsberg will be very upset and hurt personally. He will be dumbfounded, not revengeful. Van Raam will be revengeful, I figure, from knowing his personality. Krusco likes me too, very much. I'm their child. Salamander will be dumbfounded, too. They will probably try to get him to set me up or plant dope on me. They'll probably try to do the same thing they tried to do to the others: a setup, but such a good one I will have to do time for it."

Michael Metzger, who quit working for the United States of America to defend people against its laws, found his educational process a disquieting one. He was a careful, thorough lawyer, a "fact man" who did his homework diligently. As his reputation in the narcotics field grew, he began to question the justice of the Law he had devoted his life to. He came to the conclusion that most narcotics laws do more harm than good, that the policeman who specializes in the narcotics enforcement field is more often a deputy of injustice. He began musing upon the relative meanings of the word "pig." It was not an easy process for a former ace district attorney.

A forthright sort, he did not hide his conclusions from the men he drank and associated with. In court he still clung to his old coldly anchored style—Metzger never gets off his chair to ask questions, not even for cross-examination—but there was a new vibrancy in his voice, a strident hostility to the testimony of narcotics agents and their informers. He also found, after it became obvious that he was not Playing the Game, that his old D.A. associates were avoiding him.

"They waited for a while to see what kind of defense lawyer I'd be—kind of hung back and watched. Playing the Game means you never go for a cop's throat in court. You kind of put on a show for your client's money, and you don't get into the jugular of cop testimony.

When it becomes obvious that an agent is lying on the stand, you don't say that. You say, 'Well, maybe the officer made a mistake.' You don't start talking about perjury. You talk about the agent's memory. I know too many lawyers who are Playing the Game. You know, they're on a first-name basis with the agents, they have drinks with them, they're good old boys. If some clients heard what their lawyers say about them to narcotics agents, they'd fire them on the spot. A lot of lawyers view their clients, especially long-haired kids, as scum."

Attorney Tony Serra, who saw the seventeen-year-old suffer a nervous breakdown at the hands of narks, illustrates another aspect of playing the game. "For some time among older lawyers there was this tendency to try to win a narcotics case by buying the agent off. I'll periodically have a client who'll suggest it to me, and I always reject it. I personally know of one narcotics agent who has let it be known to me that he can be bought, but I won't do it. I won't pay them off for a very special personal reason. Because I'm not a double agent. A lot of lawyers are mediators. They'll be representing a client in a narcotics case. Yet they'll be on a coffee-sharing basis with the narks. That's totally hybrid. To pay a nark off is an act of treason. You become a part of it if you do that. You sink to their level. I'm not into establishment crimes. It is repugnant to my sense of morality. I consider myself a semantic warrior in a conflicting court. This is one of the few places left where you can, like, still wear the colors. On a game level, this is cowboys and Indians for me.

"The thing that galls me," Serra says, "is that the nark premises his whole existence on fraud. He lives a lie. He lives his cover story. Policemen were traditionally honest. A nark has to lie; his job requires him to lie. He gets by on his ability to lie professionally. He eats with you; he sleeps with you; he fucks you. That's the reason why there is capital punishment for treason in war. They live that thin line between reality and illusion. Sometimes a nark doesn't honestly know when he's lying. The policeman on the street is into a different thing. He's got his hat on. He knows what the fuck he is—a professional."

Michael Metzger, who once defended New York policemen facing departmental charges, now began to study the relationship of the law to police abuse. He found, for example, the ruling of a New York State Supreme Court justice, Judge Irvin Younger, who, in 1970, observed that the testimony of certain police officers in narcotics cases "should be scrutinized with especial caution." He found a Supreme Court ruling of

1905—*Weeks* v. *the United States*—particularly relevant: "The efforts of the courts and their officials to bring the guilty to punishment ... are not to be aided by the sacrifice of those great principles established by years of endeavor and suffering which have resulted in their embodiment in the fundamental laws of this land."

He began listening to his close friend Phil Ryan, a no-holds-barred political attorney, a tough, plain-spoken, and articulate black Irishman, who wears his feelings about narcotics agents where most policemen wear their badges. Phil Ryan sees, in the attempted enforcement of drug laws, "the massive corruption of law enforcement. Any propensity it might have for the fair and equal protection of the law is dissipated either through its own corrupt practices, or its own dealings in narcotics, or its own acceptance of money, or its use of informers and its expenditure of funds."

It is Phil Ryan's feeling that "we are creating a nation of informers. Drug arrests require the massive expenditure of money to scurvy and scumbag people who inform on their brothers and sisters." He sees the tactics of nark enforcement as a continuing pattern in American life, "the vesting of police officers with life-and-death powers when those very officers evidence not a love for life but a macabre lust for the death forces." Phil Ryan believes, borrowing Alan Watts's phrase, that we have created "an armed clergy," that this armed clergy is enforcing "through their arms, through their conduct, through their viciousness, through their brutality, through their courts—and they are their courts—the suppression of the strongest and most noble aspirations of people to live a liberated life."

Michael Metzger was near the end of a legal road that began with sending antiwar protesters to jail. As he immersed himself in his field—what he would call "the sea of shit" and Phil Ryan "the belly of the monster"—Michael Metzger noticed that narcotics agents were pointing to him in court, bad-eyeing him from the stand. He didn't give it much heed.

He also ran across a series of cases he never thought he'd be using, cases in which men were prosecuted by the Law for motives of revenge and vendetta. In *Lenske* v. *the United States* (1967), a man was prosecuted by the IRS because of his "unorthodox social and political ideas." In *Dixon* v. *the District of Columbia* (1968), a man was prosecuted because he wouldn't make a deal with a policeman after being issued a parking ticket. Looking at these cases, Metzger shook his head. He thought we were living in a more legally sophisticated decade, that acts of retribution and injustice wouldn't be tolerated by the public. He read the words of the Dixon decision hurriedly, words that would come back to haunt him: "The government may not prosecute for the purpose of deterring people from exercising their right to protest official misconduct. . . ."

Some of his lawyer friends were advising Michael Metzger to soften his rhetoric about narks. It wasn't prudent, they told him, to talk that way. Especially for him, a former U.S. district attorney who once had worked with them. The narks might feel betrayed. He didn't take special note of these warnings. He was, though, more and more angered by what seemed to be a continuing pattern of intimidation. The agents of the BNE were trying to stifle his business.

"They'd arrest a guy for a narcotics charge, and they'd ask the guy what lawyer he was going to use. Well, when the guy said he wanted to use me, they'd get all upset, or badmouth me—tell the guy I'd just take his money from him."

But the last straw was the fate that befell one of his clients, a young man named Richard Frink, moments after the BNE arrested him for possession of marijuana. Frink asked permission to call his lawyer; permission was granted.

"Who's the lawyer?" a BNE agent asked him.

"Metzger," the young man said.

The nark leaned back and slapped Richard Frink across the face as hard as he could.

Sometimes, when narks draw guns and crash through the night, people die. If there is an armed clergy, if there are policemen with a macabre lust for the death forces, then there are victims, the recipients of bullets, embalmed in the pursuit of law and order. The killing is always accidental. The killers always have regrets.

In the past few years nark raiding teams have participated in three star-crossed shootings. On Thanksgiving Day, 1968, in Oakland a narcotics squad composed of state / local officers burst into the home of a prominent surgeon. Somehow or other they had assaulted the wrong house. The agents apologized. They apologized, too, for a shotgun that accidentally discharged and shattered a living-room wall. A year ago in

Kensington a group of federal agents busted a man suspected of being a mid-level marijuana dealer. During the course of the arrest one of the agents' guns accidentally discharged, putting a bullet into that man's temple.

The death of Heyward Henry Dyer, twenty-two, in Whittier, California, a suburb of Los Angeles, on October 4, 1969, is a parable; a BNE-led raid that ended in death, a killing that was adjudged tragic but without criminal liability.

On the night of October 3 two BNE agents, along with four sheriff's deputies and a narcotics detective from the Vernon, California, police department, arrived at a Whittier apartment house shortly before midnight. They had a search warrant to enter apartments B and D at 8033 South Comstock Avenue. The two-story apartment house used 8031 as the address for the lower floor and 8033 as the address for the upper floor. The agents mistakingly crashed into apartments B and D on the lower floor, 8031 South Comstock Avenue. They had busted the wrong place.

In apartment D tenant Bill Corey was awakened by the sound of his door being smashed open. Corey said he woke up staring at two plainclothesmen who held him at gunpoint and searched the premises before realizing their mistake.

Agents also entered apartment B by smashing through the door. Asleep in the bedroom were Mrs. Florence Mehan, fifty, and her twelve-year-old daughter, Susan. Mrs. Mehan said she awoke to find three men in plainclothes aiming guns at her. "I saw three men," she said. "One of them grabbed me by the arm. I screamed, and I ran out. I thought they were going to attack me." Her daughter said, "They just grabbed Mommy by the arms and said they had a search warrant to look for marijuana."

The neighbors said they heard screaming and scuffling from Mrs. Mehan's apartment and ran to their doors. Among those who heard the screaming was Mrs. Mehan's son-in-law, Heyward Henry Dyer. Dyer lived in an upstairs apartment not among those listed in the search warrant. He rushed downstairs to his mother-in-law's apartment and found the agents, their guns drawn, ransacking the place.

The agents, finally realizing they had raided the wrong apartment and were in the wrong place rousting the wrong people, went to the upper floor and broke the doors down in one of the apartments listed in the warrant.

Mrs. Barbara Gurley, a neighbor, said she and her husband were awakened by screams. "The cops looked like a bunch of madmen running around. They had all kinds of guns down there. We didn't even know who they were. It seemed so strange that they were running around downstairs and doors were being kicked open, and all of a sudden, boom! they're upstairs. Then they were just all standing there with guns. It's frightening to see a bunch of people with guns, and you're really not sure who they are or what they want."

The agents were raiding an apartment directly above Mrs. Mehan's. In the Mehan apartment Heyward Henry Dyer was joined by his wife, Linda, seven months pregnant, and their twenty-two-month-old son Francis. Upstairs Detective Sergeant Frank Sweeney, a fifteen-year veteran of the Vernon police department's narcotics squad, was holding a rifle pointed to the floor. The rifle was his own treasured weapon, unauthorized for police business, a high-powered military ordnance AR–15. Sweeney's gun "somehow" discharged, sending a bullet through the floor. Heyward Henry Dyer was shot through the head as he was holding his infant son. "We were just talking and trying to calm Mother down," his wife said, "and all of a sudden a shot came through the ceiling, and he fell to the floor. I looked at him and grabbed my baby. I knew he was dead because his stomach wasn't moving. So I ran outside, and I yelled, 'You killed him; you killed him!' And this policeman said to me, *'Lady, it was just an accident.'*"

The fatal raid netted its suspect. Charles Brent Jenkins, twenty, was arrested and booked on possession of marijuana and dangerous drugs charges. Two red capsules and two white tablets were seized, along with 150 seeds of grass.

There were some mighty strange aspects to this raid. The BNE was in charge, and its agents had asked Sweeney to go along. Sweeney was not working and was not collecting overtime for the mission, but he had come for his own reasons on his own time. Somehow or other the Whittier police department was not notified of the raid, and no Whittier policemen were asked to join the party.

No one could quite understand how agents had crashed into the wrong apartments—until, that is, it was revealed that the narks had spent two to three hours at a nearby bar drinking beer, gin, vodka, and whiskey before launching the raid. On the way there one agent stopped at a liquor store and bought a six-pack of beer, splitting the beer with five other agents and an informer. The agents, it was revealed, had gone to the bar to kill time—waiting for the search warrant to be issued. A breath-analyzer test taken by Whittier police showed that Sweeney had been drinking. Mrs. Dyer said she had smelled the odor of alcohol and said the agents were "acting very loudly and moving in an unsure manner." Sweeney's eyes and those of another agent were bloodshot, she added. The arrested man, Jenkins, said he noticed that one of the agents' eyes were bloodshot and "he seemed to stumble a bit when he talked." His wife, Carol Jenkins, asked one agent about his blood-shot eyes and was told, "It's because I've been up since seven this morning." The apartment-house manager, Tony Clemente, also noticed that Sweeney's eyes were bloodshot and said it was his impression that "agents had been drinking" because of their "arrogant and aggressive manner."

No one could understand how the powerful AR–15 rifle discharged until the occupants of the apartment above Mrs. Mehan's described Sweeney's actions. Arthur Ronald DeVore, twenty-six, and Edward Gates, twenty-five, were living in the apartment. DeVore testified that he was being questioned by Sweeney when the rifle discharged. He said Sweeney was "belligerent and ornery" and had first threatened Gates when he asked why the police didn't present their search warrant before entering the apartment. DeVore said Sweeney replied, "Well, what do you know? We have another wise one here." He said Sweeney feinted toward Gates's head with the rifle butt, then turned to him and asked to see his hands. DeVore had two fingers missing. DeVore said Sweeney looked at the hand with the missing fingers, then tilted the barrel of his AR–15 at a forty-five-degree angle and "brought it down upon my hand. He pulled back one or two steps, and the gun went off." Earlier in the raid, DeVore said, Sweeney had pointed the same rifle at him, snapped the safety off, and said, "You better get against that wall, or I'm going to blow you up against it!"

In a split decision, a coroner's jury found that Dyer had been killed by criminal means and sent the case to the grand jury. The grand jury, however, voted not to indict Sweeney—ruling, in effect, that Sweeney was not negligent in the handling of his high-powered favorite weapon. The case was now up to the district attorney, who could still elect to bring criminal charges.

But Whittier District Attorney Evelle J. Younger refused to prefer charges against the narcotics agent. Younger called the case a "tragedy" but said it did not justify preferring criminal charges.

Two months after the death of Heyward Henry Dyer, his wife gave birth to a baby boy.... Charges against Charles Brent Jenkins were dropped when a judge ruled that the search warrant the narks had been waiting for in that bar was made out incorrectly: "too ambiguous".... Detective Sergeant Frank Sweeney is still a respected narcotics officer of the Vernon police department, still takes part in raids coordinated by the Bureau of Narcotics Enforcement.... Whittier District Attorney Evelle J. Younger prospered. He is now Attorney General of the state of California.

Dialogue. Sandy White, ace nark informer, and her boy friend, Ted Donnelly. Subject: narks.

Sandy: *What do you think about narks?*

Ted: *I have nothing against the bastards.*

Sandy: *You have what?*

Ted: *I said I have nothing against the bastards. It's just that some things they do are highly illegal.*

Sandy: *Some things everybody does are.*

Ted: *Yeah, but does that give the narks the right to go ahead and do it just because some things everybody does are illegal?*

Sandy: *I don't know what you're talking about. There's bad apples in every bunch.*

Ted: *Yeah, but they're all bad apples in the nark business.*

Sandy: *I don't know. A lot of them are righteous, conscientious people, and a lot are schmucks.*

Ted: *What do you mean conscientious people?*

Sandy: *I mean they really believe in what they're doing.*

Ted: *You really believe that putting a joint in someone's hand and saying, 'Ah, look, he's got something,' or walking in and planting something—*

Sandy: *No.*

Ted: *It's case history they do that.*

Sandy: *Some of them do, yeah.*

In March of 1970 Michael Metzger, who'd been warned to soften his rhetoric, formally called federal agent Kenny Krusco a liar. The same Kenny Krusco he had worked with in the Werber case as a district attorney; whom he had never trusted; who "never looked you in the eye." The same Kenny Krusco, top federal nark, who chummed with Gerry Van Raam at LaRocca's.

The charge came after Metzger was retained to prepare the federal appeal of LSD pioneer-industrialist Owsley Stanley, a gentle and likable man who believed in the spiritual power of acid and in the music of the Grateful Dead. A part of Michael Metzger's spiritual odyssey was a poignant courtroom moment when he stood before the court and asked that Owsley Stanley be allowed bond. He told the court that Owsley was not a criminal sort, that because he loved the Bay Area too much he would never exile himself to a foreign land. He expected the request to be routinely granted. When the D.A. suddenly asked to see the judge privately in his chambers, Metzger thought it curious. When, moments later, the judge returned and categorically denied bond, Michael Metzger knew he was defending not an accused felon but a man who was being persecuted for the way he lived and for the style of life he advocated.

Standing in the courtroom that day, unable to comprehend the lightninglike brutality of the judge's action, his belief in the law once again a cruel joke, Michael Metzger cried. He made no attempt to wipe the tears away as Owsley was handcuffed and taken away by marshals.

Hired to file the federal appeal, Metzger found that the central character in Owsley's arrest, the man who made out the affidavit upon which the search warrant to Owsley's lab was granted, was his old shifty-eyed friend Krusco, "who seemed to enjoy the cops-and-robbers aspect the most," who seemed most interested in putting Frank Werber behind bars.

Poring over the records, the fact man found flat contradictions between the affidavit Krusco made out to obtain the warrant and Krusco's courtroom testimony. He charges that Krusco had deliberately misled the U.S. commissioner to get his warrant, that Krusco had lied to his government superiors just to get his crack at Owsley. "Indeed," Metzger told the court, "there can be little question that, had the agent accurately reported the facts in his affidavit, a search warrant would not have been issued."

45

In his affidavit Krusco said that one of Owsley's associates told him "that he would be able to provide approximately one gram of LSD tablets, that he would be manufacturing LSD tablets at the laboratory." But in his testimony Krusco said Owsley's friend had said, "I asked him if he could obtain some acid. He said that at that time he had nothing but he was going up to the laboratory that afternoon and would make an attempt to obtain some LSD for me." Analyzing Krusco's affidavit and his statements under oath in court, Metzger concluded there was nothing in what Owsley's friend had told Krusco that provided "probable cause" to believe the place where he was going was a place where LSD was manufactured. The man told Krusco he was going to the lab. He did not say he would be manufacturing LSD at the lab. "Had the facts been revealed in Krusco's affidavit," Metzger said, "there can be little doubt that a warrant would not have been issued" and that Owsley could not have been arrested.

The allegations against Krusco were damaging—so serious that the Court of Appeals for the Ninth Circuit ordered the United States to file a supplemental brief answering them. Interestingly, when it was submitted, the response did not argue that Krusco was lying, using the words "even if the statements [Krusco's] contained therein [in the affidavit] were false. . . ."

For a man like Kenny Krusco, scaling the totem pole of nark success, an embarrassment like that was a jolt to the solar plexus; his action even more embarrassing to the government, committed to keeping Owsley Stanley, acid prophet and Grateful Dead advocate, behind bars.

As a result of Metzger's plodding research, Kenny Krusco one day was called on the thick carpet in the U.S. district attorney's office and questioned about his tactics and inconsistencies.

But Kenny Krusco would weather the rabbit punch. He would personally even the score with the attorney who was playing games with his career. Nine months after Kenny Krusco left the room with that thick carpet he was in Michael Metzger's home in Sausalito, menacing the lawyer with his gun.

"Go ahead, Kenny," Michael Metzger said to him; "shoot me."

On May 15, 1970—two months after the courtroom humiliation of Kenny Krusco—a young man named Michael Ludwig was arrested for possession of marijuana. The arrest was made in Marin County. The arresting agency was the BNE.

Under penalty of perjury, in an affidavit, Michael Ludwig stated "that he was handcuffed and ordered to lie face down on the ground; that he complied with this order immediately and explicitly; that one of the agents kept waving a revolver at him; that this same agent began asking him various questions about himself and the use of marijuana; that he was without counsel at the time and refused to answer all questions; that this same agent then repeatedly struck him very hard on the head with his gun; that all the time he was lying in a handcuffed position with his face to the ground; that, handcuffed, he could make no action, overt or covert, toward the agent; that, his head to the ground, he could make no motion that could be construed as an attempt to escape; that the agent's action was unprovoked and unnecessary and was caused by his [Ludwig's] refusal to answer questions without benefit of counsel."

The young man identified the agent as Gerritt Van Raam. In court Gerritt Van Raam, he of the pearl-handled gun, did not deny hitting Michael Ludwig while he [Ludwig] was in a handcuffed position. But Gerritt Van Raam said Michael Ludwig threatened him by making a motion with his head.

The attorney who would represent Ludwig in court, whose sensibilities would boggle at the grand-guignol image of a prone and handcuffed man being pistol-whipped, was Michael Metzger.

Dialogue. Sandy White, ace nark informer, and her boy friend, Ted Donnelly. Subject: busting Santa Claus.

Sandy: *They want me to bust the Grateful Dead.*

Ted: *They do, why?*

Sandy: *I said I can't. They're my idols. They said, "Well, what the hell? Do it for the prosperity. At least you'll get their autograph." I said, "I don't want their autograph." If I bust them again, they'll go to jail.*

Ted: *They're good people.*

Sandy: *I know. I hate to do it. I'm torn.*

Ted: *Have they been busted before?*

Sandy: *Twice. One more time, and that's it.*

Ted: *Really?*

Sandy: *They always manage to get out of it. None of them are my cases.*

I don't have the balls to do it. I would be the outcast of every kid in the world. I couldn't do it. I keep on telling Elsberg, "But they're my idols."

Ted: *Tell them that's like busting Santa Claus and you can't bust Santa Claus.*

In the summer of 1970 Michael Metzger, armed with the Ludwig case, went after BNE agents Gerritt Van Raam and Robert Luca. He accused both men of perjury. The perjury charges shocked the court-room: a flagrant violation of all the nice-guy commandments of Playing the Game. Indeed, the district attorney, Joshua Thomas, would criticize Metzger for just that: for attacking an agent's character and not his memory. Thomas fumed, "To attack the memory [of agent Luca] is one thing; his capability to observe and recollect the events that occurred is one thing. But for an officer of this court to come out, under the circumstances of this case, and accuse a witness of committing perjury.... Your Honor, for that statement I would almost ask the court to hold Mr. Metzger in contempt. I really think that any attorney, whether he's representing a defendant or the people, has a certain duty to exercise responsibility and temperance in the statements that he makes, and for Mr. Metzger to feel justified in making statements like that, I think, is the height of irresponsibility."

Thomas's outburst was prompted by Metzger's charges that agent Luca's report, used to justify his entering Ludwig's apartment, was "a complete fabrication." Metzger said, "I think it should go into the record to show the quality and the nature of his testimony and his reliability as a witness—purely for the purpose of impeachment. I accuse him of direct perjury in this courtroom. He is lying, in my humble opinion, after reading and rereading the facts."

Notwithstanding the district attorney's fulminations, the judge agreed, saying of Luca's actions, "There is a discrepancy there.... I think the report can be received into evidence for impeachment purposes. There is a difference between the report and the testimony."

"Fine," Metzger told the judge. "That's all I'm interested in."

In the same case Metzger dissected the testimony of Gerritt Van Raam, who had claimed that an ordinary citizen, Wilbert Harris, had approached his agents and given them information about Ludwig. Metzger tracked Harris down, and Harris's testimony flatly contradicted Van Raam's.

Metzger's summation was a categorical indictment of narcotics enforcement tactics, with asterisked attention to the BNE and Gerritt Van Raam. "I respectfully submit," he said, "that the court try to put together the number of miracles that took place in the period of the BNE's investigation. And remember what Jack London said about miracles. 'You have to prove them.' This case is full of miracles. There are more 'in plain view's,' if you look at the police report, than I have ever seen in any ten cases put together. And you may reflect on the fact that this concept of 'plain view' has come into favor by police since some recent Supreme Court cases limiting the scope of searches. You never heard of 'plain view' three or four years ago. In this case every officer has 'plain view's from the beginning. They had 'plain view's of wallets lying open at the pictures of the defendants. They had people inviting them in and saying—taking them right to rooms full of marijuana that was 'in plain view.' They drove up a driveway there; somebody ran away, and it was 'in plain view.' The door was open with the lights on, and it was 'in plain view.' If you add up the number of 'plain view's in this case, you would really get an idea of how the police have become educated by recent cases. And I want to point out one other thing about this case that makes it a somewhat unique case—and I would really appreciate it if the court would bear in mind that this has been one case that hasn't gone through, bim-bam, you know, two hours. This is one of the few cases where witnesses—"

Joshua Thomas, the assistant district attorney, interrupted Metzger. He didn't want to listen to any more of this. He wanted to be excused. He had, he said, using Matthew O'Connor's ploy, "appointments to keep."

The judge admonished him. "We're not through yet," he said.

Metzger continued, "This is one of the cases where disinterested witnesses have come in, like Mr. Harris. Frankly, I was completely lulled as far as Mr. Harris is concerned. I assumed all along the police were telling the truth in their affidavits. And it just occurred to me late in the case that he ought to be interviewed. And Mr. Thomas is going to say that Mr. Harris was lying for some reason or another, lying under oath, but that his police officers were never lying. He heard Mr. Harris's testimony. There is an example about officer credibility in this case. There is a citizen who's not facing time in jail—has no reason to lie—who unequivocally says that what these officers testified to in this court and

49

what they put in their search warrant is untrue. But, if you will just bear in mind, if you will look over the search warrants and affidavits the police used as supports that are marked in evidence, and count up the number of miracles, the number of really fortuitous things that happened to these police, you are going to come to one conclusion, if nothing else: *that the Bureau of Narcotics Enforcement, represented by Mr. Gerritt Van Raam, is one of the luckiest bunch of police officers the sun has ever shone on.*"

The die had been cast. In a matter of a few months Metzger, within the legally sticky courtroom arena where the stakes were high, had threatened the cop careers of three of LaRocca's best customers.

But Gerry Van Raam, though Michael Metzger didn't know it, was not going to let him get away with calling him a liar, calling Bob Luca a liar, calling Kenny Krusco a liar.

On September 24 Douglas Edward Rambo was arrested in Mill Valley in Marin County for possession of marijuana. The arresting officer was Gerritt Van Raam. In an affidavit, under penalty of perjury, Rambo described what happened: "At the sheriff's office in San Rafael agent Van Raam offered to procure the release of Rambo on his own recognizance if he would help Van Raam *get Metzger*. Van Raam stated to Rambo that he, Van Raam, wanted to get Metzger. Rambo agreed to help Van Raam, and pursuant to said agreement Van Raam procured a release for Rambo upon his own recognizance a few hours after [he had] brought [him] to jail, without bringing him to court. After his release from jail, Rambo was driven by agent Van Raam back to his automobile in Mill Valley. During said trip, agent Van Raam continued to discuss with Rambo his plan to get Metzger and stated on several occasions his desire to do so."

(The reporter asked Van Raam about his alleged deal with Rambo. "When we arrest people," Van Raam said, "certainly we try to ask them, Do you want to cooperate? And we may ask them about specific individuals. Generally we ask them about a whole bunch of individuals."

("But you asked him about Metzger," the reporter said.

("I probably did," Van Raam answered.)

When, a few months later, the plan to "get Metzger" unfolded, a BNE agent drove an informer to Michael Metzger's home. The BNE agent who did the driving that night was Robert Luca—"purely for the purpose of impeachment," Metzger had said—who would be inside

Metzger's home in a few nights, rifling through his possessions, frantically searching for contraband.

On September 29, 1970, at a preliminary hearing before Judge F. J. DeLarios, Michael Metzger accused Gerritt Van Raam, to his face, of perjury. The charge came five days after Van Raam had asked Douglas Rambo to help him to "get Metzger." By making that charge and by making it as skillfully as he did, Michael Metzger unleashed a chain of events that almost cost Gerritt Van Raam his job and reputation and almost cost Metzger a jail term.

The charge involved the sale of a package of LSD to a BNE agent from San Diego named John Miles. Gerritt Van Raam was the only other agent present and one of the arresting officers.

Agent Miles testified that around July 23, 1970, he had made contact with a girl in San Diego named Toni Radford and had made a deal with her to buy some LSD. On July 25 Miles and the girl flew to San Francisco International Airport, where the buy was to take place. At the airport the girl told Miles to wait for her. She walked down a concourse, where she met a man named Gerald Lipinski. Some twenty minutes later she returned and met Miles at an airport bar. She opened a purse and removed "a brown-and-white paper bag." Miles identified himself and arrested her. Since Miles had not seen what took place between Lipinski and the girl, no charges could be made against Lipinski—based on Miles's testimony.

But Van Raam testified that he had followed the girl and had seen her meet Lipinski inside the terminal. He testified that he then saw them go outside the terminal to a Jaguar sedan. He testified that Gerald Lipinski leaned into the Jaguar and handed the girl a "white cylindrical object with brown-and-orange markings on it." This same object was later found to contain LSD. Van Raam provided the missing link between the girl and Lipinski. Without his testimony Lipinski could not have been charged with anything.

Metzger charged that Van Raam's version of the events was "a complete fabrication and was patently perjurious." To put punch behind his charges, he pulled an astounding courtroom ploy: the unvarnished truth. The girl, Metzger said, did in fact contact Gerald

51

Lipinski concerning a sale of LSD. Arrangements really were made to take "the buyer" to the San Francisco airport.

On July 25 Lipinski, with the LSD in his possession, drove to the airport. He got there about two hours before the girl and her buyer. Since Lipinski had never met the buyer, he didn't want to keep the LSD on his person or in his car. He knew that, if the buyer was a nark, there would be searches. So Lipinski placed the package of LSD in a public locker. He went back to his car and left the key in it. Then he waited for the plane. He watched the girl and Miles as they came down the ramp.

He talked to the Radford girl in the concourse and told her he didn't like the looks of the buyer accompanying her. He thought he looked like a nark. He told her to go back to the buyer and ask him to front the money (hand over the cash before any acid was shown). The buyer refused. Lipinski told the girl he didn't want any part of the whole thing. He was sure the guy was a nark. He and the girl started walking out of the terminal. She argued. She thought Miles was not a nark, and she needed the money and wanted to make the deal herself. Fine, Lipinski said, if she wanted to make the deal herself, that was her business. But he wasn't going to go near that locker. The two walked over to the Jaguar, and he gave the girl the locker key. She went to the locker, removed the LSD from it, went back to the bar to meet Miles, and was arrested there. Lipinski never went back inside the terminal but drove away. He was arrested near the Golden Gate Bridge.

"At no point," Metzger said, "did Lipinski ever hand any bag whatsoever to the girl. The simple fact of the matter is that the agents failed to observe the locker scene. Had there been proper surveillance, Lipinski would have been seen putting the bag into the locker and Radford would have been seen taking the bag from the locker. With such observation the agents could legitimately have put together a fairly strong case against Lipinski. The truth is that they failed to see this, and Van Raam took it upon himself to manufacture the evidence needed to make a case against Lipinski."

Metzger's argument was strengthened by the testimony of Van Raam's fellow BNE agent Miles, who said that, moments after she was arrested, Toni Radford told him she had taken the acid from a locker and Lipinski was her accomplice.

But this was not just another accusation. This one had an extra bite. Prior to the hearing and the testimony, Metzger met with Judge DeLarios in his chamber. Metzger told the judge that, if testimony followed the police reports, perjury would take place in his courtroom. DeLarios made the following decisions: If Van Raam testified that he saw Lipinski hand the girl a "white cylindrical object," Lipinski and the girl would be directed to take lie-detector tests. If they passed their tests, the judge said, he would direct Van Raam to take a lie-detector test.

After the hearing ended that day, Michael Metzger, once again striking blows for the people, was pleased. He had his quarry trapped, he thought. The quarry was a familiar one, a throwback to the Hogan days: a public official.

The stakes were high for Gerry Van Raam. His career had already sustained one strike when he resigned under a cloud from the San Francisco police department. Now, if Lipinski and the girl passed their lie-detector tests, his reputation, his career, could be put on the line again. All because of this man Metzger, who seemed to find some crucial symbolic commentary in the way he did his best to maintain law and order.

But the counselor didn't realize in the pursuit of his quarry that he was hunting a hunter, a man whose agents were scouring the jails trying to find someone . . . anyone . . . who would sell them Michael Metzger.

It is relatively easy to buy men in jails, where convicts desperately grab for freedom by doing policemen favors or copping information. That these jailed men turned down their freedom rather than sell Michael Metzger to the BNE attests to his respect as a lawyer.

While Lipinski and Toni Radford took turns taking their lie tests, the agents of the BNE were busy making deals to "get Metzger."

On October 6, 1970, Metzger received a letter from Timothy W. Butler, an inmate of the Mendocino County jail in Ukiah. Butler wrote him that a BNE agent was "trying to make a deal" with several inmates who would receive "special consideration if they will help in supplying information which could lead to your arrest."

Around October 6, BNE agent William Filben visited Mendocino County jail inmate Michael Aylwin, awaiting trial on an LSD charge. Aylwin had been arrested by the BNE.

"Well," Aylwin says, "Filben came up and started talking about the hopelessness of my winning my case, you know, me doing about five to life in state prison. Well, I wanted to talk to Filben about my case because I knew that we were about to have a search-and-seizure hearing coming up, and I knew that he had smashed through the door and several other things, and I was trying to reason with him, you know, to get him to try to tell the truth."

Did he propose a deal to you? Aylwin was asked.

"Correct. What he said was that, if I would be willing to give him enough information to bust the attorney, Michael Metzger, or give him any kind of information that would lead to Metzger's arrest, he would personally guarantee that I would never go to prison."

"What was your reaction to that?"

"First of all, I was shocked, you know. I mean, I just—it shocked me that the whole thing would come down. But then, after the initial response, I asked him, you know, what he thought I could do? And he said that he thought that I was close enough to Metzger and I had been to his house and I ought to be able to give him enough information to make a bust on Metzger."

"Did you give him any information?"

"No, I didn't," Aylwin said.

"Did you have any information to give him?"

"No, I didn't."

On November 10, 1970, Christopher McDougal was arrested, allegedly for selling LSD to an undercover agent of the Federal Bureau of Narcotics and Dangerous Drugs. After his arrest, McDougal was taken by federal narcotics agents to the office of the BNE in the Federal Office Building. That's where he learned that the feds were also in the bidding for Michael Metzger. In an affidavit, under penalty of perjury, McDougal described what happened next: "During this interrogation, I was asked whether I could give the narcotics agents information about Michael Metzger. I was told further that, if I could give information about any of these people, I would be given lenient treatment from the courts in my case and bail would be substantially reduced. I told the narcotics agents that I had no information about Metzger except that I knew he was an attorney in the Bay Area."

On November 18, 1970, a Berkeley attorney, James H. Newhouse, was at the Alameda Municipal Court representing three clients. Gerrit Van Raam was a witness for the prosecution. Before the hearing, Newhouse told the district attorney, Wright Morton, the circumstances surrounding Van Raam's testimony in the Lipinski case. "I further informed Mr. Morton," Newhouse swore in an affidavit, "that, based on my experience with agent Van Raam, I was distrustful of his testimony, as were numerous attorneys who also had experience with agent Van Raam's testimony." The affidavit continues: "At 4 P.M., during the recess of the preliminary hearing, agent Van Raam spoke to me and informed me that, if I related the circumstances of Metzger's case to anyone else as I had to Mr. Morton, he would sue me. I suggested that he be my guest. He said, 'Don't you worry about that, and Metzger will get his, too.' "

In early October, as the BNE was searching for a man who'd sell Michael Metzger, Toni Radford took a polygraph examination, passing it with flying colors. The test, by George W. Harman of San Francisco, showed without doubt that she was telling the truth.

On October 21 Gerald Lipinski took the Harman polygraph. The result that came back was "inconclusive"—meaning not that Lipinski had lied but that test conditions were "faulty." Metzger sent Lipinski to Chicago, to take the polygraph from the man who invented the machine, John Reid, the ultimate lie-detector authority in the world. Lipinski took the Reid test on October 27. The test showed conclusively that Lipinski was telling the truth.

That left Van Raam.

On November 19 Judge F. J. DeLarios of the Municipal Court of San Francisco sent Gerritt Van Raam's superior, Matthew O'Connor, excerpts from the two polygraph reports. The judge reminded O'Connor of his directive telling Van Raam to take a lie test.

On December 1 Metzger wrote Matthew O'Connor, telling him he was aware Judge DeLarios had sent him the excerpts and asking "whether or not agent Van Raam is willing to be examined by an independent polygraph examiner." Metzger gallantly offered to pay the costs.

Matthew O'Connor, the bureaucrat with the pink cheeks, received that letter on Thursday, December 3.

That same day John Storer, head of the state of California BNE, announced that he had ordered agent Van Raam to take the lie test.

Curiously enough, it was also on that day that Gerritt Van Raam found the informer who would sell him Michael Metzger. The informer was an ex-convict, a former heroin addict, a gun freak who had recently been busted in possession of an arsenal of weapons. The price for Michael Metzger, a nark later admitted, was $50. The informer admitted a bonus: dismissal of all charges.

Dialogue. Ted Donnelly, BNE informer Sandy White's boy friend, and Judy Simmons, BNE informer and Sandy White's girl friend. Subject: a schizo trip.

Ted: *Yeah, but how in hell can you say, like we said last night, that you and Sandy smoke or whatever, grass and hash and speed or whatever you guys use? And I know both of you use it.*

Judy: *Yeah.*

Ted: *But how can you go out and turn around and fuck people for using it?*

Judy: *It's a schizo trip. A lot of it is. And there are a lot of people I can't do it to, and there are a lot of things I will not do it for.*

Ted: *Yeah, you say it's against the law, and you still go ahead and smoke or whatever. Why do you really do it?*

Judy: *You want to know the real reason?*

Ted: *Yeah.*

Judy: *Experience.*

Ted: *Experience in fucking over people?*

Judy: *Well, that's part of it.*

The way Marin County narcotics agent Al Teixeira finally told it, Gerry Van Raam came up to his office one day—the same day his boss ordered him to take the polygraph—and just happened to bump into the man who would sell Michael Metzger. The man was Gerald Noel McDonald, thirty, a chunky, bearded professional U.S. Customs informer who had been paid $18,000 for services and information rendered the government between April and September of 1970.

Gerry McDonald was a soldier of fortune, a man who talked about violence all the time, who was "into a 'Terry and the Pirates' " trip, as an attorney would later say. He was a bounty hunter, a professional informer for indiscriminate hire, who was being paid $18 a day for information provided the Customs people (besides his $18,000)—$18 on the very day in July when, surrounded by an arsenal of weapons, he was arrested by two narcotics agents who did not know of his valued government connections. The agents were Gerry Van Raam and Al Teixeira. But weird things always seemed to be happening to McDonald, crawling around under thunderclouds of intrigue and spine-chilling mystery. His best friend disappeared one day, and

McDonald wound up with his friend's wife, inheriting the man's yacht. When his friend's body was found, McDonald was the sole prosecution witness against the man who was charged with his murder. After the sale of Michael Metzger, Gerry McDonald would himself shortly disappear, last seen near Salt Lake City, Utah, driving another friend's car. The other friend had vanished into thin air the week earlier.

On that Thursday, December 3, as Al Teixeira would later tell it in court: "Well, McDonald came into the office, and he wanted—he came in. I didn't see him when he came in. I didn't even know he was there, and agent Van Raam came back to my office and said, 'Hey, I want you to come up and hear something.'" According to Teixeira, McDonald told him and Van Raam that in May he had been at Metzger's home with two other men and had seen marijuana and cocaine "but never in large amounts." "McDonald," Teixeira said, "stated that Mr. Metzger would go down some stairs with some keys, come back up, bring little bits of narcotics on a plate, and would put it on the table, and people there would partake of it."

Teixeira admitted later that, in fact, McDonald had given him this same information in September. Why wasn't action taken against Metzger in September? Why did Teixeira wait until the day Gerry Van Raam, on the brink of his lie test, told him in the office that he wanted him to "hear something"? Teixeira would dodge that question on the witness stand until the judge, saying it "loomed large," asked it: "Why did you wait till December to pursue this lead? Or why did you pursue it at all, if the latest information you had related to the presence of narcotics in May?"

Teixeira's answer: "Never got around to it at the time, I suppose."

Did Teixeira and Van Raam discuss the lie test that Van Raam faced? "Yes," Teixeira would admit. "He didn't really come out and say anything. What he said was—and just common knowledge—that some judge in San Mateo County wanted Mr. Van Raam to take a lie test."

Did Van Raam ever say he wanted to "get Metzger"? "Absolutely not," Teixeira said. Interestingly, months later, during the hearing of another case in Los Angeles, Gerald McDonald, the informer, would tell two attorneys "that Van Raam had said to McDonald that he hated Metzger, wanted to get Metzger, and would see that all of the criminal charges pending against McDonald would be dismissed against him if he could get any information whatsoever that would aid agents in arresting Metzger."

Was there a deal made with McDonald to drop the charges against him for his help? First Teixeira said, "We didn't specifically tell him." Pressed, Teixeira said, "I had stated to Mr. McDonald that, all right, he was arrested by me. He had a case pending. I told him that, if he would be an informer for me, I would do what I could. I couldn't promise him nothing, and that's exactly what I said." (Two months after McDonald had sold Metzger, the district attorney, meeting with law enforcement officials, decided to drop all charges against him. The officials? Agents Van Raam and Teixeira.)

(When the reporter asked Van Raam about the charges against McDonald that had been dropped, he said: "We didn't have anything to do with dropping the charges against McDonald."

("But you did go to the D.A.'s office with Teixeira days afterwards, right?"

("Yeah, well, we go there frequently."

("But you didn't discuss the McDonald case?"

("No. In fact, I was mad that the case was dismissed. We weren't consulted at all. It was an independent action by the district attorney."

("You mean you argued against the charges being dismissed?"

("It was already done when I found out about it. We went in and, so to speak, raised hell.")

In that meeting between Van Raam and Teixeira and McDonald on December 3 the problem was: How to set Metzger up? The answer was simple. Metzger was an attorney. McDonald would ask to be his client. Who came up with the idea? "Van Raam and myself," Teixeira was to say. "We just asked McDonald to see if he could go over and see Metzger," Teixeira said. To see Metzger where? "At his house." Why at his house? "Well, we wanted to see, while he was there, if he would see any of those narcotics again." The meeting broke up that day. McDonald was told to come back the next day at four o'clock.

The next day McDonald called Metzger from Teixeira's office. Van Raam was there, taping the call. McDonald began the conversation with the informer's bread and butter, the Duke-In name, asking if Metzger had heard from a mutual friend. He told Metzger he needed help with a case and asked to see him. Metzger said, according to Teixeira, "He would be glad to take the case and stated that he was going to Crete the first part of the week following." Metzger told McDonald he was busy and suggested he see one of his law partners.

"I'd like to drop over by your house," McDonald said.

"You know the weekend is coming up," Metzger said, "and you know you can make it over to the office next week."

But Van Raam and Teixeira couldn't wait that long. Metzger was going to Crete. If the plan they suggested to McDonald was going to yield its victim, they had to work fast. McDonald was told by the two to meet them at seven o'clock that night. They'd see whether they could get Metzger then. The rendezvous was to be at a motel near Sausalito, and a Fargo, a transmitting device, was planted on McDonald.

McDonald was driven to Metzger's house from the motel by Teixeira, Van Raam, and BNE agent Robert Luca, whom Metzger had accused of perjury in March. "McDonald went up to the front door," Teixeira would say, "and knocked. You could hear him knocking, and you could hear him come down and walk around, and I heard him say 'Mike' a couple of times, and then he came back to the car. He said, 'I can see Mike up there. He's barbecuing. He's got a girl. But he won't answer the door.' So we said forget it." Forget it, that is, for the night. McDonald was told to meet them again the next day, at the Marina in San Francisco.

The meeting was at 1:30 Saturday afternoon. It was the same crew—Teixeira, Van Raam, and Luca—but this time, coincidentally, there was a federal agent there, too. "But it wasn't prearranged or anything," Teixeira would say. After a fifteen-minute delay McDonald once again was driven to Metzger's house. What was the subject of conversation during those fifteen minutes? According to Teixeira, nothing: "We just sat there and looked at boats."

McDonald was again rigged with the Fargo. The agents were parked in a nearby driveway, eavesdropping. This time Metzger let McDonald in. What happened inside the house? Teixeira, who was listening to the Fargo, couldn't hear too much. "It was kind of broken. The Fargo wasn't working good. We could hear some talk, and then it would go dead."

But an oral statement that McDonald gave Teixeira and Van Raam, and that Van Raam taped, gives a detailed picture of what McDonald claimed took place inside.

McDonald: I walked up to the door and said hello and walked inside, and Metzger asked me if I wanted any orange juice, and his three girls were in the house. And I approached him like, like I, like we were talking with Mr. Van Raam, as to hiring him to represent me. And so we were talking, and at that time Mike got up and rushed off, walked off to a coat over by the wall, and pulled out a joint, a marijuana cigarette, and lit it.

Teixeira: Exactly what did he do with it?

McDonald: Oh, he just got up and walked over to his jacket like he was going for a pack of cigarettes and pulled it out and sat down and blowed [*sic*] it.

Teixeira: Did he consume the whole thing?

McDonald: I didn't notice if he did. To my knowledge, he took the greatest percentage of it.

McDonald came out of the house and got into Luca's car. Teixeira and Van Raam, in another car, followed them to the Army Corps of Engineers building in Sausalito. McDonald then got into Van Raam's car, and, according to Teixeira, "when he came out and he got in the car with us, you could smell it [marijuana]. I was sitting in the back seat, and Luca said, 'Man, you smell him?' And I said, 'Yeah.' "

Now Van Raam and Teixeira had what they needed to bust Metzger: McDonald's contention—in return for the $50 and the bonus—that he had seen Metzger smoke a joint. But even now, strangely, they had problems. It wasn't easy to procure this search warrant.

Josh Thomas, the assistant district attorney who had branded Metzger "irresponsible" for calling Luca a liar, didn't want anything to do with this bust. Teixeira called Thomas Saturday night, hours after McDonald left Metzger, and asked his help in getting a search warrant. Thomas, according to Teixeira, refused. "He [Thomas] said he was tied up and didn't have the time. He was currently involved in a very heavy case load in Solano County, and he could not take the time to do it."

Teixeira didn't much like it but decided "I'm not going to argue with the man." He finally got his search warrant, early Sunday afternoon. By that time Van Raam had met him at the sheriff's office. Van Raam, Teixeira said, was "right there" during the difficulties with the search warrant. He was "right there" again when, warrant in hand, the raiding party drove from the sheriff's office to the Sausalito police station.

But as the narks pulled into their cars to head for Metzger's home, Van Raam, who had been "right there" all along, stayed behind. Why did Gerry Van Raam, who had told several people he wanted to "get Metzger," stay behind at the critical moment? "He didn't want to go," Teixeira said.

The question was asked in court: "Did he tell you the reason he did not want to go to the arrest was that he felt he might be open to

criticism? Because Metzger had put pressure on him to take a lie test?"
A D.A.'s objection saved Teixeira from that thorny question. "I asked
him if he wanted to go," Teixeira repeated, "and he said no."

(Months later the reporter pressed the point with Van Raam.

("The point that I can't understand is: You were there all along, in
getting the search warrant, meeting McDonald, and then you don't go
to the bust."

("Well, I was working on another case," Van Raam said, "but I
specifically didn't go there."

("The question is, Why?"

("Motivation? So I wouldn't be accused of what you are accusing
me of?"

("I'm not accusing you of anything. I'm just throwing a question at
you."

("No," Van Raam said, "what I have been accused of, the vendetta
thing. . . . Let's face it. *Like a doctor doesn't work on his own son.*")

As the raiding party, in a winding cop-caravan, left the Sausalito
police station, Al Teixeira was leading the way. Al Teixeira, who said
Gerry Van Raam was his "father" in the narking business. Al Teixeira,
who dreamed one day of becoming a BNE agent.

As Al Teixeira was hand-carrying his search warrant to the bust,
Gerry McDonald, professional informer, was lolling in his murdered
friend's boat. Two months later he would tell two attorneys that, in fact,
he never saw Michael Metzger smoking a joint.

As the posse neared his plush $100,000 home with the heated swim-
ming pool, Michael Metzger was having a drink. He was tired (he had
spent the weekend with his three children). He wasn't worried about
anything. Some of his friends, hearing that Gerry Van Raam had to
take his lie-detector test, warned him, "Be careful, Mike; you'll get
busted."

"Bullshit, you guys," Metzger would say, "that's paranoiac. I'm not
doing anything illegal."

He was settling down with a book when he heard the knock on the
door. The book was Ramsey Clark's *Crime in America.* He went to the
door, opened it, and blinked. Wow!

Al Teixeira did the talking. Behind him stood a phalanx of narks and of uniformed cops. Michael Metzger flashed on the warnings that his friends had given him. So this was it. The posse had come for him.

"Paranoia," he had said.

Shit.

Naiveté.

He looked at the agents on his landing, standing around the redwood home he had bought to free himself from New York's jungle, and he thought: It takes them a whole army to do this. His mind still couldn't absorb the fact it took nearly a dozen state / local / fed agents, backed by uniformed officers of the Sausalito police department, to do this. To bust a lawyer, a former D.A. He scanned the faces in the posse and saw a galaxy of his court cases. He knew most of these men. They had been his cross-examination victims. Krusco, whom he had called a liar. Luca, the BNE man he had accused of perjury. Teixeira, boy wonder, creepily crawling for his guru.

But where was the guru? As the posse fanned out around the house, sneakily keeping him in sight, beady eyes peering, he understood why the guru hadn't come. Why—after all the foreplay with Rambo and the other guys in jail—Van Raam couldn't come for the climax. He had a twinge of compassion for Gerry: It must have been tough to stay away. But the guys in this posse were too polite, too gentlemanly, observing some foreordained protocol. He realized that somewhere, sitting around some fluorescent neon campsite, the posse members, deputized and armed, had said, "We won't make any mistakes. We won't give him any outs." He knew then that, when these men left, he would leave with them in handcuffs.

He knew that, if you are a nark, playing this kind of deadly game, you don't come into this place, to his place, in the climate of the polygraph, and walk away without the victim. The stakes are too high. He knew that they knew: If they left here on this night without him, Michael Metzger would be armed with his most potent public argument against nark excess, about the groundless prosecution of innocent men. "When I looked at the search warrant, I couldn't fucking believe it. I couldn't believe they had gone that far. They had made it up. It was based on blatant perjury. It fucking floored me. I had underestimated them. All the things I said to my friends came back in great detail, my pooh-poohing the possibility of this. This! They just busted me! Wow! I had really been foolish. I had blessed the bastards with the tiniest amount of ethical practice. The tiniest amount was giving them too much credit."

An hour passed. They were lovingly fingering his dirty laundry, spreading his soiled underwear on a table, item by item. They were taking his curtains down, pulling the rods apart, holding them to the light, looking for pills. They were taking the Ramsey Clark book and splitting its pages, peering under the binding. They noticed his sunken swimming pool's year-round heating and wondered whether anything could be hidden there.

He asked whether he might wander around the house "to keep an eye on you" since he was not under arrest. Teixeira said he might. An agent followed him around as he followed the other agents around. He was given momentary comfort by the expressions on the faces of the Sausalito policemen, overwhelmed by what was happening. They kept calling him "Sir"; they politely asked for a drink of water. They seemed to have a hard time accepting him as a suspected criminal. They remembered him in another context: Michael Metzger had given them the keys to his house a long time ago, asking them to go inside when his burglar alarm went off.

Luca, he noticed, was a man possessed—scurrying from one room to another, angry that the search was yielding nothing, rummaging through his books feverishly. Krusco said nothing, glared at him, stayed steps behind, made sure he wouldn't escape.

About an hour after the search began Al Teixeira came out of the bedroom and placed Michael Metzger under arrest. He seemed pleased. He had a knapsack in his hand and a fistful of what appeared to be weed. There was more weed in the knapsack. Metzger laughed. It was a belly laugh that resounded throughout the house. "I knew they'd resort to the plant, and this was it. I took a look at that knapsack, and I couldn't stop laughing. I had never used the damn thing. It was brand-new. I had bought it because of a weakness in my character. I was talking about camping and health, but it was always talk. I never got around to it. I had satisfied my obsession by buying camping things. The knapsack had been a constant reminder. You're always talking about it, Metzger, but you never do it. I couldn't stop laughing because I couldn't believe they'd resort to a ploy as crude as this."

There was jubilation among the agents. For the first time since he had come into the house, Kenny Krusco was talking. Metzger was his. He had himself a man under his arrest.

"Get over there," Krusco yelled, "get over there." He pushed Metzger up against a kitchen cabinet.

"Cut it out," Metzger said.

Krusco looked at Metzger, pulled his jacket back, and showed him the gun on his hip.

"Go ahead, Kenny," Metzger said; "shoot me."

Krusco had him spread-eagled against the wall. He asked him for his wallet and his keys. One of the keys was an odd-shaped size.

"Ah-ha," Krusco said, "what do we have here? This looks like it's for opening vending machines." Metzger regained his sense of humor. He was laughing again. The son of an industrial magnate was being accused of having a key that would open a vending machine: of being a petty thief. The key was for a suitcase.

Some time later in his garage they found a safe. The safe contained 4½ ounces of marijuana and hashish and ¼ ounce of cocaine. Teixeira threw his hands into the air. The raid was over. Michael Metzger, former district attorney, was accused of a felony. He was driven first, in handcuffs, to the Sausalito police station, then, still in handcuffs, to the Marin County sheriff's office.

Luca drove. "They made sure to keep me in handcuffs. The handcuffs were cutting off my circulation. Every now and then Luca made sure he stepped on the brakes too hard. I'd get jostled and hit my head against the dash." At the Marin County sheriff's office he was booked and fingerprinted, and his mug shot was taken. "Take some extras," he heard an agent say. "We'll need souvenirs." The minute he got inside the office Teixeira ran to a telephone, trembling with excitement, and dialed a number. "We got him! We got him!" he yelled.

That night Michael Metzger was free on bond, facing decades in jail. He now knew what the word "Kafkaesque" was all about. His metamorphosis was complete: from prosecutor, to defender, to defendant. The defendant needed an attorney like Michael Metzger to remain a free man.

When he got home that night, he found that the agents had left behind the knapsack with marijuana in it that they had planted. It was his final pale laugh of the evening. The contraband that had led to his arrest had been left behind on the living-room couch.

That night Al Teixeira met his "father" at the family hearth: LaRocca's, the bad-vibes bar where Vic Damone tunes sugar-coated the air. How did it happen that hours after Metzger's arrest Al Teixeira met Gerry Van Raam at their mutually favored watering hole? Was there a prearrangement? Teixeira would be asked that question in court, and he would get rattled. Finally, Judge Joseph J. Wilson, his patience gone, asked it: "Was there some arrangement to meet?"

"No," Teixeira said, "there was not no arrangement [*sic*]."

"There was not no arrangement [*sic*]?"

Van Raam, Teixeira said, "just happened" to be there.

Courtroom testimony of ace nark informer Sandy White. Subject: cowboy boots.

Q: *You had a conversation with Pat Wolfe* [an undercover narcotics agent]?

A: *Yes.*

Q: *Tell us that conversation.*

A: *I asked him why he wore such pointed, extremely pointed cowboy boots.*

Q: *What did he say?*

A: *He said, "They are good for kicking in doors."*

Q: *Did you say anything to that?*

A: *I said, "Oh, do you kick down a lot of doors?"*

Q: *What did he say?*

A: *He said, "Yeah!"*

Attorneys' toilets were flushing all over the Bay Area, the joke went, after the Metzger arrest. Bootleg copies of the Metzger mug shot were the hottest items around the Hall of Justice since *Playboy*'s first mons veneris issue.

Michael Metzger found himself most troubled, not by the bust itself, but by the lack of public reaction to it. "People avoided the whole issue like the plague. That really hurt me. It was an obvious railroad job, an obvious injustice, but most people didn't give a shit. Part of it was due to the fact that people didn't have all the details. You have to know the whole interweaving fabric of the thing to know what happened. But the main reason is that people are too cynical. They figured: 'Well, if you want to attack that hard, you have to accept the consequences.' So my arrest was 'the consequences,' and according to that logic I brought the whole thing down upon myself. A lot of lawyers I knew just backed off and became very neutral. They were waiting to see who would win."

Those who know him say this was a most difficult period in Metzger's life. "He was really fucked up," says his friend Phil Ryan. "His whole existence was threatened. He had devoted his life to the law, becoming a really brilliant lawyer, sinking everything into that one basket, and now finding it all—disbarment, prison, the whole trip—in jeopardy. And we're not talking about any charismatically outgoing guy, a sportsman, or a playboy. We're talking about a guy who sank a lot of his frustrations into the study of the law."

He began the hunt for a lawyer to represent him in court (he'd been stung by a partner's initial reaction: "How is this going to affect our business?") and talked to Ryan about a choice. "Well, it was clear that I couldn't be his lawyer," Ryan says. "He and I were close friends, and I couldn't, really, direct him. He needed a good, tough, respected lawyer who would brook no nonsense."

The choice was Patrick Sarsfield "Butch" Hallinan, in his thirties, the son of one of the greatest lawyers in San Francisco's history, Vincent M. (Big Vince) Hallinan, still active in the firm at the age of seventy-four. The legendary Big Vince, the product of a Jesuit education, one side of his face paralyzed by an old gridiron injury, still ranks with the greatest lawyers in America; a man who once one-upped Percy Foreman, F. Lee Bailey, and Melvin Belli on the same television program (he called Belli "Belly"). Big Vince, a very tough *hombre*, once the Progressive candidate for President, the victim of McCarthyite witch-hunting, once spent two years in a federal prison for what the government claimed was income-tax evasion.

Butch Hallinan, in almost every respect, was his father's son, right down to the way he smiled. "Big Vince smiles crooked," Ryan says, "because part of his face is paralyzed. Butch smiles crooked because Big Vince smiles crooked." Along with his brother, Kayo, Butch Hallinan cut a mean swath through legal circles, where there is no argument that Butch Hallinan has the most wicked right hand of any lawyer in the Bay Area.

Not only does he smile like his father, but he is also as colorful. In 1952 a high school boxing champion, he was in Ross General Hospital (in Marin County) recovering from a severe beating. His arm was broken in two places. He'd been mauled by two guys, he said, each weighing 200 pounds. He became a conscientious objector. ("That boy," his father said, "has the heart of a lion.") He married a rather attractive Mexican girl, but the marriage was annulled shortly after the wedding night. The girl's father said he discovered Butch's "radicalism and atheism." The whole Hallinan family was once arrested for participation in a civil rights demonstration.

When San Francisco's Mayor Joseph Alioto called his brother, Kayo, "a street punk and an extremist," Butch petitioned a judge to order the mayor to prove why his remarks were not in contempt of court. He once got into a shouting match with a judge, calling the judge a "nut" and a "little sadist." The outburst cost him five days in jail.

His haymaker style would be perfectly suited for Al Teixeira.

"Run that by me again," Teixeira would tell Butch in court, asking for a repetition of the question.

"I didn't mean to run that by you," Butch Hallinan said. "I'll try to hit you between the eyes this time."

He is a pipe-smoking, gnomish little man whose face looks as if it's taken its quota of upper cuts, but which also is that of a scholar. He once quit the law for three years to pursue a doctorate in anthropology. Everybody knew Butch Hallinan, and most people respected him. Even the people who did not respect him were afraid of him. His political views were not radical. "Butch is a civil-liberties liberal," Phil Ryan would say. He was undoubtedly hard-nosed enough to run the Metzger case his way, to be able to tell his client, if need be, to shove it.

But, if Michael Metzger, client, was pondering his attorney, so, it developed, was Gerry Van Raam. Four days after Metzger's arrest, when it appeared that Phil Ryan would be Metzger's choice, a tape-recording between Gerry McDonald, the $18,000-a-year informer, and Gerry Van Raam reveals this exchange:

Van Raam: Do you know anything about Mr. Ryan?

McDonald: He is one of Metzger's partners.

Van Raam: Do you know anything about him prior to that?

McDonald: The only thing I know about him is that, while he was going through law school, he had something to do with the Trident down in Sausalito. [*Ryan was that restaurant's manager.*]

Van Raam: Did you ever see him at the Trident?

McDonald: No, I didn't.

Metzger resolved, the week after his arrest, to keep the heat on nark tactics. He viewed his arrest, strategically, as an attempt by arrest to muddle the issue, to put him on the defensive, to make him expend his energies defending himself instead of crusading against narks. He was disturbed also by the intimidating effect his arrest seemed to have on other lawyers. "I'm going to watch how I talk to that guy [Van Raam]," one lawyer told him. "I don't want him coming to my place."

Three days after Metzger's arrest Van Raam told his superior, John Storer, BNE head for the state of California, he was refusing his order. He would not take the lie-detector test. He appealed Storer's order to the Attorney General of the state of California, who took it under advisement—meaning months would pass before a decision would be made.

The weekend after Michael Metzger's arrest Butch Hallinan, of the mighty right hand, went to a party.

Coincidentally, Gerry Van Raam would lead a raiding team of his BNE agents into that same party. But the posse got there too late. Butch Hallinan left just before Van Raam got there. He left because his wife, as Phil Ryan said, "took him by the ear and dragged him away." Her husband had created one of his classic scenes.

Butch Hallinan got pissed off and threw one of his fabled right hands at an assistant U.S. district attorney. The punch—columnist Herb Caen would describe it as "the most fantastic right cross you ever saw"—hit the mark. The assistant D.A., his eyes rolling, lay flat on his ass.

The D.A. flat on his ass was Jerry Eisenberg. Butch Hallinan, the conquering warrior, who had learned to be a good sport about his living-room KOs, lifted Eisenberg off the floor. A flaming Irishman, who is Jewish by marriage, Hallinan tried to smooth things over with an ethnic witticism. "Hey," he told the D.A., "don't we Jews have enough trouble without fighting each other?"

But the party had unnerved him. It was at the Mill Valley home of a young, easygoing, long-haired attorney who specialized in drug cases. Mark Susnow, twenty-nine, was also president of the San Francisco Federation of Young Democrats.

A week after Metzger's arrest Butch Hallinan, whose ring experience had taught him some things about sucker punching, was a bit wary. When, moments after he got there, a man he had never seen before walked up to him and started asking him detailed questions about the Metzger case, his radar showed a distinct bleep.

He told the man he didn't want to talk about it. When the man persisted, Butch Hallinan told him to "fuck off."

Half-joking, he went up to Susnow, pointed to the stockbroker-type, and said, "He's the informer."

Susnow didn't know the man either. He hadn't invited him to his party. The man showed up with a girl named Kathy Zaloz, a girl who had joined the Young Democrats only two months earlier. Susnow was a bit relieved when Kathy Zaloz left with her "boy friend" at about 10:30.

Al Teixeira would say, later, in court, "At approximately eleven:thirty on the eleventh of December, I received a telephone call from Gerritt Van Raam. He advised me that he had made contact with a confidential and reliable informer. The informer stated to Mr. Van Raam that he had been at a party and had seen, on the premises, at least nine persons smoking what he believed to be marijuana."

Butch Hallinan was uncannily right. The informer was, in fact, a stockbroker, Peter Gilbert, in his mid-twenties, a man who worked with Gerritt Van Raam because he believed the use of marijuana to be evil, a man who, Teixeira would say, "has given me information in the past that led to the arrest of at least ten persons and the seizure of at least twenty kilograms of marijuana and an ounce of cocaine."

Where did Gilbert "make contact" with Van Raam? Kathy Zaloz would say, later, "After we left the party, he went to LaRocca's Bar in North Beach," the place that is Gerry Van Raam's official hideout, the place where he bumped into Al Teixeira only hours after Metzger's arrest.

But the action quickly moved from LaRocca's to Susnow's house, where Teixeira teamed up with Van Raam, who brought Gilbert along. "I found the residence," Teixeira would say; "there were several cars parked on the front area of the street. The house was, in fact, a hillside. I could hear music coming from inside and could see shadows on the windows of the people milling around. Also, just as we drove up to the front of the house, there was a person staggering in the street who appeared to be under the influence of *something*."

The plot now was to send Gilbert back inside the house. "The guy came back around one:thirty," Susnow says. "I opened the door and told him the party was over. The guy pushed right past me and started looking around. I went after him, kind of grabbed him, and told him to get the hell out."

Teixeira said, "The informer did in fact go back inside the residence, was admitted, returned shortly, and stated there was an odor of marijuana smoke still on the premises."

Susnow says, "A moment later there was a knock on the door. I opened the shade and saw four men on the other side of the door. Either Teixeira or Van Raam said, 'We have reason to believe you've committed a felony.' Without warning, they kicked the door down."

A party guest, Ted Worchester, dating one of Susnow's secretaries, said, "Several people identified themselves as police officers and crashed through the door. They started pushing us down the stairs into the dining room. Mark asked whether they had a warrant. They pushed him aside and said they did."

"When I first looked out the door," Susnow says, "I didn't believe they were policemen. They looked like holdup men. Real bad karma."

Moments later Gerry Van Raam pushed Mark Susnow to a wall and handcuffed him.

"We're going to ruin your reputation," Van Raam said.

"Hey," Susnow said, "have you taken your lie-detector test yet?"

"I don't have to take it," Van Raam said.

"He kept looking around the place," Susnow says, "like he was looking for somebody."

The raiding party, it turned out, did not have a viable search warrant. "I asked to see the warrant," Susnow says, "and Van Raam put it on the kitchen table. At the bottom the judge's name was typed with a space left for his signature. But the signature wasn't there."

"Guess what," Susnow told the people in the room. "Van Raam has a warrant, but it isn't signed."

"I don't need a signature," Van Raam said; "I got the judge's permission."

"They were all over the house," Susnow says. "They were turning everything inside out. They had rifles out. The mood inside the place was okay, though. We figured, 'Well, fuck, they're on their trip. This is their trip.' Some people were strumming guitars."

As Mark Susnow looked at those rifles and found the handcuffs cramping his circulation, he remembered a client's experience with the BNE. "It was a horror story, really gothic. The guy told me they came into his house and put a gun up against his temple. Then they sat around for an hour, eating his food, drinking his beer, and watching his television. They were waiting for the judge to give them another warrant for another place.

"About an hour after they got there and started searching," Susnow says, "Teixeira came running into the living room, all excited. 'Look what I found. Look at this!' he said. He was holding a 'roach.' "

"I went into the kitchen area," Teixeira would say, "to check for other persons who might be in the residence . . ."

(Butch Hallinan, having picked his D.A. off the ground, was gone, passing the narks' headlights as he drove out.)

". . . and at the time," Teixeira said, "noticed in a dish, laying on the sink, two partially smoked suspected marijuana cigarettes."

"They searched us," Ted Worchester said, "kept us in the living room under guard a couple hours, and finally took us away."

The experience would play games with Mark Susnow's head. The day he was arraigned he had a jury trial and, in his final summation, told the jurors of his arrest. "This is no longer my America," Mark Susnow said, "this is no longer the country I grew up loving." He would leave the Young Democrats, alter his life style, and find his respect for the law fading. Within a year Mark Susnow was thinking of quitting his law practice. He was getting into music. He was trying to sing. He'd sit at his desk, still piled with affidavits and legal briefs. A tape recorder was pointed at him. He'd play the tape periodically and, a faraway look in his eyes, nod. The tape was the voice of Mark Susnow singing "Suzanne."

He'd sit at that desk, listening to the sound of his own voice, and one detail of that bad karma night would crystallize over and over again, flooding his consciousness. He was in handcuffs, and the circulation in his arms had been cut off, and he told Gerry Van Raam of his pain.

"Could you take 'em off a bit?" Mark Susnow asked.

And Gerritt Van Raam looked him squarely in the eyes, smiling, and said he had lost the key.

(Van Raam denies it. According to him, he had used another agent's handcuffs and said, "I don't have a key. You'll have to ask that other officer.")

After Mark Susnow's arrest most young lawyers in the Bay Area became harried victims of paranoia. Their fears were warranted. Gerry Van Raam wasn't through yet. He was, for instance, trying to set Michael Metzger up for another bust.

A few weeks after he was booked and handcuffed, not long after

Butch Hallinan missed the Van Raam party at the Susnow house,
Metzger got a letter from an inmate of the Mendocino County jail.

Dear Mike:

*It is urgent that I see you as soon as possible. I have great reason
to believe you are in imminent danger of another bust. I have great
reason to suspect the BNE is setting you up again, this time outside
Marin County.*

*Today, Chuck Hall, the BNE chemist who works under Van
Raam, mentioned various totally diabolical schemes to set you up.*

I told him he was crazy.

*He talked to me for over two hours. What the hell's going on
anyway? The BNE men keep insisting that I get you busted.*

*The BNE will let me walk if I agree to set you up. They're
planning to bust you. Van Raam will stop at nothing and from what
I hear from Hall, it's about to happen any day.*

Mike Aylwin

It was the second time the BNE tried to deal with Aylwin for
Metzger. Before Metzger's arrest, in October, it was BNE agent William
Filben who promised to drop all charges if he'd help the BNE nail
Metzger.

A few days after Metzger's arrest Hall came to see Aylwin. "We
talked about a whole bunch of chemical stuff, and then he said that they
had the goods on Metzger, you know. They had him firm, and he said
there was a running battle between Van Raam and Metzger, and that's
about all he said at the time."

Then, a week later, Hall came back to see Aylwin again. This time
Aylwin was only a few days away from his trial. "First of all Hall came
up here, and he told me that he had been talking to the district attorney
and the D.A. had been interviewing witnesses for my case all week long
and that they had come up with at least ten different ways of convicting
me during the trial. He said that it was completely and totally hopeless
for me to even consider winning the trial. Then he told me he was
interested in getting Metzger again. I think his exact words were, 'We
believe you have enough information to set Metzger up in a bust

outside Marin County.' And I asked him, 'What do you mean by out of Marin County?' And he said, 'Well, anybody that gets busted in Marin County isn't a bust at all because the courts are too lenient.' Then he said Gerry Van Raam wanted to get Metzger on a bust out of Marin County, hopefully Sonoma or Mendocino or San Francisco County, something like that. He said that if I arranged for Metzger to get busted again, he would see to it that I was on the street before my trial began. He said that he wanted me to contact Metzger immediately and ask him to represent me at my trial. And to tell him that I had the base chemicals for LSD and cocaine and that I would give him these base chemicals in payment. I told him he was crazy, that Metzger would never go for anything like that. Hall said that, see—he told me that first of all he didn't know too much about it. He said that Van Raam had told him, had approached him one night at a bar and told him that he had information that Metzger would be interested in receiving large quantities of chemicals in payment for attorney's fees. I told Hall that Van Raam was crazy too. Metzger wasn't like that. Hall told me it would be just a matter of time before they found somebody that would set Metzger up for another arrest, this time outside Marin."

Why did Van Raam want to bust Metzger again?

"Chuck Hall told me," Aylwin said, "that Metzger had become a *menace to the BNE.*"

(Asked about that statement, Gerritt Van Raam looked evenly at the reporter and said, "I don't know what Chuck Hall said.")

Phil Ryan, his flaming Irish-Italian temper in full fury, had put up with about as much as he could take. Metzger, his best friend, faced a prison term. Butch Hallinan, his Irish-Jewish crony, was saved from handcuffs by his own self-preserving tomfoolery. Now Ryan kept hearing about Van Raam readying to bust Metzger again. Well, not if Phil Ryan could help it. He had an especial dedication he had picked up the hard way. He learned a potent lesson one day about social conscience and the lawyer's responsibility to pursue police excess. The lesson was personally searing. "I had a case where a cop claimed a kid assaulted him. The kid told me the cop had beaten the shit out of him. I got the cop on the stand, and he lied his head off. I knew he was lying because I had some films which clearly showed the kid was telling the truth. So I finally called the D.A. and the judge together and showed them the films, and they agreed to drop the charges against the kid. I thought my case was over. I didn't bother to go to the trouble of preferring charges against the cop. I thought that was the D.A.'s responsibility. But the D.A. didn't do anything about it. The fact that I didn't do anything about it will haunt me to my grave. Because two weeks after that the same cop killed a black man in Hunter's Point."

Phil Ryan, who paid his dues in Mississippi working in an SNCC (Student Nonviolent Coordinating Committee) legal aid project, a white man who went out of his way to go to Howard University, who matured legally at the right hand of Big Vince Hallinan, has never been short on guts. With the storm cloud of the BNE above him—Van Raam had already asked McDonald about Ryan—he threw himself into the fray, appointing himself an angel of justice, a good guy of retribution, a one-man Truth Squad.

When Matthew O'Connor pursed his lips through a talk show, gurgling vagaries, it was Ryan who conjured images of Hitler and Goebbels in rebuttal. The show was an illuminating public peek into the things the BNE did not want the public to hear.

"What percentage of your arrests for narcotics result in convictions?" O'Connor was asked.

"It's not, ah—*can we delete this part from the tape?* I don't have the data with me. I just couldn't come off the top of my head and give it to you."

"Not even generally?"

"No, our track record is a little bit different," O'Connor said.

Asked about Van Raam's refusal to take the lie test, O'Connor went to great pains to point out the judge's directive was not a "court order."

"What if there had been a court order? Would it have been obeyed?"

"If there was a court order," O'Connor babbled, "it would be delivered to the bureau, and *we would comply as much as we possibly can.* There may be a restraining order or a writ enjoining the court order until such time as policy could have been determined."

"What about BNE agents engaging in drug dealing? Selling 'contraband' to line their own pockets?"

"If I heard any word [like that] of any of our agents, he would be the *exception.* He would immediately come into focus and be the subject of a full investigation. We certainly do our own dirty wash, and we don't try to whitewash or cover up."

"Is it common for an agent to deal?"

"No, it's not. There's an excellent understanding. The men understand immediately. . . . If there is any involvement, they will be prosecuted, and I would be glad to serve the warrant myself."

"Are deals made with informers to dismiss charges in return for their cooperation?"

"No promises are made to them. No deals are made along those lines," O'Connor said.

Phil Ryan was champing at the bit to reply to the commissar's comments. "Well, listening to what he said, I was reminded of the dialogue that took place between Hitler and Goebbels," Ryan said. "Hitler was very concerned about his image in Nazi Germany, and Goebbels discovered the formula that would ensure Hitler's good image. And he told Hitler, 'You tell a lie often enough, everybody will believe it.' "

He replied to O'Connor's assertion that the BNE does not make deals with informers this way: "I could almost laugh at that. Anybody who's been involved in the criminal practice, a judge, knows what O'Connor says is not true. And what is disturbing about that kind of statement is it's sort of arguing against the obvious. That he would state on radio, in plain view of anyone listening that might possibly believe it—it shows the kind of credibility the man has." But Phil Ryan's juggernaut assault on the BNE did not end with Hitler-Goebbels imagery.

Sandy White says, "We had a court case, and right in that part of the case before it started, out of the clear blue sky, Ryan turns to the D.A. and says, 'I don't want any BNE agents in this room. They're all liars.' Elsberg gets all upset by that comment. So Elsberg goes back to Van Raam and tells him, like a good little boy, what happened. Tells everybody in the office about it. Van Raam says, 'That figures, that son of a bitch.' "

Some time later Ryan was examining Van Raam on the stand. The cross-examination was so vigorous that the district attorney objected that Ryan was "badgering" Gerry Van Raam.

Face to face with Van Raam, Ryan, his complexion purple, asked, "Are you investigating me, Mr. Van Raam?"

Van Raam, taken aback, could only say, "I can't discuss any investigations currently under way."

The badgering would keep up outside the courtroom. Phil Ryan, who had learned his lesson about social conscience the hard way, was on a

75

holy crusade. Whenever he'd spot Van Raam in a lobby, Ryan would yell, "Hey, Gerry, how are your eyes today? Got any plain-view evidence?" He'd go on search missions to LaRocca's to see how often Van Raam drank there, and, whenever he wouldn't find him, he'd leave a message with the bartender: "You tell that son of a bitch Phil Ryan was looking for him."

His friends were warning him, the way they had warned Metzger, that, if he pushed his luck, he'd become the next victim. Ryan kept it up ceaselessly and made sure to keep clean. He remembered the advice his friend Bill Kunstler, the Chicago Eight attorney, once gave to a lawyer smoking a joint, "That's the cheapest arrest in the world."

One day he spotted Van Raam outside a courtroom and ambled up to him, friendly, grinning. When he got very close to him, Phil Ryan said, "Now let me give you some advice. If you bust me, you better have that search warrant pinned to your lapel, because, if I don't know who you are and you come crashing through my door, I'm liable *to blow your fucking head off.*"

Van Raam stood there, the whites of his eyes showing, his mouth a panorama of his tonsils.

Dialogue. Sandy White, ace nark informer, and her boy friend, Ted Donnelly. Subject: the nark motto.

Sandy: *I talked to Elsberg after I talked to you, and we both have a groovy plan to get our rocks off. We're going to make you an operator.*

Ted: *I just got drafted, huh?*

Sandy: *Yeah, you even get paid for it.*

Ted: *What do I get to do? Make love to you?*

Sandy: *No. If I tell you, will you keep it to yourself? You're going to set Phil Ryan up on a search warrant. We're going to make you reliable. That means you're going to work with me on one case, but that will be good, baby, 'cause you'll meet all the guys and you'll know the system. I can tell you all about it, but then knowing them yourself is even better, right?*

Ted: *Yeah.*

Sandy: *Then you can go over to Ryan's house and smoke a little dope with him.*

Ted: *Do what?*

Sandy: *Smoke a little dope with him. "Get high, get paid"—that's our motto.*

In the spring of 1971 Matthew O'Connor, the maestro of double-talk, was trying to devise ways to hype his public appeal. He had just decided that he would run for sheriff, and he had just been figuratively kicked between the navel and the kneecap: the pit of his image. Being in that kind of straining, bent-over position, it is understandable that he wanted the talk-show tape deleted when it came time to discuss the record of his bureau's convictions.

The man who did the kicking was supervisory field agent Van Raam. The two most celebrated busts in BNE history—the arrests of Michael Metzger and of Mark Susnow—were thrown out of court. The search warrants in both cases, judges ruled, were invalid. In his zealous haste to make the busts—Metzger was on his way to Crete; Hallinan couldn't be expected to stay at the party all night—Van Raam made simple mistakes.

The Metzger and Susnow camps picked their dramatis personae with great care. Helping Hallinan defend Metzger was William Weissich, silver-haired and in his sixties, a Nixon Republican, a member of Marin County's elite establishment. Representing Susnow were Tony Serra, the long-haired "semantic warrior" and student of nark brutality, and the legendary great old man himself, the King of the Hill, seventy-four-year-old Vincent M. (Big Vince) Hallinan.

For Michael Metzger it was in most ways a hollow triumph—perhaps not much of a triumph at all. The case was not dismissed because Van Raam had gone on a vendetta. It was dismissed because Gerry McDonald, Van Raam's informer, obtained his information by "fraudulent representation," his ruse to hire Metzger as his attorney. "Information obtained in such manner," the judge said, "is fruit of the poisonous tree, and any evidence procured under the search warrant must be suppressed."

The charges against Mark Susnow were thrown out on an even more irrelevant technicality. A new California statute held that, before a search warrant was issued, there had to be either a written statement attesting to the "probable cause" of illegality or a recorded statement with a transcript attached. In Susnow's case the recorded transcript was not transcribed until five days after his arrest, a violation of the letter of the law.

"When we got the verdict," Metzger said, "some of my friends started calling me again. Like, one guy that I had worked with in the D.A.'s office called me and said, 'Gee, I was meaning to call you all along, but I thought it'd be inappropriate.' A lot of guys called up and said, 'You know, I was pulling for you all along.' One thing the whole thing taught me: You don't have as many friends as you think. I know I'm not the first guy to say that. It's like the client of mine who saw his best friend the day after he got busted, and his friend said, 'Well, buddy, I hate to tell you this, but it's about that statement I made out last night implicating you.' "

Mark Susnow thought he saw some shimmering hope. "It was really rough on my family, you know. My wife's folks are pretty straight, and they heard about what happened and really freaked. But a couple of times after the arrest a bunch of us younger lawyers got together, and we said, 'Hey, they're fucking around with all of us.' It developed into a brotherhood kind of thing. We realized in a sense that we were brothers and we had better stick up for one another."

What made the dismissal hollow in each case was the refusal of the judge to condemn Van Raam's tactics formally, to strike a blow against police excess by dismissing the cases on those grounds.

In Metzger's case Judge Joseph J. Wilson was ready enough, strangely, to admit Van Raam's vendetta but would not dismiss the case on that basis. He chose to slap Van Raam on the wrist rather than hit him where it would have hurt. "The evidence would warrant," Judge Wilson said, "the rather obvious inference that this particular prosecution was instigated for motives other than just the obtaining of marijuana in someone's possession. . . . The timing between Mr. Metzger's charges against Mr. Van Raam and the subsequent search of Mr. Metzger's house is—one had to be naive to think there was no relationship."

But it is doubtful that Gerry Van Raam heard Judge Wilson's words or even was listening to them very closely.

The Attorney General's office had made its ruling about the lie-detector test. Van Raam didn't have to take one.

The Attorney General of the state of California had already ruled upon the tactics of narcotics agents in the past. He was Evelle J. Younger, former Whittier D.A., the same man who in 1969 had ruled that the killing of a twenty-two-year-old black man in a BNE-led raid (by a nark who'd been drinking) was "tragic" but "without criminal liability."

The Attorney General's office said Gerry Van Raam did not have to take the polygraph test for two reasons: 1) It would cost the state of California too much money; 2) It would prove "deleterious to law enforcement."

As far as Gerry Van Raam's status inside the BNE was concerned, nothing had changed. He was off the hook. The BNE gravely listened to Judge Wilson's high-toned critique of Van Raam's conduct, but the BNE did nothing about it. Gerry Van Raam weathered another storm and remained field supervisor. His actions, for those discerning enough to notice, may have bespotted the BNE's image just a bit, but what the hell? He wasn't running for sheriff; O'Connor was. "Besides," Sandy White says, "Van Raam didn't want O'Connor as sheriff. He wants him right there, as his boss."

The only thing that the two rulings officially said about Gerry Van Raam was that he wasn't careful enough about getting his search warrants. By the time the charges against Metzger were dismissed, Gerry Van Raam was too busy, too involved on other fronts, to get very upset about a few critical words. He had busted Metzger; he had almost busted Hallinan; he had busted Susnow; he was investigating Ryan.

And now he was trying to set up a new target: a razor-thin, freaky-looking twenty-six-year-old private eye with the spaced-out eyes of a young Basil Rathbone; a weirdo who wore his hair down to his shoulders, looked as if he was the last survivor of an Old Testament famine, slouched around in a Panther leather jacket, and actually wore a peace symbol right on his shirt sleeve.

Granted, Michael Murphy didn't much look like Mike Hammer, but then Mike Hammer didn't have Murphy's tenacity, either. Mike Murphy didn't have a gun because he didn't believe in violence. Never mind all that *Kiss Me Deadly* stuff. He believed in the cerebral.

His brains were more than enough to quickly infuriate Gerry Van Raam. Murphy got involved with Van Raam through that other Irish hardass Ryan, the guy liable to "blow Van Raam's fucking head off." The case involved Frank Werber, owner of an organic food haven, the Trident, in Sausalito; the same man who had been Michael Metzger's one and only drug case as a federal D.A.

Frank Werber was busted, for the third deadly time, by the BNE, through a "confidential and reliable informer." Murphy was paid to learn everything about the informer and everything about Gerry Van Raam.

He made one big mistake. In Idaho, tracking Van Raam's past, he left a card. The card got back to Van Raam. Van Raam was not happy to hear his past was being tracked in that particular state. The battle was on.

Trouble was, Murphy didn't look like he could handle any kind of a battle. He looked like the slightest breeze could sweep him aloft. He had arms that made John Lennon look like Steve Reeves; his chest looked like a scale-model replica of Rod Stewart's. He lived in Oakland with his wife, Pam, another gentle sort, and a ménage of cats. He didn't own a weapon, but he did own a stereo. He didn't read cops-and-robbers stories, he read Hesse and underground newspapers and plugged himself periodically into his headset. He lived simply. He didn't make very much money, and obviously he didn't eat very much.

He specialized at drug-case investigations, was a Haight graduate, knew drugs, and knew some of the people who dealt them. (Van Raam took one look at Murphy and put him down as a speed freak; Murphy, gumshoeing around Van Raam, stayed so clean he shone.)

When he was hired to do the Werber case—at a paltry $5 an hour (Frank has never been loose with his cash)—he had one special ax to grind. He knew about "confidential and reliable" informers. "The first case I ever did involved an informer who was living at a commune and wanted to save his chick just before the bust came down. The chick wouldn't go. The guy went berserk and shot three people. So say I knew the kind of people they were using."

The informer who set Frank Werber up, he discovered, had an aura of mystery around her. Her name was Sandy White. That's all he knew. He got one quick glimpse of her at a court appearance in Marin County.

"The first time I was ever aware of Murphy," Sandy White says, "was after Frank Werber was busted by my search warrant and I was informed by Elsberg that Werber had a lot of money and would probably have an investigator out snooping around and to be on guard. Okay, so I went to the court that morning in Marin. I spent much of the morning in Teixeira's office. I was just waiting and making calls to dope dealers that I had deals going with at the time. Van Raam and I were joking around, and I was playing with a nine-shot revolver. So then I got the call and walked down, and I had to wait a few minutes. So for about five minutes I was out there in the hallway. I saw Murphy sitting in there. And Elsberg says, 'Be careful of that guy; he's an investigator.' Van Raam says, 'Take a good look at him and run out of there. Don't let him take a good look at you. Put your glasses on.' So I put the sunglasses on, and I really stared Murphy down. Van Raam says, 'I know that dude, and I'll tell you about him later.' "

Murphy didn't get a good look at her that day, but he became very curious about Sandy White. He looked through old court cases and pored through public records, hoping to find a lead. The research took him more than two months. All he found out was that she had set up more than 350 people. In the third month of his search he found a guy who'd been busted by her in Berkeley. The guy knew Sandy White's boy friend.

His plan, from the beginning, was to convince her to talk to him. Murphy was not a ruthless sort, and he didn't want to hurt her. He knew, too, that, if he could befriend Sandy White and convince her to inform on the BNE, he would be striking blows not only for the case but for the Big Picture.

The risks were high. Metzger and Hallinan were friends of his. He had worked for Ryan. He knew that the informer system was the ingrown toenail of the BNE and the nark establishment. By trying to pump an informer, he'd be jitterbugging around that toenail: Van Raam would like him even less.

There was a very immediate physical danger. He felt that, even if he did get close to Sandy White, chit-chat with her in her living room, she would be perfectly capable of planting a joint on him and bringing about his arrest. He had a mental picture of sitting in a room, talking to her, when Van Raam would lead his troopers storming through the door. Murphy, who liked playing with his cats, was playing with dynamite.

He didn't know then that Ted Donnelly, Sandy White's boy friend, would become his valuable ally, that Donnelly had no love for narks either, that he was already telling Sandy White she was being used.

Murphy genuinely liked Donnelly. For more than two months before he ever met Sandy White, Murphy talked to her boy friend, first on the telephone, then as a drinking partner. Murphy got to be a friend.

81

As he got to know Donnelly, he realized that the girl he was tracking was pathetically neurotic: not the evil lady he had envisioned but an emotional hulk, a psychic casualty with very few friends and almost no friends she really trusted. The girl, Murphy found, had a twisted love-hate relationship with another BNE informer who imitated her, Judy Simmons.

He found out, too, that the spooky relationship between Sandy White and Ted Donnelly was a direct reflection of the life style she led, the kind of "rat" she had become when she teamed up with the BNE. She was just like one of Salamander's lizards: meeting Ted in a gas station, falling in love with him, while she was trying to bust him.

Love Story: A/K/A Bonnie Parker + the Grease Monkey

Ted: Were you planning to set me up at first?
Sandy: Yeah. They told me you'd turn me on to a good lead. When I first met you in the gas station in my car, the cops were there. To stake. All around. I don't go nowhere without cops.
Ted: How did you get into Werber's?
Sandy: Well, I'm a good undercover agent. I'm damn good. I'm a pro. I can do anybody.
Ted: Aw, shit.
Sandy: Now, look it, it was hard doing Tommy Smothers.
Ted: Was it?
Sandy: Yeah, I was nervous. You know, I'd seen him as a TV idol.

Ted: Yeah, Sandy needs help. After that talk we had last night, far out!
Judy Simmons: I don't remember specifically what she said.
Ted: She said she had no feelings, live day by day, fuck everybody.
Judy Simmons: Well, that's pretty much the way she is. In fact, I think, I don't know her. I'm not even sure where I stand with her. I don't think I'd ever place my life on it without any reservations, but I think probably I'm just about the only person in the world that she wouldn't screw unless

I screwed her.

Ted: I kind of feel she would screw me if she got the chance.

Judy Simmons: I know she would.

Ted: Like, she was trying to set me up the first time I met her.

Judy Simmons: I don't know if she'd do it now or not, but I wouldn't trust her.

Sandy: What else did Judy tell you? Did she tell you I was screwing other guys?

Ted: No.

Sandy: She didn't?

Ted: I said: Whatever Sandy does, man, she's free to do whatever she wants to. If she wants to screw someone, fine and dandy.

Sandy: I told you what happened the night we went out and this guy, this guy looked like a real greasy pig, he looked like a Hell's Angel, he's a pig with a beard, kind of long hair, leather vest, you know the type. He started fooling around with me, and I couldn't stand him. So I walked away. So Judy latches onto him—"Oh, he's so intellectual." So he says, "Do you want to come over to my house for a party?" And I go, "Well, I don't know." And Judy goes, "Come on." So it was just her and me and him.

So he calls over this other guy, he's an expert pool player. He was a longhair. He plays bass in a rock band, real cute guy, about twenty-five. So I said, "Oh, yeah, I know you." So the four of us went to his house. He didn't even start the party or do nothing. He went right upstairs to the bedroom and left me with this guy I hardly know in the living room. Just walked right up to the bedroom and shut the door. And what am I supposed to do? Listen to music and talk? So that put me in a very bad situation. Half an hour later Judy comes walking out with nothing on.

Ted: Kind of sickening, wasn't it?

Sandy: Yeah, so at the time she thought we'd be sitting there talking, the other dude and I. Well, you know me, he was a pretty good fuck, too. I fucked the shit out of him. So I said to her, "Why did you do this? Why did you make me do this? Why did you go straight to the bedroom? You know that's not nice. Who do you think you are, some kind of whore? You think I'm going to play whore games, too? I'm not going to do things like that, God damn it. That's not my trip. My husband was the son of an ambassador. He had more class than that."

Sandy: Judy is really a bitch. There's things that I would do to fuck her up. Like blowing up one of her suspects and blowing a case for her. She was going to bust a guy for five pounds of grass, and I didn't think it was worth it. The guy was a good friend of mine. So I just gave him a little call.

Sandy: Where did you go?
Ted: Went up to Ryan's office on Union Street.
Sandy: Is it a nice office?
Ted: Ain't too bad.
Sandy: Did you see any dope in there?
Ted: No.
Sandy: Did they say anything against me?
Ted: No.
Sandy: Did they insinuate anything? Did they think I was ugly?
Ted: No, they said you were kind of an attractive woman.
Sandy: Is that what they said, or are you just saying that?
Ted: No, really.
Sandy: They said I was attractive, no kidding?

Ted: What's your ex-old man up to these days? You never told me anything about him.
Sandy: He's a graduate student at the University of Chicago, working on his master's in market research. His father is in the State Department. He's in a very high-class family. I was married to him for three years.
Ted: So, look what you've accomplished? You've got a lot of big names under your belt, don't you?
Sandy: Yeah, what? Busting people?
Ted: Well, that. And making a name for yourself with people you work for.
Sandy: How about my grades in school and all that? Plus I was a big dope dealer. Plus I was the best screw in town. Plus I have my head together.
Ted: Yeah.

Sandy: Oh, give me some heroin, man. I want to come down.
Ted: Come on over. I'll get you down.
Sandy: I don't mean that way. I want a roll of heroin. Shoot it up in front of you so you can throw up. You could dig it. You'd probably be a good junkie.

Sandy: Let's run away.
Ted: All right.
Sandy: Where do you want to go?
Ted: Let's go to Utah.
Sandy: What would we do for dope?
Ted: Oh, they got it down in Utah.

Ted: I had an argument with Judy.
Sandy: Yeah? What were you talking about?
Ted: A case.
Sandy: A case?
Ted: Yeah, because we got on this big hairy trip about why did she bust people, you know, even though they did have grass. She said, "No matter what it is, it's illegal." I said, "Listen, bitch, I've seen you do your dope, and then you fuck people around."

Ted: We used to have a good time together.
Sandy: Yeah, we used to.
Ted: Too many people got big mouths, big ears.
Sandy: Too many people playing stupid games.
Ted: You're playing cops and robbers and screwing everybody. You're screwing everybody but me, babe.
Sandy: Ted, come on. I love you.

A few days after Gerry Van Raam spotted the Idaho traveler, Michael Murphy, in court, the hunter was sitting in his office talking about setting him up. Sandy White says, "Van Raam asks me, 'When are you gonna see Salamander? I have a case I want him to do for me. This Murphy's been harassing me, and I want him done good.' And I said, 'Let me do it.' I went into one of my song-and-dance routines. 'All right,' Van Raam says, 'let Joe try it first.' So I said all right, but, if he fails, I can do it? Please? Please? Please? And he says yes. So Joe called Van Raam later that week and got the info that he gave me later on—which was Murphy's license plate number on his yellow Volvo and a couple of Duke-In names. And also that Murphy was considered dangerous because there was an investigation and we were to watch our step. Van Raam had heard that Murphy was looking into me, and he said, 'You don't want to talk to Murphy; you don't want him to find out your identity because the Werber case is in full force now and every time you open your mouth you're going to give info that might help him in the case; you want to keep your mouth shut.'

"So I talked to Joe Salamander. I said, 'Well, I can't really do him because he's seen me before.' And that's what I thought in my mind. So this goes on for four or five weeks, and I kept bugging Salamander about Murphy, you know. Did you get the motherfucker? And Joe says, 'Well, I keep on driving by the house, but his car is never there. So I never go in.' Okay, so then Joe has to go to Europe to look for snakes. So I run into Van Raam at the office again, and I say, 'Well, it looks like Joe didn't do that thing for you.' And he says, 'Yeah, you go ahead, Elsberg will give you the info.' The next day Elsberg says, 'Just a minute, Van Raam wants to talk to you.' Van Raam gets on the line, and he gives me the information. I write it all down in my black book. So then one night we were in Oakland fooling around on other things. I had a big case going, and Elsberg says, 'Well, let's go to Murphy's, now is a good time.' And I said, 'Okay.' So he dropped me off halfway up the block and parked. Murphy's car wasn't there. I walked up to his door and met his wife."

Pamela Murphy knew all about Duke-In names and Gerry Van Raam by then, and, when the strange and nervous woman who said her name was Kathy Thompson came to the door, dropping names, asking to have a drink of water inside, Pam made sure she didn't take one step in.

"I went back to the car," Sandy White says, "and I told Elsberg I could only get up to the porch, and I said the girl was friendly but crazy paranoid."

Pam called Mike, told him about Kathy Thompson, and Murphy, his scarecrow head speeding, decided a swift and disarming ploy against the BNE. He told his wife to call the Oakland police department. Pam Murphy, her voice shaking with fear, called the police department's emergency number and told the dispatcher she feared a burglar was readying to strike her home. She said a strange woman had come to the door, probably to case the joint.

The Oakland police department promised the house would be given special surveillance the rest of the night. The tactic was effective. If they busted him, Murphy thought, he'd make the BNE look bad. Someone who had dope in the house was not likely to call the police department and ask for special attention.

Nevertheless, Murphy feared the bust would come anyway and he would be planted. He called Butch Hallinan.

Hallinan said, "Well, kid, the next time I'll hear from you, you'll be in jail."

But he wasn't busted that night. He was, however, being constantly followed. Sitting one night at his favorite bar, Thomas Lord's on Union Street, he scanned the faces and saw—guess who—agents Dick Violet and Robert Luca, Metzger's old nemeses.

"A few minutes after they got there," Murphy said, "Violet goes down to the john. Then he comes back up. Pretty soon I had to go to the john. I mean, I really did. I wasn't playing a game. So I walked into a stall and sat down. I heard the door close and then some footsteps, and then I saw this pair of wing-tip cordovans stop directly outside my stall. My friend watched Violet come down after me, and he decided to come down, too. He figured: 'Hell, I'm not going to let them hassle Mike while he's taking a shit.' So when my friend came down, there was a confrontation outside my stall and finally Violet gets out of there."

What happened then?

"I wiped my ass," Murphy said.

The incident would lead Violet to tell Sandy White the next day, "*We know every time Murphy takes a shit.*"

By then, Sandy White says, Van Raam had issued a general order within the department to "get Murphy." Another directive advised the agents to "follow and harass" Murphy in their free time. Van Raam told Sandy that, since she had failed and Salamander had failed, he had found a new finger: a North Beach belly dancer would get Murphy. (Murphy promptly started tracking the belly dancer.)

How often did she hear Murphy's name mentioned in the narcotics squad? Sandy White was asked.

"At least twenty. Maybe fifty."

How many times were threats leveled against him?

"Every time," she said.

(Van Raam denies it. The two agents were not following Murphy, he said. They were in the bar "socially." There was no order, Van Raam said, of any kind to "get Murphy." "I would suggest," Van Raam said, "that Murphy is paranoid.")

On August 18 Murphy got a call from Ted Donnelly, Sandy's boy friend. He put her on the line.

"I just talked to Van Raam," she said. "I'm not gonna work for them anymore."

She wanted to meet Murphy. Murphy was scared. It sounded too good to be true. Was she setting him up again? Or had Donnelly really convinced her?

And so it happened that Sandy White, ace informer, spent a night at the funky little home of Mike Murphy, ace cerebral private eye.

"It was one of the weirdest things of all time," Murphy said, "inviting a nark into your home when you know she's been assigned to bust you."

But within the confines of Matthew O'Connor's Big Picture, it was just one of many all-time weird things coming down. As Gerry Van Raam zeroed in on the goblinlike private eye, his fed and local nark cohorts were lining up their own targets.

Coincidentally, both their targets were lawyers, both militantly young. The feds went after Brian Rohan, flashy rock attorney. The locals aimed at, and missed, Tony Serra, the semantic warrior who wouldn't pay them off and who was running for mayor of San Francisco as the Platypus Candidate, campaigning for the abolition of narks.

If Serra's attempted arrest was an act of blatant vengeance, then Rohan's bust was a bit more sinisterly devious. Back when Gerry Van Raam was still hunting Michael Metzger, two of the prison inmates the BNE tried to deal with said that the agents had also shown special interest in one other attorney, Brian Rohan.

Some six months after the initial curiosity Rohan was named in a federal indictment. The indictment charged him with conspiracy to import, smuggle, receive, conceal, and transport marijuana. It was a brand-new, all-encompassing federal statute, tailor-made for the newly created Justice Department Task Force on Narcotics Enforcement. The charge went back three years.

It is surprising they didn't go after Rohan earlier. Rohan, a fortyish, rococo, and raucous-voiced man with a penchant for technicolored peacockry—envision this: a football jersey with red-and-white bellbottoms—made his reputation by freely representing many hippies caught in the original police crackdowns on the Haight. He became a people's" drug lawyer who soon began specializing in the legal end of the mazelike rock industry, acting as adviser to the Airplane and the Grateful Dead.

Butch Hallinan, who by this time was suffering shell shock from too many hours spent in the nark combat zone, was hired to represent Rohan. What he saw was more of the same pattern: Krusco tactics on a grand scale.

Essentially Rohan was indicted for a standard attorney's practice. When some of his clients wanted to buy a ranch near Phoenix, Arizona, and feared their references weren't good enough, Rohan acted as trustee. He made out the forms; the ranch was technically listed in his name. But he never spent time at the place, never even visited it. When his clients were nabbed trying to truck a large quantity of marijuana to the ranch, Rohan was indicted along with them. It was clear he had been on the list long before that.

The feds, working out of San Diego under the direction of a sawed-off lady named Elizabeth Meiers, were having some rough times. If Rohan's luck holds—he was arraigned in December 1972—his case will become part of a pervasive fed pattern: high-powered bungling.

One of the Justice Department's greatest enforcement fiascoes since J. Edgar Hoover began walking the streets took place a few months before Rohan's arrest: the search and seizure of a veritable *Queen Mary*-ful of evil weed, the *Mercy Wiggins*. The *Mercy* is a sixty-foot Louisiana shrimp boat that almost succeeded in smuggling a Gargantuan quantity of grass into the Bay Area—333 bags of weed, weighing from fifty to seventy pounds each, jammed into her every nook and cranny.

The feds had been wiretapping the phones of a well-known San Diego hairdresser for weeks when they pieced out a conversation telling them the *Mercy Wiggins* was Bay-bound with her record stash. The hairdresser, a typically fey and attractive man, was the Mr. Big of the operation. The pursuit of the *Mercy* created one of the greatest nark dragnets in California history. It was like a nark convention: Sandy White was there as an observer, so were members of the San Francisco police department, and the BNE was there in force.

The Coast Guard was tailing the *Mercy* from Mexican waters, except that somewhere out of San Diego the Coast Guard got too close. The *Mercy*'s crew, ever alert, noticed the big cutter about a mile behind them and decided to forget about San Francisco. They stayed well out of the harbor, comfortably past the three-mile international limit, and decided that, if they had to, they'd go all the way up to Canada. The narks got nervous and decided to forget about the three-mile limitation. A task force assault was launched on the shrimp boat—two cutters, three patrol boats, three planes, and a helicopter. The cutter *Point Barrow* was picked to tag the *Mercy Wiggins* and sounded a siren command for her to stop. The *Mercy*, no naive craft, speeded up. The cutter raced off after her and, a mile-long Keystone Kops game of tag later, came up alongside. An oral warning was sounded, "Belay. Shut down your engines." The *Mercy* shut her engines down. A boarding party of sixteen Coast Guardsmen and six narks with guns drawn paraded on deck. They must have been flabbergasted. The shrimp boat was sailing on her own cloud of marijuana, and "marijuana debris" even caked the deck.

"Don't flash those guns, man," a *Mercy* crew member said. "We ain't nothin' but professional smugglers."

But the fiasco was only beginning. When the case came to trial, the lawyer representing Mr. Big found out about the wiretaps. He wanted to hear the tapes. The minute he decided to listen to those tapes, his clients were off the hook—because the tapes were filled with sensationally racy suck-fuck dialogue, enough material for six new Jacqueline Susann novels. The hairdresser provided boudoir services for some of the fanciest ladies in San Diego society. And the ladies did not hesitate to give their names in their eagerness to "see" Mr. Big while the admirals toasted each other at the officers' club.

Okay, the attorney told the D.A., you want to enter the wiretaps as evidence? Fine. We'll enter *all the tapes* as evidence, making those ladies' horny requests a matter of public record. Even the government doesn't have that much bullheadedness (there were, after all, *admirals* involved). A quiet deal was worked out in the judge's chamber. Everybody got off after six months, including Mr. Big. He could go back to his admiralty; everybody was happy.

The attempted arrest of Tony Serra by members of the San Francisco nark squad was about as zany, but filled with more Van Raam touches.

The week his Platypus Party dump-the-narks campaign went to the polls, Tony Serra was involved in a jury trial, defending a black man who had been arrested by San Francisco narks Arthur Gerrens and James Hampton, periodic LaRocca patrons and men with infamous reputations. Gerrens, in his early thirties, a strikingly handsome Germanic type, was known as the Gestapo of the Haight. Hampton, his partner, another sleek, well-groomed man, part Filipino, was alleged to have stuck a lighted cigarette butt into a suspect's navel. Serra's client, Nathaniel Harrington, was charged with assault with a deadly weapon upon a police officer. Harrington was a poet, a student, an alleged user of heroin. Hampton charged that, while he pursued Harrington during a heroin bust, Harrington pointed a gun at him and it misfired. Serra contested Hampton's charge and called him a liar. When Gerrens backed Hampton up, Serra called Gerrens a liar, too. On the morning of November 1 Serra put Gerrens through an excruciating cross-examination in which he made Gerrens "look silly" and referred to him continually as the Gestapo of the Haight.

That night, the day before the election, a dozen San Francisco narks crashed into Tony Serra's house—or what they thought was his house, the address that Serra listed as his official residence. The raiding party was led by Arthur Gerrens and James Hampton. Gerrens had signed the search warrant.

Serra, however, wasn't there; he had just moved. But neither was owlish Dale Metcalf, who was living at the house. "Within the few months before the bust," Metcalf would remember, "I had had a case where two other San Francisco narks busted one of my clients and ripped him off of $4,000. The man even gave me the denomination of the bills. Formal complaints were made to the police complaints bureau." The two alleged nark-thieves also participated in the bust. Since neither Serra nor Metcalf was there, the posse found only John Wike, a young law student who had only recently taken his bar exams. "It was the usual stuff," Metzger said. "They came in and searched everything, my clothes, my bedding, my bureau drawers."

The search warrant alleged—through the use of an unidentified "confidential and reliable informer"—that a person "named Dale" at that address had 800 pounds of marijuana in a Z paper-towel box on the first floor. The warrant alleged there was a large quantity of cocaine on the second floor. There was one serious problem: The building had no second floor.

The agents filed a misdemeanor charge against Wike, finding four-tenths of a gram of marijuana in a back room. They confiscated Dale Metcalf's wallet, containing all his identification. They then tried to file a "joint possession" charge against Metcalf—all for four-tenths of a gram of weed. But even the district attorney couldn't buy that. He refused to file charges against Metcalf. Strangely, when D.A. Harry Clifford filed the charges against Wike, he said he was filing only because he wanted to give Serra and Metcalf a "forum to attack the search warrant."

Gerrens and Hampton, meanwhile, like other LaRocca's patrons in the past, were free to administer "due process" to other victims.

The week after the bust the jury found Serra's client innocent. Jurors said it was their opinion that the narcotics agents were lying.

Under oath and under penalty of perjury, Bureau of Narcotics Enforcement informer Sandy White, in an affidavit, attested to the police conduct of her superior, Gerritt Van Raam. The affidavit should have been cause for a full-scale investigation.

"I was served with a subpoena to appear in the Superior Court of the county of Marin. I did appear pursuant to the subpoena and was called as a witness by the defendant's attorney.

"After being excused from the witness stand, I went upstairs to the cafeteria of the Marin County Courthouse to meet a friend. While in the cafeteria, I saw agent Van Raam. Upon seeing me, Van Raam approached me and asked me what I was doing at the courthouse. I informed him that I had been served a subpoena by Mr. Michael Murphy and that I had testified in connection with the Werber case.

"Van Raam questioned me about my testimony and then stated that he was definitely going to send someone to Murphy's house and that he would get a search warrant *whether or not the individual sent there saw any contraband.*

"His exact words were as follows: 'You should have told us about the subpoena. Now you know what it means to be riffed by those motherfuckers. I'm really going to get Murphy and those guys now. I'll send Joe Salamander to Murphy's. I don't care *if Salamander sees something or not.* I want to get Murphy good. He's really got my goat.' "

The charges were the gravest imaginable against a police officer: that, for personal reasons of vengeance, he would arrest a man even if there was no criminal violation.

Once again Gerry Van Raam got away with it. The court admonished him for his tactics in the Metzger case, but his superiors looked the other way until the Attorney General got him off the hook. Now one of his star recruits, an informer he had called "reliable" in more than 350 court cases, swore under oath that Gerritt Van Raam was using the law in furtherance of his own vendetta.

And once again the Bureau of Narcotics Enforcement looked the other way. The same officials who had paid Sandy White to send people to jail now looked the other way.

(Asked about the charge by the reporter, Van Raam "absolutely and categorically" denied it.)

Sandy White admitted in court that she had used illegal means to gain entrance to the residence of Frank Werber. The charges against Frank Werber were dropped.

That same day Joe Salamander—who, Van Raam had said, would be used to handcuff Murphy—made a phone call. The snake expert called Mike Murphy and said he wanted to meet him.

"No thanks," Murphy said.

"What really gets you," Michael Metzger is saying, "is the judges. Time after time they see Van Raam or his men lie. Time after time they don't do anything about it. Oh, I don't know. Maybe some of them will be more careful about Van Raam. I think some people got burned with my case. Some people in the D.A.'s office in Marin County. They didn't realize it was a personal thing.

"A lot of lawyers, though—they tell me, 'I'd never do what you did to those guys. I'm going to be very careful. I don't want the hassle.' I suppose in that sense Van Raam won."

The telephone rings in Michael Metzger's office. It is the Sausalito police department. The burglar alarm in his house has been tripped.

The muscles twitch in Michael Metzger's face. He gets on the phone and calls a friend. "I don't care if you're busy," he says; "just get up there. I don't know who in hell has been poking around."

Paranoia?

Sure.

Michael Metzger, man of boyish ideals, isn't naive anymore.

"A lot of us," Tony Serra would add, "we live like fugitives. We move around to different places. We check the rear-view mirror all the time. We switch phone numbers. It's crazy, yeah, but it's *survival*."

Sandy White sits in her suburban home, watching the sea gulls skirt the tide outside her window, remembering her betrayal of the BNE.

"Well, I was really lonely about six months ago. I mean, you know, like for a boy friend relationship. And I was very, you know, like I was doing cases, and like I wasn't meeting new people, and like it wasn't satisfying anymore.

"And I wanted to smoke a lot of grass again, and I couldn't cop from anybody. You know, I had a desire for it. And, ah, I ran into a guy named Ted Donnelly. And, ah, he ripped me off. He was a low-class, ignorant, but very intelligent con artist. And I fell for it. He said he wanted to marry me, and then he just split.

"I don't know why I fell for it. Maybe because he was available. If you had been available, you know, it could have been you. It could have been anybody. It's just that he was available at the time. And I'm glad I went through that experience because I'll never fall for another bum like him again.

"Well, you know, he was someone to talk to, and he gradually persuaded me to talk to Murphy. He convinced me that I'd been such a bad girl when I'm really a hippie at heart. And that I really don't belong in the conservative corporate structure of the BNE."

What are you going to do now? she is asked.

"Well, there's just one thing they can do to really hurt me, and that's get my teaching credentials away. Okay, what could I do if I couldn't teach? What could I do?"

The question, which hangs in the air for a moment, gets a fateful and immediate answer. The phone rings, and Sandy White's mother whispers to her that it is Gerritt Van Raam.

She disappears for a few minutes and comes back smiling.

"You're still in the family, honey," Gerry Van Raam told her. "Maybe we can work together again."

You mean, she is asked, that after the betrayal . . . after the court statements . . . after the affidavit . . . he'd still use you?

"That's water over the dam," Sandy White says. "None of that hurt his reputation or anything."

There is a lightning-bug twinkle in the electrode casualty's eyes. "See," she glows, "I was a really *good* operator."

March 2, 1972

[AUTHOR'S NOTE]

The charges against Michael Metzger are still pending—more than two years after his arrest. He is still trying to feel his way through a deadly and seemingly infinite legal mine field. "Sometimes I don't think this will ever end," he sardonically tells his friends. "I'll still be going to court to defend myself when I'm an old man. I'll be sixty-five and still be writing briefs for my own case." Unvanquished, he has done his best to build his law practice.

Gerritt Van Raam, scaling his career ladder, finally found the inevitable banana peel. Not because of the allegations surrounding the Metzger case—his superiors claim—nor because of allegations surrounding any other bust. Rather, it was alleged at a departmental hearing that Gerry Van Raam supplied confidential information involving a man's arrest record to a defense attorney. Van Raam denied the charge but was stripped by the BNE of his "field supervisor" status and was demoted to an ordinary street agent.

"I don't believe a word of it," said attorney Phil Ryan. "There was an awful lot of heat about the Metzger case and about Van Raam's tactics, and I think the BNE finally couldn't take it anymore. So they chose a graceful way out and used the other charge."

Ryan bumped into Van Raam on a street corner in the spring of 1973 and described the meeting this way: "The guy was standing there looking pretty abject. I'd heard about what had happened to him. I went up to him, and I said, 'Hey, Van Raam, still harassing me, huh? Still following me everywhere like the Goddam Gestapo?' He got very nervous and said, 'I don't do that, Mr. Ryan! I'm not following you! You have to believe me. I'm just waiting for a ride!' He looked almost desperate that I believe him. I just smiled to myself and walked away."

LaRocca's still prospers as a nark hangout: Vic Damone and Frank still monopolize the jukebox, guns still bulge, but a few patrons don't come around anymore.

Matthew O'Connor, top nark linguist, was promoted to a very high-level and cushy narcotics enforcement job in Sacramento . . . and Sandy White, code name Bonnie Parker, suffered another nervous breakdown and spends much of her time eyeing the sea gulls in the back yard.

2. The Strange Case of the Hippie Mafia

"I live for the enforcement of narcotics laws. It used to be in 1961 that, if you got a single joint, it made headline news. I'm convinced, and I was at that time, that this was not going to be a passing fad, but that this was going to be a giant subculture, and it flat out is."

—Sergeant Neal Purcell, Chief of Detectives,
Laguna Beach police department.

They are crouched high in the eucalyptus trees, these hippie/surfer/*mafiosi*, bootleg traffic cop whistles in their mouths, infrared Swiss binoculars to their eyes, on the lookout for The Law. Down in the dense chaparral on the Laguna Beach hills their German shepherds are living radar devices, diabolically trained to raise bleeping yapping hell at the first sniff of enemy gun oil. Laguna Canyon is their lair, a nearly inaccessible place where they can boil pea-green hash oil and stockpile saccharine-sized tabs of Orange Sunshine and Xmas acid; where their refined Ohaus triple beam scales and Hershey cocoa cans of Afghan hash are tucked into camouflaged panels alongside gym bags filled with $100 bills.

Their driveways are lined with Land Rovers and Volkswagen campers, outfitted with "dead space" and "trapped" with chopped-out wheel-wells, into whose frames Pyrex bottles of the hash oil they call "greasy kid stuff" have been welded. They rotate their women, holding perverse waterbed orgies, facing each other nude in contorted lotus positions, passing joints and pipes and body fluids until they collapse upon expensive Persian-rugged floors. Their women, naturally, are but dope molls, sources of ass and money, runaways whose parents actually pay them to stay away from home.

Caves in the canyon are arsenals of dangerous drugs, crammed with redwood vaults of million-dollar stashes. Tucked among the lush hills are eight-foot-tall marijuana plants and *Clavis purpurea*, a ripe LSD fungus that takes a year to culture. Vitamin-E bottles in their medicine chests are filled with Costa Rican cocaine; dope is everywhere in their shrewdly chosen shacklike homes, though it is hard to find ... hash inside walnuts, hash oil hidden in shoe polish, butter, and pumpkin pies. And sometimes they lick lollipops that are mindfucking candy canes of highest-velocity LSD. The surfboards against their walls have hollowed skegs, stuffed with the finest primo hash available from the Russo-Afghan border. They keep so much loose cash around their hovels that, when one of the treebound sentries blows a police whistle, or when one of the radar dogs starts acting crazy, they run thousands of illegal dollars to their toilet bowls. And start flushing. Sometimes their toilet bowls are clogged with a soggy mixture of hash oil and dirty money.

They wear fourteen-karat brushed-gold rings with the word "LOVE" carved into them. They carry water pistols dripping LSD. They operate a "Spy School" on an Adirondack mountaintop, which trains them to elude even FBI, even Interpol arrest. They own a roving beat-up school bus, which is really a clandestine printing press mass-producing phony passports and Social Security cards. They rent the snazziest Cadillacs to drive cross-country and wear crewcut wigs to set up their deals. They are "tied into the Mafia and the Weatherman." They have a ruthless high command, which views underlings as "expendable people." They have a Board of Directors chaired from a remote Alpine peak in Switzerland. They are experienced enough smugglers to know that tinfoil triggers secret Customs detectors; so they pack their contraband in styrofoam. Their courtroom mouthpiece is a "gangster type." They make millions of dollars a year and are the single biggest source of LSD and hashish *in the world*!

They are all members of an underground countercultural syndicate, the Brotherhood of Eternal Love ... corrupted flower children who once preached the teachings of Jesus Christ ... now a cold-blooded family of criminal materialists ... a denim Cosa Nostra! Timothy Leary is their godfather; Jimi Hendrix was one of their soldiers.

That, at least, literally and in detail, is the way the Orange County Grand Jury sees it.

On Sunday, August 6, 1972, the district attorney of Orange County, Cecil Hicks, a man of weighty political promise in the state of California, announced he had "broken the back" of the Brotherhood of Eternal Love. The day before, a task force of some 200 narcotics agents made a series of lightninglike predawn arrests, acting on twenty-nine indictments handed up by the Orange County Grand Jury. Most of the arrests took place in Laguna Beach, a picture-postcard resort town with a century-old artistic repute just a few miles down the Coast Highway from the Western White House and some thirty miles southwest of Disneyland.

Hicks called the Brotherhood of Eternal Love "the biggest dealer of LSD and hashish in the world," and Laguna Beach Police Chief Joseph J. Kelly, the former provost marshal of the Marine Corps' Pendleton and Quantico bases, known as Old J.J., chorused that his town was "the biggest receiving and distributing center of narcotics in the world."

Timothy Leary, the world-renowned apostle of LSD, was identified by the district attorney as "a key figure" of the brotherhood and was one of those indicted. His bail was set at $5 million, and Hicks said he would demand Leary's extradition from Switzerland. "Leary is personally responsible for destroying more lives than any other human being," Hicks said. "The number of his victims destroyed by drugs and LSD runs literally into the hundreds of thousands." Hicks claimed Leary was directly benefiting from the brotherhood's alleged "drug racket" affairs: "He appears to live comfortably and travel from place to place without any money problems."

The investigation, Hicks said, took more than a year and netted 1.5 million LSD tablets, 2.5 tons of hashish, 30 gallons of "exotic hash oil," $20,000 in cash, and "innumerable" sets of identification papers. Some of the suspects were arrested at a dilapidated ranch in Riverside County on barren desert land east of Los Angeles—"Leary's Ranch," Hicks called it—and three suspects were arrested on the island of Maui in Hawaii.

Forty persons were arrested in all, although the grand jury indicted only twenty-nine. Hicks explained the eleven extra arrests as "a bonus." The grand jury, the district attorney laughed, "has more work to do."

Money to finance the brotherhood's "smuggling and dealing" activities, Hicks said, came from a "number of sources, and investigators may never be able to pinpoint the actual backers." The smuggling operation, he said, was headed by a "Mr. Big," who "coordinated the traffic." He did not identify Mr. Big, who was still being sought, but referred to the brotherhood as "the Hippie Mafia."

The astute district attorney, being a man of political savvy, took care *not* to provide certain relevant details. He did *not* say that, while all of those arrested were supposedly members of the brotherhood, most of them did not even know each other. He did *not* say the year-long probe was launched through the whole-hogged supersleuth efforts of the Laguna Beach police department. He did *not* say that for many months the federal government refused to become involved in this globally far-flung probe and that officials in Hawaii had so many doubts they initially refused even to grant search warrants.

Nor, significantly, did Cecil Hicks say that the investigation was really led and triggered by the zealous efforts of a single Laguna Beach narcotics officer, Sergeant Neal Purcell, the same man who, in 1968, while still a patrolman, arrested Timothy Leary on the marijuana charge that led to Leary's imprisonment . . . and Purcell's promotion to head of the detective squad.

On the day after the district attorney's dramatic announcement, through some convenient bureaucratic mixup, Sergeant Neal Purcell identified the Mr. Big whom Cecil Hicks had refused to name. Purcell gave mug shots of Mr. Big to the Laguna Beach newspapers, the *Daily Pilot* and the *News-Post*. Mr. Big, according to Purcell, was Robert Andrist, twenty-nine, a Laguna rug merchant who liked to taunt policemen by smoking sacrilegious joints on the public sidewalks. But when Purcell pointed the finger, it caused whooping belly laughs among Laguna street people. Sure, they said, Bobby Andrist was indeed Mr. Big: He weighed almost 300 pounds, and his nickname was Fat Bobby.

None of it, of course, made much sense to the taxpaying residents of Laguna Beach, whose sun-reddened eyes were gradually becoming accustomed to the glare of the gothic. They suddenly found themselves on the front page of the *New York Times,* internationally portrayed as some sort of criminal doper's haven. Worse, their own police chief, Old J. J., was saying his little town was more notorious than Marseilles, New York, or Istanbul.

It seemed to be "Goony Beach's" season in the redhot media sun: Just as the brotherhood headlines ebbed, Laguna made the front page again. In a hospital down on the south side of town, Hopalong Cassidy was dead.

It doesn't look like any Sicilian lair or doper's haven; it is a town rooted in jabberwocky, a page out of *Alice in Wonderland*; it seems worlds away from "the biggest receiving and distributing point of narcotics in the world." In some ways Laguna Beach is a refuge from the rest of Southern California, a village that has seemingly little to do with cancerous urban sprawl and the freeways that straitjacket the rest of the area. There are no freeways here. As a matter of fact, there are only two roads leading into town—Laguna Canyon Road and the Pacific Coast Highway.

The ocean is edged by a semicircle of hills, and the canyon itself is almost a canyon of caves, its sides from base to 1,200 feet cut and bored with fine sandstone rock chiseled by nature. Hyacinths, tulips, and dwarf citrus dot the hills and the freeform gardens. Houses from a bygone age, like the Witches' House on Wave Street, make parts of town look like a time-warp, a monument to serenity. You get to the Witches' House, for example, by crossing over a wash and find gabled roofs of contrasting heights with mullioned windows. The topmost gable peaks sixty feet from the ground. The door into the house is of heavy wood, and there is another massive Norman door inside, with a circular stairway curling beside a fireplace of magnesite rock.

Laguna's soul is the Pacific Ocean, the glory of eight- and ten- and twelve-foot surf. Early in the morning you can hear seals offshore and watch sea gulls divebomb the beaches in search of spare food. Sandcastle architects spend long hours constructing ornate Moorish marvels that are then shattered by the tide. But it is the surf that is the town's bloodstream, the salt foam and the riptide which sometimes banish tourists onto contemplative rocks. Sometimes a storm will whip out of Baja California on Mexico's west coast, and the surf will rise majestically to twelve feet. To get a twelve-foot surf takes perfect conditions: Sometimes it is hot inland and the ocean is cold; at other times it is hot inland and the water is nothing but red tide and jellyfish; when a riptide sweeps in, surfers take their boards and go righteously crazy, crashing heads and boards into each other.

In the past few years, as the little town found itself in pained metamorphosis, as Tim Leary came and so did the provost marshal from the Marine Corps, as the surfers started hanging out at places like the

101

Mystic Arts headshop and the smell of grass and patchouli swept over moon-kissed beaches, strange new visitors strayed to Goonyland's shores. Hardnosed cops were swinging bigger sticks, sun-bleached kids were turning on to heavier drugs, and from the coalblack caves of the Laguna Canyon green-eyed mountain lions strayed to the beaches and left clawprints, karmic clawprints, in the sand.

Timothy Leary came to the beaches in the summer of 1968, a kind of psychedelic antichrist who had founded his own "church" and was fleeing an irate "old-fogeyism" that had forced him from the state of New York. He was already a notorious media figure when he arrived, repeating, with toothy smiles and fervid enthusiasm, the same evangelistic message he had proclaimed all along the East Coast. "LSD is a sacrament," he told everyone within earshot in Laguna, "and, like every great religion of the past, we seek to find the divinity within and to express this revelation in a life of glorification and worship of God." He called his new church, whose formation he had announced at a press conference at the New York Advertising Club in 1966, the League for Spiritual Discovery. Members of his congregation, he said, designate a room in their homes as a "shrine."

Leary's every sentence seemed to make shrieking headline news, and each headline seemed to cause him further problems. He had taught at Harvard, organized psychedelic celebrations at the Village Theater in New York City, and had moved, finally, to a large private estate in the village of Millbrook near Poughkeepsie, New York. He left Millbrook when police and townspeople started harassing him with the aid of an ambitious prosecutor named G. Gordon Liddy. He was already facing a possible thirty-year prison sentence in Texas, and the villagers of Millbrook echoed their town's historian, who wrote a letter to the village newspaper, saying: "Leary's attitude will draw drug addicts here and when the money runs out, they will murder, rob, and steal to secure funds with which to satisfy their cravings. Then the crime wave will have reached Millbrook." Leary shrugged, closed up the leather, jewelry, pottery, sculpture, and carpentry shops on his borrowed estate, and left.

He came to Laguna because he liked the town's peaceful and artistic atmosphere and because his new wife, Rosemary, a striking, auburn-haired ex-model, had slummed on Laguna's beaches as a teen-ager. As soon as he arrived, of course, he and his wife and his nineteen-year-old son, John, with hair even longer than his silver-haired father's, were besieged by newsmen and admirers.

By this time news of Timothy Leary's League for Spiritual Discovery had already spurred dozens of similar cults in all parts of the country. One of these cults was formally born in Laguna Beach on October 26, 1966, just a month after Leary announced the formation of his group in New York, and almost two years before Leary came to Laguna. Incorporated under the laws of the state of California, it was called the Brotherhood of Eternal Love. Its articles of incorporation stated: "The purposes for which this corporation is formed are: The specific and primary purposes are to bring the world a greater awareness of God through the teachings of Jesus Christ, Buddha, Ramakrishna, Babaji, Paramahansa Yogananda, Mahatma Gandhi, and all true prophets and apostles of God, and to spread the love and wisdom of these great teachers to all men, irrespective of race, color, or circumstances. The general purposes and powers are to buy, manage, own, and hold real and personal property necessary and proper for a place of public worship and carry on educational and charitable work. This church recognizes that all obligations are to God, and acknowledges God as its head and all great religious men as the guiding light to faith, love, and understanding in all matters. Each member shall have the undisturbed right to follow the Word of God according to the dictates of his own conscience, under the enlightenment of the Holy Spirit. The following statement of faith, therefore, is not a test, but an expression of the spirit in which this church interprets the Word of God. We believe in God, the Father of all mankind in whose love we find purpose and salvation. We believe in the brotherhood of man, in the creative quality of the human spirit, and in the immortality of the human soul. We believe this church to be the earthly instrument of God's will. We believe in the sacred right of each individual to commune with God in spirit and in truth as it is empirically revealed to him."

The primary force behind the Brotherhood of Eternal Love was John Griggs, known to his friends as Farmer John, an intense twenty-six-year-old who shared Leary's beliefs in the psychedelic enlightenment of LSD, marijuana, and hashish. When Timothy Leary and his family arrived in Laguna Beach, Farmer John and the half dozen of his friends who called themselves members of the brotherhood treated him as

103

their private heaven-sent prophet. Leary and his wife and son and Farmer John and his friends spent a lot of time along the beaches, watching the surf and smoking grass, sitting around bonfires, and dropping acid, spreading the Word. Since Laguna is a surfer's paradise, there were many young people who heard the Word and turned on. Leary enjoyed his Laguna stay. He spent long hours in the sun, and, as more and more young people adopted alternate life styles, he found himself the guru of the town's burgeoning head colony, a respected elder statesman, wearing bells and beads around his neck, who was friendly with everyone, even policemen, and preached Love and Enlightenment to the police chief himself.

But some of the residents, and particularly some of the policemen, were growing a little jumpy. The beaches were crowded with glassy-eyed longhairs who scared the tourists, a whole Freaktown was building up in the canyon, and the smell of marijuana floated everywhere. When Leary's war-weary station wagon passed through the center of town, traffic seemed to come to a standstill.

Neal Purcell, a squat, dark-complected man with puffed cheeks and a contrasting pencil-thin Gilbert Roland mustache, joined the Laguna Beach police department on September 1, 1969. He came from the Newport Beach police force, a town just a few miles from Laguna on the Coast Highway, where his duty had been to entice and entrap homosexuals hustling the beaches. Purcell was a gung-ho, rule-book cop who proselytized among his colleagues and warned them about the moral decay of America. He didn't like long hair. He didn't like girls walking around with their tits popping out. He considered marijuana and LSD near the root of a generational corruption. And he could not comprehend why the city of Laguna Beach allowed a man like Timothy Leary to pollute its beaches, infecting the young with that contagious rot. But, while he often voiced these lofty concerns, Neal Purcell was just a beat cop, a rookie on a new police force driving a cruiser and handing out parking citations.

On December 26, 1968, Patrolman Neal Purcell, cruising the Woodland Drive–Freaktown area of Laguna Beach, noticed Timothy Leary's station wagon blocking a roadway. He contended later that, while most poeple in Laguna knew the station wagon by infamous sight, he didn't know its owner until he checked the man's driver license. He contended that, as he approached the car, Timothy Leary rolled his window down and a cloud of marijuana smoke almost knocked Purcell off his feet. Leary's wife sat next to him, and his son, John, was in the back seat. This, said Neal Purcell, is what he saw: "Just prior to my placing him under arrest, I observed John Leary in the back seat on all fours. By that, I mean on his hands and knees, and he was attempting to get over into the front seat, and his father was turning in the seat, trying to push him back, and John kept trying to come over. It reminded me of a dog jumping from the back seat to the front seat, and this continued until I approached. Now, after I approached and identified myself, John would bring his face up close to the window, make faces at me, bring his hair forward, brush it down in front of his face, and then part his hair and peek out with one eyeball and stick his tongue out, making noises with his mouth." Purcell called for assistance and searched the car. ("If anyone was on his hands and knees like a dog," Leary would say later, "it was Purcell. I thought he was going to lick the floor.")

"What did you find?" Leary asked him when the search ended. Purcell waved two joints in the air.

"Big deal," Leary said.

Leary and his family were charged with possession of marijuana and dangerous drugs and released on $2,500 bond the next day. But Neal Purcell had just begun. Two days later, once again on routine traffic patrol, Purcell watched Leary's station wagon pull into a motel driveway on South Coast Highway. Purcell parked his cruiser and waited. Leary came out of the motel minutes later with two friends. He carried a rectangular package. Purcell followed them. Driving north on the Coast Highway, he noticed a burning cigarette being passed back and forth in Leary's car. He thought that was suspicious. He noticed, too, that the tail lights on Leary's station wagon were faulty. He flicked on his cruiser's cherrytop, wailed his siren, and tried to pull Leary over. Leary kept driving and Purcell finally pulled him over half a mile away. Purcell saw one of Leary's friends flick the butt away. Once again Purcell thought he would be overcome by the cloud of "marijuana aroma" coming from the car. He was getting ready to arrest Tim Leary for the second time in three days when a police sergeant arrived on the scene and gave him a direct command: Don't arrest Leary or search the car! Neal Purcell was plenty pissed off and told some of his friends that the police chief (Kenneth Huck would soon be replaced by the Marine Corps provost marshal) was "coddling" the Learys.

Timothy Leary had more than a year's wait until his trial. He spent most of that time in Berkeley, but he also spent several months at an isolated ranch off a serpentine two-lane in Idylwild, near Riverside, a ranch owned by his friend, Farmer John Griggs, and the Brotherhood of Eternal Love.

It was way back then, early in 1969, that Neal Purcell, the street cop who had busted the bigshot Dr. Leary, began investigating the Brotherhood of Eternal Love. He started gumshoeing on his own time, in the days when he had no paid business being a detective. But it was an investigation that, almost four years later, would put Neal Purcell on the front page of the *New York Times*.

At the arid base of the Santa Ana Mountains, four miles south of Highway 74 outside Idylwild, California, two miles southeast of the Lake Hemet Grocery Store in the sunworn village of Mountain Center, a dirt road winds past two padlocked fences to a fallow steppe of land and ramshackle property: a one-story wooden frame ranch house painted pale yellow, a mobile home trailer, three twelve-foot Navaho canvas tepees, and a jutting wooden tower with a fish-shaped windsock. It is a desolate whitehot landscape of cactus, mesquite, and calcite.

According to a police informant and former Oregon deputy sheriff, the Brotherhood of Eternal Love purchased this particular acreage "because it is high on a flat area and backed up by mountains on the back side, and the front side of it faces miles of open ground. They picked it for this reason: that they wouldn't be spied on and surveillance would be almost impossible." The wooden tower, the informant said, had a paramilitary function. "Twenty-four hours a day there would be a man up there watching the road, and he'd sound an alarm if anybody came." The purpose of this land, according to police theory, was to provide Brotherhood of Eternal Love members with a combination lamasery / rest home / orgy center. It was the place, police believed, where occult brotherhood initiations were held, where acid converts got their first liberating doses of holy Orange Sunshine.

Timothy Leary came with his family to his friend Farmer John Griggs's ranch after his arrest, and Neal Purcell soon noted a tantalizing piece of police "intelligence" in his file, intelligence he was later to convey to a top-level strategy session of narks: "As a matter of showing the close-knittedness of the organization, during one party where they all sat around in a circle, they swapped hands and everybody swapped partners. Then everybody held hands in a nude position, the females astraddle their male counterparts, and *had at it.* It was approximately at the time that one of the other members was shacking with Rosemary Leary and Leary was shacking with this man's wife. These orgies, in sitting in the circle, were quite common."

On July 14, 1969, Dr. Arman Leon Dollinger, Riverside County's pathologist, veteran of more than 6,000 autopsies, a highly skilled body-cavity Sherlock, was summoned to examine the dead body of a beautiful seventeen-year-old girl. She had drowned in an opaque pool of water on Farmer John's Idylwild ranch. She was Charlene Almeida of Laguna Beach, known to her friends as Dolcino. Timothy Leary had tried to give her mouth-to-mouth resuscitation.

Dr. Dollinger's investigation found detechial hemorrhages of the serosal surfaces of the lung, bloody mucus in the air passages and the bronchi. The stomach and bladder were distended by gas but empty—the girl hadn't swallowed anything for the previous twenty-four hours. Dr. Dollinger took two blood samples; both samples showed a "significant amount" of LSD in her bloodstream.

That same afternoon John Hamilton, a crusty Riverside County homicide detective, drove to the Idylwild ranch. He spoke for more than an hour with Timothy Leary. "Leary said he didn't know anything about the girl except that they called her Charlie. He said he'd seen her off and on for some time, first in Laguna Beach. He said she'd been brought to the ranch about ten days before that by Leary's daughter, Susan, and she'd been living with some of the people in the tepees, but the last few days she'd been sleeping on the ground outside. He said he'd heard some of the children hollering, and he came outside and someone had pulled her out of the pond. He tried to revive her and then drove four miles and called us." Hamilton recounted a surreal insensate conversation with Leary during which Leary, standing by the pond where the girl had died, said, "There's nothing wrong with drugs; they do more good than harm." "He also told me," Hamilton remembered, "as we were standing out there, that he was going to run for governor of California and that he liked policemen, except for narcotics officers. In fact, he said that every policeman should get a $1,000 bonus for every arrest he makes and that, if he was governor, he'd pass a law saying whatever property a policeman recovered, the policeman should get half of it."

A few weeks after Charlene Almeida's death, Dr. Dollinger and Detective Hamilton rushed to the ranch once again. Farmer John Griggs, the man who had informally founded the Brotherhood of Eternal Love, was dead from an overdose. Moments before he collapsed, he told his wife he had taken too much psilocybin, a drug of the mushroom family. The pathologist discovered that Farmer John, whose two-year-old son had collapsed from a mushroom overdose months earlier, had 108 milligrams of psilocybin in his urine, causing one sardonic clerk at the Lake Hemet Grocery Store to tell his friends, "All these hippies out there are dying of acid indigestion."

With the drug-related deaths of two young people occurring within three weeks, many area residents panicked, and so did the dozen inhabitants of the tepees and the ranch. They fled, calling Idylwild a "bad scene." Leary, still facing his Laguna trial, was charged with contributing to the delinquency of the seventeen-year-old drowning victim, charged with causing her to lead "an idle, dissolute, and immoral life" by "threat, command, and persuasion." Some street people in Laguna said that Farmer John's overdose and the temporary abandonment of the Idylwild ranch marked the end of any formally organized Brotherhood of Eternal Love.

But Neal Purcell, who would be the star witness at Leary's Laguna trial, didn't believe it. The Brotherhood of Eternal Love, he insisted, led by Timothy Leary, was directly responsible for Laguna's problems. Laguna taxpayers, enraged and frightened by the senseless death of one of their seventeen-year-olds, started paying closer heed to what Neal Purcell was saying.

Timothy Leary went to trial in October of 1969 and was found guilty of possession of marijuana. The judge sentenced him to six months to ten years and called him "an insidious and detrimental influence on society." The courtroom was packed; older Lagunans cheered; Leary's followers carried palm fronds and yellow jonquils, and one kid held high a Bible and yelled, "Behold, there is no law in this court! I have testimony here for this court—the word of God! Lord God! Come down! Come down!"

In September of 1970 Timothy Leary walked away from the California Men's Colony near San Luis Obispo, after scaling a ten-foot chain-link fence; Neal Purcell added another piece of "intelligence" to his file. An informer told him, he said, that the Brotherhood of Eternal Love had planned and financed the break. "The brotherhood had the

Weatherman spring him. They paid the Weatherman $25,000. They were waiting with cars. His clothes were piled into another car by the Weatherman and taken south that day. Leary was taken north under pretty heavy armed guard in another car. The Weatherman were armed, and supposedly they would have done you under if you tried to stop them. The passport was waiting, the plane was waiting, and they took him abroad."

By that time a kind of psychic riptide had swept through Laguna Beach. Neal Purcell was a traffic cop no longer. He was a detective and Old J. J., the Marine Corps provost marshal, was his boss. A councilman was even suggesting that all the canyon's caves be dynamited "to clear the long hairs out." And all because of events that took place on two national holidays ... days that became known as the Christmas Invasion and the Fourth of July Insurrection.

In the days before Christmas of 1970 dayglo-rainbowed posters, circulated in California and as far east as the Alleghenies, invited "all wise beings" to Laguna Beach on Christmas Day "to celebrate the birth of Jesus Christ." The posters promised a funfilled Aquarian nativity complete with cosmic light shows and celestial music and advised visitors to "bring musical instruments and plenty of food." The posters were signed: "The Brotherhood of Eternal Love." The "love fest" was to be held in the Sycamore Hills triangle of the Laguna Canyon, a mesalike area near Freaktown on Woodland Drive.

Police Chief Kenneth Huck, a good-natured moderate with progressive ideas (he wanted his men to wear navy-blue blazers instead of police uniforms), didn't think the proposed love fest was too much to fret about. He talked to one of the organizers, the owner of a local record store, and was told: "A lot of us just casually came up with the idea of getting a lot of people together. Christmas is the time of year you should be with your family." Huck viewed the brotherhood as a loose-knit, informal group of young people without any specific leadership or criminal intent. His biggest worry was a paralyzing China wall of bumper-to-bumper traffic.

But City Councilman Ed Lorr, a bluff, fiery-eyed right-winger, talked about a "shameless orgy" and "left-wing revolutionaries intent on burning our town." Ed Lorr was elected to office thanks to Laguna's political demographics—4,974 Republicans compared to 2,919 Demo-crats—and was well known for his blowhard rhetoric. ("A woman's place is in the kitchen," Ed Lorr said, "not in politics." And: "Women do not have the nervous system to serve on committees." And: "If we want to get rid of this hippie problem, we ought to go on up to the canyon and dynamite their caves." And: "You look at one of these longhairs and it reminds you of a gunsel in the Capone mob.")

Big Ed's ideas reflected the furious crosscurrents of Laguna Beach. Goonyland, suddenly the gathering place of bare-footed hippies and Leary-lovers, was traditionally proud of its artists and its sleepy-hollow pace. Ice-cream socials, bridge parties, and the American Legion's Potluck Dinner were always well attended. The Patience Wright Chapter of the Daughters of the American Revolution was still hyperactive. At the same time long-haired artists like Skip Richardson, a scrimshaw wizard who etched bucolic scenes on whale ivory, found the town a profitable place. The high school football team, even, was called the Laguna Beach Artists. In pre-Leary days town scandals revolved around people like the drunken pilot who buzzed the town in his light plane and finally landed on the beach. But now the town was divided not only by cultural but also by local political / ideological issues. Some people felt the city council and the city's bigwigs were interested only in suckering more and more tourists, building cyclopean motels, hustling new money, and thereby ruining Laguna's treasured tranquillity and uglifying its harmonious vibe. Others like Ed Lorr felt the town was threatened not by new business but by the long-haired hordes who mobbed the beaches, headshops, and bars, and frightened away all too many fat wallets.

So that when Ed Lorr heard about the Christmas Day love fest, he thought the hippies were trying to close down his town. Paranoid crowd estimates fevered the bridge party grapevine—30,000 or 40,000 hippies, ads in the *Los Angeles Free Press*, Laguna as the West Coast Wood-stock. When he talked to Chief Huck and the chief didn't seem adequately perturbed, Lorr took his case to the people, telling everyone that command decisions had to be made "to save Laguna."

As the kids started trucking to Laguna the rainy week before Christmas, Chief Huck suffered a mysterious "respiratory collapse" and removed himself from authority. There were those who whispered that the council had put too much pressure on the police chief, strong-arming him to take a big-stick stand, and he simply decided it would be wise to duck the line of fire. The council, led by Lorr, deputized itself and called in a posse of policemen from all over the state.

The kids came in record numbers, and Chief Huck's worst expectation was confirmed: traffic jammed up all over town. A 50 × 30-foot platform was erected, as well as a helicopter landing pad. It was not a rock festival, although there was unexciting music, and the fest was highlighted by the appearance of General Hershey Bar, a whey-faced war critic who came dressed up in mock-military uniform and distributed pornographic cartoons of Selective Service Director Hershey cornholing Uncle Sam . . . and Uncle Sam cornholing God. Some of the organizers got on horseback to monitor the crowds, and, after police roadblocks stopped new visitors, one kid leaped out of a plane and parachuted to the site. There was a lot of grass and a lot of acid, but the hospitals reported no serious casualties. One kid got up to say he had called the Vatican and invited the Pope. When the festival ended, a crew of kids went back to the site and cleaned it up. One of the organizers, a serious young woman who has lived in Laguna most of her life, said, "There was no real organization. The brotherhood was more a vibe than a group. It symbolized love, understanding, and dope, and it symbolized freak power in Laguna Beach. So a bunch of us got together and called ourselves members of the brotherhood and had the posters done. It was that simple."

But even though Christmas Day ended without damage, Ed Lorr held a New Year's press conference and announced that "hard-core revolutionaries intended to provoke a confrontation between hippies and police, start a riot, and burn down the town." Lorr said he was making his statement to allay any feeling that the council had "encouraged the hippies." "This was a drug festival," he said, "attended for the most part by youngsters turned loose by irresponsible parents. Young people," Lorr said, "were turned into freaks and subjected to degradations of mind and body. This council knew in advance that the city would be invaded by unknown numbers of hippies, and there was no conceivable way to prevent it. Hard information from our police revealed that SDS members were in town."

The long-haired influx and Lorr's saber-rattling, along with the hovering images of Leary and acid death, freaked the town. The frenzied feeling was apparent when the Mystic Arts headshop, a "drug haven," according to Lorr, burned to the ground during a heated council election in which three councilmen won office on a platform that the editor of the Laguna *Daily Pilot* characterized as a proposal to "drive the dirty, drug-crazed hippies out of town."

The brotherhood tried another love fest the following Easter to bemoan the Crucifixion and celebrate the Resurrection of Jesus Christ, but the happening, this time in Death Valley, was blocked by rattlesnakes, scorpions, and bone-chilling night-desert cold.

In Laguna Beach, meanwhile, now governed by the 3–2 anti-hippie council majority, City Hall was undergoing an "evacuation." Many city officials, uncomfortable with the tactics of witch-hunt and police harassment, were leaving town. Police Chief Huck, the *Daily Pilot* said, left for "an area more receptive to his progressive ideas of law enforcement." So did the city manager, the city attorney, the finance director, and the city treasurer. The new council was considering a number of "urgency resolutions"—like banning singing in the streets and on the beaches, prohibiting long-haired young people from renting motel rooms. At the same time the police department initiated a "crackdown on hippie housing" and "hippie loiterers" who dared to stand in one spot on a public sidewalk for more than two minutes. The crackdown was to climax on the Fourth of July, when the Laguna Beach police department, led by Neal Purcell, attacked the residents of Freaktown—for setting off patriotic firecrackers, which, naturally, disturbed the peace.

Woodland Drive, out in the Laguna Canyon, is about a mile from the beach and twists into another meandering road called Victory Walk. It consists of four streets in a single-block area, a makeshift colony of some fifty funky anti-suburban homes, most of them adorned with megalithic peace symbols, grinning Buddhas, and yellowed posters of Timothy Leary and Che Guevara. Laguna Beach's Freaktown butts a hill that rises several hundred feet and is thick with flora, thistles, and crag. One of the homes on Woodland comprises three addresses—237, 245, and 247—and is known to police as The Red House, The Leary House, and The Brotherhood Headquarters.

Detective Sergeant Neal Purcell sits behind his cluttered desk at the Laguna Beach police department headquarters, his hair spray-netted and dry-look ducktailed, and talks about Freaktown: "When I first arrived there, and going through that area for the first time in 1968, I found out quickly that it wasn't the conventional-type setting. When you talk about a one-block area with fifty homes on it, you might think that it's, you know, curbs, sidewalks, gutters, fire hydrants, and so on, but that's not true. There is one streetlight in that whole area, two paved roads approximately twenty-two feet wide. Off of this are several paths. The paths are only made of dirt, and they are only six feet wide, and there are houses on both sides of the paths. The surrounding hills are made up of nothing but deep holes, small caves, heavy vegetation, and a lot of other dirt paths.

"Now, where I found that the area was different than the other neighborhoods in Laguna Beach is, I quickly found, for the most part, it was young people who lived there. They openly smoked marijuana out in the streets. They openly sold LSD. I would find that trying to surveil the area was almost an impossible task. They had what was known as a bicycle patrol made up of many of these people where they would ride bicycles and carry a police-type whistle, and every time they saw someone who looked like a policeman they would blow the whistle off and the whistle would be heard throughout the colony there, and after a while it sounded like a bunch of crickets in there with those whistles. They also had platforms up in the large trees where I have observed on many occasions people standing, some with binoculars, some without, and they also had whistles. They had more dogs in that area than I have ever seen in the normal-type block. I was told this several times: that the dogs were trained to smell the gun oil. I didn't believe this at first, but, unless a police officer has a certain odor about them, every time we would go in that area, you might manage to get in there and be in there five minutes, and all of a sudden a dog would sniff you out, and then you would have several dogs on you trying to get you out of the area. We would see where strangers would come into the area and the dogs wouldn't bother them at all. Then the first time one of us would go in there, the dogs would get all excited.

"The setting there, I have watched them many times, the people there smoking dope out in the street. I have also found other peculiar things. On the outside there is a frontage road that runs along parallel to Laguna Canyon Road. The road would line up with individuals sitting in their cars, and maybe the driver or one individual in the car would be missing. I would sit back in the shadows and watch a car drive up, one individual getting out, go into the area, and he would come back in about five minutes, and I have made several arrests, into the hundreds.

When the person came back they would put on some type of ego trip that they had to show the dope they had just bought from someone inside, and as they would be showing it to their friends in the car, I would walk up and see the dope and place them under arrest."

On the night of July Fourth, 1970, the freaks of Woodland were having a block party. Roman candles and firecrackers were exploding everywhere, and a high-decibel rock band served as accompaniment. Some 250 freaks sat around, danced, and smoked joints. Police went into the area, claiming they were responding to "noise complaints" and, using a bullhorn, ordered the celebrants to disperse. A kid yelled, "What about the firecrackers in the other parts of town?" But the party ended, and two of the police cruisers left the area.

One cruiser stayed behind. Narcotics Detective Neal Purcell sat in his car and watched as a kid sitting on a stoop smoked a marijuana cigarette. Neal Purcell arrested him. He spread-eagled the kid against a car, frisked, and handcuffed him. It was at this point, Purcell claimed, that "a pack of hippies" attacked him with fists and bottles. Purcell issued a 999 call on his police radio: "May Day, officer needs assistance!" Five police agencies responded: forty-four policemen, twenty-three cruisers, and the Costa Mesa police helicopter.

The freak Fourth of July turned into chaos and madness. Purcell set up an emergency command post and coached the assault; policemen used billy clubs and Mace, chasing some kids through houses and into the canyon, which was brightly Klieg-lighted by the chopper. Seventeen persons were arrested, eight of them on narcotics charges. A Vietnam veteran who had lost an eye in combat was Maced at point-blank range. Purcell displayed a loaded German Luger, which he said he'd found at the scene; he said three wine bottles had struck his command cruiser. Another police car suffered $150 damage.

The ACLU filed a protest and, singling out Purcell, accused the police of brutality and overreaction. Purcell replied, "Drugs are Laguna's biggest problem, and they've been the biggest problem ever since I've gotten here." The former city manager, James Wheaton, issued a report saying that, if Purcell had not made his marijuana arrest, "the party atmosphere would probably have continued." The mayor, issuing a separate report, noted there had been "some overreaction," and quoted a witness who had watched policemen billyclub a girl and drag her by the hair while other policemen grabbed her boy friend's ponytail and sprayed Mace into his face. Purcell replied, "Taking of prisoners by hair-holding is not uncommon."

Neal Purcell was praised for his "decisive action" by many residents, particularly by Councilman Ed Lorr, and soon became his new police chief's number one gun. Neal Purcell and J. J. Kelly got along just fine. The provost marshal of Pendleton and Quantico had quite a reputation himself. Old J. J. had busted more homosexuals ("fruits") in the Marine Corps than any other cop-commandant and was the first cop in America to train grass-sniffing narkdogs.

When fifty-three-year-old J. J. Kelly—father of eight, walking carica- ture of the B-movie Irish cop, founder of the U.S. Marine Corps Military Police School—took over as provost marshal of Laguna Beach, Neal Purcell finally got his "green light" to go after the Brotherhood of Eternal Love. J. J. got Purcell the most modern electrical snooping gadgets available: a videotape recorder, which would dramatically capture narcotics transactions; a sensitive two-way Japanese listening device, which could be hidden on the body and had a four-mile "ear range." J. J. Kelly blustered the week after he took over that he would not "coddle" drug addicts of any variety. A reporter asked him whether he had ever smoked grass and the chief scowled that he had not. "When I was in the Marine Corps," he said, "I was trained to detect the smell. I sat in a room where it was smoked for educational purposes. I thought the smell most unpleasant." He recalled, too, with swelling pride, that while at Pendleton he had been the liaison with Secret Servicemen guarding Richard Nixon at nearby San Clemente. He had been invited to meet the President at the Western White House and had been photographed with the President on the golf course. The picture, J. J. Kelly explained, was one of his most prized mementos, though, lamentably, he could not show it to anyone because Richard Nixon was dressed in his golf clothes and photographers were not allowed to snap the President in Arnold Palmer attire.

Weeks after J. J. Kelly took office, Ed Lorr's council majority passed a series of new statutes at the chief's behest. Skateboarding was prohibited; all parade permits were to be personally granted approval by the chief of police; jaywalkers and homosexuals would be prosecuted vigorously.

Shortly afterwards, a sixteen-year-old boy was arrested, frisked, handcuffed, and, as his mother watched horrified, taken to jail. The offense? Skateboarding. The skateboard was taken from him and tagged as evidence. Two long-haired eighteen-year-olds were arrested, handcuffed, and jailed for crossing Coast Highway at Cleo Street against the light. They were released the next morning on $5 bond.

On Labor Day, 1971, Chief Kelly's men, once again led by Neal Purcell, arrested sixteen persons for taking boisterous part in a fifty-year-old Laguna tradition, the Walkaround. Each Labor Day in Laguna the folks mourn the end of summer by walking from bar to bar on the Pacific Coast Highway. This time, when some 100 staggerers reached the Orphanage Bar and couldn't get in because the place was too full, eight plainclothesmen came running across the street in flying wedge formation and ordered the pixilated walkers to disperse. According to Chief Kelly, his men were attacked by these pot-valiant mourners. The mourners claimed police flailed them with nightsticks and flashlights. An ex-Marine captain and Vietnam veteran said he was billyclubbed by three policemen and told "you found out what happens to people who argue with policemen." He said he was pressed face down onto the redhot hood of a police cruiser with an overheated engine and searched. An officer directing traffic held a can of Mace and, as the cars passed, raised the can and nonchalantly sprayed the drivers.

Some Laguna natives were getting just a trifle upset. One man got up at a city council meeting and sarcastically asked when certain other measures would be adopted. Measures like: mandatory removal of vocal cords of all resident dogs at birth; prohibition of consumption of alcoholic beverages between consenting adults; immediate construction of permanent police barricades at both roads leading into town. A local columnist proposed another law—conditional use of permits for the building of sand castles. "No sand castle may be built if the shape deviates from the established norm for sand-castle construction. A copy of the norm is on file with the chief of police. No castle may be erected to represent anything resembling a phallic symbol. All offensive castle plans will be destroyed by the chief of police."

But J. J. Kelly's most controversial move was his offensive against homosexuals. He set up a "Gay Squad" in a town having one of the

116

proportionately largest gay colonies in the state. Heading it was that veteran gay-hunter from Newport Beach, Neal Purcell. Purcell donned a disguise, practiced the art of the limp wrist, and wore tight pants to act the part of a fiftyish roué enticing tourist gays. He was armed with his new Japanese two-way listening device. He arrested several homosexuals, handcuffing them on the beach for making lewd advances. When gays banded together to protest the harassment, Chief Kelly replied, "I do not condone homosexuality." The crackdown had a wild irony: Laguna Beach's newest celebrity-resident was Christine Jorgensen, forty-six, one of America's pioneer transsexuals.

While Neal Purcell dressed up in his gay disguise at nights, he was still investigating the Brotherhood of Eternal Love by day, cracking down on dopers . . . and collecting brutality charges. Purcell raided a canyon home, armed with a warrant suspecting possession of marijuana, and found the homeowner swimming in his pool. The owner claimed that, while he was still in the pool, Purcell grabbed a metal pole and beat him over the head, then sprayed him with Mace as he tried to get out of the water. The man's wife claimed she had been hurled against a wall and then into her bedroom, causing a severe lump on her head. When Neal Purcell was beaten into the surf trying to arrest a Marine smoking a joint on the beach, a lot of gays and dopers were delighted.

But Purcell was happy, too. The man who had begun investigating the Brotherhood of Eternal Love while still a traffic cop had finally struck paydirt. He had tried, through the years, to garner other agencies' funds and support. He had failed. "Our toughest job," he'd say later, "was selling everyone, including our supervisors, on the idea that an outfit like the brotherhood, in bare feet and long hair, could actually exist."

Now he had convinced the Bureau of Narcotics Enforcement, Attorney General Evelle J. Younger's infamous raiders, to take part. The BNE had a powerful ally, Orange County District Attorney Cecil Hicks, who recruited cooperation of the Federal Bureau of Narcotics and Dangerous Drugs.

The district attorney of Orange County loved it. The brotherhood was perfect. He had prosecuted bottomless dancers and porno bookstore owners. He had denounced the Supreme Court, sexual freedom, draft dodgers, and the President's Commission on Marijuana. Now freckle-faced Cecil Hicks, who aspired to be Evelle J. Younger's successor as Attorney General of the state of California, drew a bead on his most custom-tailored target: the "Hippie Mafia."

A main link in the case against the Brotherhood of Eternal Love is a thirty-four-year-old former Oregon deputy sheriff named Bob Ramsey, who swore, under oath, that his own brother-in-law, Glenn Lynd, was "Timothy Leary's number one assistant."

Bob Ramsey, who was once a deputized narcotics informer for the Josephine County sheriff's department, claimed that his brother-in-law trusted him implicitly, as a member of the family, and spilled his innermost secrets "whenever he got high." He said he was revealing the details of these "intimate conversations" because of a heartfelt concern about "everybody going to the dogs." He said his brother-in-law had gone to the dogs, and he denied Glenn Lynd's claim that Bob Ramsey was doing his best to put him behind bars because Bob owed him several thousand dollars he couldn't pay.

Bob Ramsey traced the Brotherhood of Eternal Love's trail to 1957, when Glenn Lynd was fifteen years old. "I was maybe eighteen or nineteen, and Glenn was about fifteen, when I met his sister. He was running around just like a school kid, and I started going around with his sister. Then we got married and got a place over in Anaheim. I was working for General Motors, and Glenn started hanging around with a fairly fast bunch of kids. He came to me at GM one time. I guess he had already been smoking marijuana; he had picked it up somewhere. He came to me one time when I got off work and asked me to buy some for him. And I said, 'I don't know where I could get any.' And then I remembered a guy at GM that had pretty good contacts with people, and I introduced Glenn to him. He was from East Los Angeles, and Glenn got to be friends with him and went to Los Angeles and started buying marijuana and reselling it. Then Glenn kind of drifted off by himself for two or three years, and he was going around with a girl at that time who is now his wife, and he would show up periodically and he would leave again. He wasn't working. And he appeared maybe three years later when he was growing his hair a little longer and trying to grow a mustache, and then he came up to me one day and told me that he had tried something. It was different and strange, and I asked him what it was, and he said it was a substance known as LSD. He said it enlightened his mind and gave him an insight on things. And I asked him, 'Like what?' And he said, 'Jesus or God.' This was around 1960.

"Then he kind of drifted off again. He'd take off and go places and come back and then be gone again. He had been running around with a group that I didn't know, and finally he came back and said these other people he was running around with, they could see God too, and that all their lives, thoughts, and feelings were the same, that they should form a family or group that live together. Then, in 1962, he was becoming heavier and heavier involved in the acid, and he went to their meetings, and some of these people, the group he was in—it wasn't actually formed yet—had listened to Leary speak, and Leary was speaking on the use of LSD and Glenn was talking to Leary all the time. Then he drifted off again.

"He came back around 1965, somewhere around there, and he had kind of whiskers then and his hair was getting down on his back a little bit—never on his back, but on his shoulders—and his clothes were the hippie type. They were dirty, and his shirt had patches on it, and stuff like this. Then he said they were talking about forming this family and also forming a kind of business where they could sell beads, leather goods, and other stuff the hippies would be interested in. And he said these people had the same feeling he did. They wanted to do this, the same people he had been with over two or three years—these were still the same people with him now. Then I saw him later, and he told me that they had their shop going and it was really good. Well, he went on to explain to me that the name of his, or their name—he told me it was not only him, but these other people behind him at that time—he still didn't tell me any names yet, but the people living in the family, the group, or this religious cult, had formed this business, and he said the name of the shop was the Mystic Arts. He told me also that they had formed their own religious group at this time, and he said, 'We'll start our own religion,' and it would be based on LSD, and it would be called the Brotherhood of Eternal Love. They were going to sell stuff here—all types of stuff here pertaining to the heavies or the hippies—and with this money they were going to buy land where they could go out and do their own thing. At that time he didn't call it a commune, but this church would finance this because the hippies were becoming very strong at that time; they were coming on pretty good.

119

"Well, he kept asking me to come down to this Mystic Arts Shop. Well, I didn't go down there then. It was a period of time after that, a few months, and then I finally went down there and went in, and Glenn was there, and he showed me around, and they did have quite a place there. They had one area that was all leather, one was all tapestry and what have you. They had hash pipes and everything like this. Well, then he took me to the back. They had a back room behind there where people stayed. They sat around, and they had a large hookah there, and he said that the heads come in and out of there, or the hippies or the heavies and the good friends, and sit in the back room and smoke a little dope, you know, and get relaxed and buy what they need and then leave. And Glenn said, 'This is where the people, the brothers, come in.' He didn't call them the heavies, he called them the brothers. And also where the people who run the shop sit around and smoke their dope. Now, this hashish, you know, you can, by smoking enough of it, it just puts a person down. Later in years I have seen, with these people, that where they have smoked it, they couldn't even get up, they would just lay—it takes years of practice to become a real good hash smoker, your lungs have to develop so you don't choke or cough or throw up, and I have seen people smoke this and just lay on the ground and not even move. It would be a big problem just to smile.

"Well, I didn't have any more contact with Glenn for a while. Just every now and then I would see him and hear of him, and in mid-'67 I moved to Oregon and was up there about six months when Glenn showed up. It was probably around September of '67, and just one day in the morning he came driving up, and he had this Volkswagen bus, a brand-new one, and he had the beard and everything like this. He had his wife and his two kids with him.

"I told him it was a nice-looking Volkswagen bus there he had, and he said, 'Yeah, it is. I bought it while I was in Germany. A friend and I were over there.' The bus was the expensive kind where on the inside you make a camper, and it had a stove you fold up, bunks, and electrical heating, and it was a very expensive vehicle. One thing I noticed about it, it had oversized tires on it, tremendously large tires in the back, and I seen that the sides of the wheel-well on both back sides were cut out, and I said, 'Glenn, what did you mess up a vehicle like that for?' He just laughed about it and said, 'I get better traction on it.' And I said, 'Come on, Glenn, you didn't cut it up for that.' And he said, 'I'll show you,' and he took me around to the back of the vehicle and showed me back up under the tires, and there was a real wide place which was a false bottom put in under this Volkswagen on both sides, and he had to take a torch and take that piece off because, when they bought this bus, they drove it across Europe and one Soviet-held country and ended up in Afghanistan, and at that time he said they loaded it up with hash over there. So they put the false bottom on it, and that's the reason they didn't have no undercoating sprayed on it in Germany, because he said if they put an undercoating on there and then they had to scrape it all off again, put the new bottom in there, and respray it, it might not match up or [might] peel off or something. So when they got it to Afghanistan, they would weld this piece up in there—put the hash in, weld it, and then undercoat it, and it would look just like it was done in Germany. That way, when they came through Customs and Customs officials looked at it, they would show their bill of sale and title, and it would look like it came from Germany.

"He said he got the hash in Afghanistan, through these two brothers; he only talked about these two brothers, they controlled the whole town in Afghanistan. They controlled everything; they were the wealthiest men in the city, and the hashish market was theirs, and they also controlled the law in that town; they were the law. He told me that in the beginning he just bumped into these guys, he was over there for the Mystic Arts, the headshop, and he went over there to India and Pakistan and some of these countries looking for tapestries and silverware and brassware and stuff. He was over there and buying that stuff, and he happened to come through this town, and it's a custom over there to smoke hash when you are making a deal, of any kind. Over there hash is like getting a cup of coffee here. So Glenn is telling me this, and he said they got up one morning fairly early and they took three donkeys and they took off, and he said, 'We went for a couple of hours maybe from the city and up pretty high, and when we got up to a place that was kind of like a plateau or a terrace, it looked like corn had been planted there the way it was laid out in rows, with the exception that these plants, some would reach eighteen or twenty feet in height, and the stalks would be as big around as your wrist, and the leaves would be two or three feet in length. Glenn decided then that he was going to buy his stuff standing, and he said there was acres and acres of this stuff growing. So he stayed there while the stuff was harvested, and he said the people would go along and they would pull this up by the roots, and these stalks then would be taken in and hung upside down in these buildings and the top of the plants, he said, a thing grew out that kind of looked like a pod or a cattail—similar to a cattail, and when a cattail gets dry it gets kind of fluffy and powdery. Well, that's the way the top of this hashish plant would be, and all the resin, by hanging it upside down, all the resin in the plant would run to the head of this thing, and it would dry out, and then they would take sticks and put plastic underneath it and they would beat this plant and beat it until the pollen would fall on this plastic and all the pollen is the hashish. Well, you couldn't ship it like that because it was just powder. So they would ask, 'Do you want animal fat, vegetable oil, or water mixed with it to pack it?' And then you would pick one of the three; you would pick what form you wanted it in—soles, slabs, or if you were going to smuggle it in some other form, say, in vases or dishes, whatever shape you wanted. I know one guy that had some vases made and painted, and they were pure hashish, and it came through Customs as pottery, and they would just bust it and sell it then.

"So after Glenn got the stuff he went back downtown in Afghanistan to see these brothers who got the stuff for him, and their names were Hyatullah and Amanullah. And Amanullah told him not to worry about getting the stuff back to the States. He said, 'Just put your car here, and we'll take care of everything.' And then the false bottom was put in and the hash was put in and the bus was undercoated. There was no worry about being ripped off by any of the local officials because Amanullah controlled the officials. So the vehicle could sit there and nobody is going to break into it, because, he says, over in that country death is very common, and if a person was breaking into your vehicle, they would just execute him right there, kill him right there, and that's all there was to it, because it was Amanullah's property and you didn't do anything against Amanullah because he was the power. And he didn't have to worry about any of the checkpoints out of the country because they had all been paid off by the two brothers, and when he got to the port the vehicle was put aboard the boat and there were no problems, papers were waiting, and the vehicle was shipped to the States.

"Then after a while Glenn started telling me all kinds of things about the brotherhood, about the dodges they used to beat the law. Like the names, for instance. The names are real important—like, one person would have three names. Say, here's three people and these three people have three names. All right, at a given time these three people would pick one of those three names; they would do three different jobs at one time—meaning one guy would take off for San Diego, one for Oregon, and one for New York, with loads of hash. All right, one climbs out in New York and he's using the name Christopher Leake. Yet another Christopher Leake was in San Diego with a load, and the two agencies would get to arguing, and then a third organization would get into the act saying there was another Christopher Leake in another place. All they know is three different people, three different areas got a load that day. Christopher Leake brought it in, and they don't know nothing about it. They run the record back and go to a town that doesn't exist in Utah. They have a driver's license, and it comes up at the Department of Motor Vehicles a dead end.

"Glenn told me that the brotherhood has its own moving identification system. It's still in existence the last time we knew. This is a bus with the windows painted, and at any one time the brotherhood knows where this bus is. They contact this bus—it's on the move—and need a birth certificate printed up right away, a Social Security card, or, if you have to leave the country, a passport is available, but they take the birth certificate and the Social Security card and take it to the Motor Vehicles Department in the state they are in and get a driver's license to match this person, even though there is no such person.

"Another thing he said was that the brotherhood had strict orders not to use anything over a $100 bill, because it would attract attention. The $100 bill was very familiar in California. So it would be tens, twenties or 100s. The fives they didn't use too much because they were too bulky. Glenn told me of this one particular deal he made. He made this deal and he took a brand-new Cadillac. He rented it from an outfit in L.A., a brand-new Cadillac. He bought very expensive clothes, kind of in the Western style; he took his wife and two kids and loaded the trunk of the car with hash in boxes. He was clean-shaven at that time. He took off for Newark, New Jersey, with this big supply of hashish. He said he was in Arizona. It was in the winter, and he had to stop by a restaurant, and he was going to put some chains on because it was snowing, and two highway patrolmen helped him, took all the boxes out, helped him put the chains on the car, put the boxes back in the back of the car. Glenn thanked them and offered them a $20 bill, and they said no, they couldn't accept it, they were police officers, and he got in his car and drove off."

Sergeant Neal Purcell must have liked Bob Ramsey's description of the "brains" behind the Brotherhood of Eternal Love.

"Timothy Leary was their god," Ramsey said, "their god and Glenn's god. So at the time a lot of the stuff that Glenn did, the plans he had—Leary taught them how to watch people and what to do and how to be different so people wouldn't look at you. A lot of plans laid for the smuggling came from Leary . . . . Leary kept telling them, 'Don't be like the everyday rumdums.'"

Neal Purcell and the Orange County Grand Jury accepted Bob Ramsey's every word as gospel truth. Even when Bob Ramsey horrified the jurors by saying he had often watched brotherhood members snort so much cocaine that "their eyes bled."

In May of 1971 Patrick Brennan, twenty-three, who intends to devote his life to the study of cancer and viral disease, was arrested for possession of 7.5 kilos of marijuana. "When you get busted," he'd say later, "you try to talk the cops into believing you can lead them to something bigger if they go easy on you." He was arrested because two others, also arrested for possession, told police Pat Brennan was a heavy dealer. The two who snitched got a break. After his own arrest, Pat Brennan told police he could lead them to something bigger—if, of course, he got a break. Like what? the cops asked. Like the Brotherhood of Eternal Love, he said. The cancer scholar got his break and immediately implicated his best friend.

"I'd have to start around 1966 with Danny Caserta, a guy I grew up with. We continually went surfing together, and he was always in some sort of drug activity, and, as it went, everyone moved into the New-port-Laguna vicinity and became what we called brothers. At that time Timothy Leary and Ken Kesey and several other people had got the publicity, had started this new turned-on era of people, and so everybody sort of decided to protect one another and call each other the Brotherhood of Love and use the same attorneys and keep it a secret clan in order to prevent any of them from being busted. So everybody stuck together and knew one another from taking drugs. The main drug was LSD, and to be a member of the brotherhood you had to be with several persons and usually take a very large dose of LSD. Well, I was in school most of the time, and they could see that, you know, I didn't want to take that many drugs because they could see maybe a future in me helping them by going to school in chemistry. So I was sort of not into taking drugs, say every other day or every week, which most of them did.

"For example, Danny always asked me questions about buffing LSD and what would be the most stable solution to put it in and at what temperature would it degrade, where should we keep it, things like that, useful information, and I was always a friend and I would always give them helpful advice. I can remember on several occasions at Danny's places, one of the brotherhood places, maybe there would be usually five to ten people, we would take maybe a large dose of LSD and go up to the Ortega Hot Springs and spend the night there and, you know, supposedly have a spiritual enlightenment and become better brothers, things like that. And my observation is that there was some enlightenment. If everybody wants to say they are brothers and hold maybe their hands and believe they are really seeing God or being more spiritual, that can happen.

"So finally they asked me to help synthesize LSD from lysergic acid. On several occasions they had the lysergic acid and they wanted somebody to furnish the place to do it, make several grams of LSD. Well, I never had the time to do that. If they needed some advice or any—if they needed the name of a drug that they might have to order or something, I would help them in that respect. They did ask me to make a drug called DMT, and on several occasions I did do that. On several occasions Danny Caserta asked me to drop out of school for a while and become another Owsley. Right now the brotherhood is obtaining their LSD from their own manufacturer. There is also another way of getting it. They grow the lysergic acid from a fungus, and it takes maybe a good year to culture—it's a ripe fungus and they can obtain that through underground ways, and then get someone like myself to do the final steps. And they manufacture it at a very low cost. Of course, it's buffed out first, which means it is diluted with something like lactose. They're tabbed into saccharine-sized pills, usually orange, which is where the Orange Sunshine stuff comes from because it is known to be very potent. I remember Danny Caserta with gloves on one time, surgical gloves, and he was jokingly dosing—or he had capsules—small number-five gelatin capsules, and he was buffing it with lactose. Most of it was being distributed through his brotherhood friends in Laguna Beach, and that's all I know. It could have gone all over the United States.

"Sometimes they capped it, which is a very easy technique. What they do is, they buff out or make a bowl of 4,000 hits of LSD powder, and they take a capsule with their hands, you know, with surgical gloves, tightly, and the large end of the capsules, keep tapping it into the powder until it is compressed, and put the little cap over it. Then they got their tabbing machines. I don't know where they got machines, maybe from the old pharmaceutical warehouse or the underground people they know. Then they stain it orange and put a small amount of strychnine into it, which gives a more vivid or colorful hallucination.

"A lot of brotherhood guys have gone to Maui, in Hawaii. There's a lot of them there. There's a very factual movie called *Rainbow Bridge*, about a lot of people who live in Maui and the north shore. It's a documentary of Jimi Hendrix, and several brotherhood people are in it, including Hendrix.

"I got busted because two of the brotherhood guys snitched on me. They called me at work and told me that, you know, being I'm a brother of them they wanted this marijuana and had to have it there right away. I could get it easily because, being a part of the brotherhood, there are several people I could call and get it within a few hours. I paid $130 a kilo for it, and they were going to pay me, you know, whenever they could. And they were setting me up all the time, working for the cops after they'd been busted. I didn't know they'd been arrested or I'd never have talked to them because you don't deal with anybody, even if they're in the brotherhood, after they've been arrested.

"They're not dealing in acid that heavily anymore. I know because I used to get these postcards from Danny Caserta from Afghanistan and I heard he was into hash oil, that they were doing most of their operating in hash oil."

The way Patrick Brennan told it, brotherhood members got the red-carpet treatment whenever they went to Afghanistan as the guests of two brothers who owned half the country. It was shortly after Brennan took his revenge on the "brothers" who had betrayed him that Laguna Beach Detective Neal Purcell requested permission to travel to Afghanistan—before it was discovered that one of those two mysterious Afghan brothers was a longtime employee of the American Embassy.

Neal Purcell didn't get to Afghanistan. A bunko artist and part-time hypnotist went in his stead, and it didn't even cost the narks any money.

Owen Caldwell, fifty-eight, was in the Orange County jail on May 5, 1971, charged with grand theft in a phony real-estate transaction. He wound up in the same cell with a "hippie-looking kid" named Michael Theodore.

"While I was awaiting my hearing in court, Michael Theodore told me that he was in there for possession for sale of narcotics, and he asked me if I ever had used any, and I told him no. He tried to turn me on to acid. I told him that, because of a heart condition, I wasn't able to use drugs and wasn't particularly interested, but my profession at the time, I was a hypnotist, and he was very much interested in that. So I started working with him on hypnotism.

"In the course of the ten days that I was in custody, Michael Theodore told me—he had invited me out to a ranch in Idylwild that he told me was owned by this brotherhood and that he and Dr. Timothy Leary were close friends, and he said that we could go out into the woods and drop acid and turn on. Theodore and I had agreed that, when he got out, he could use my car. At the time I was buying a mobile home in Huntington Beach, and I asked him if he wanted to stay at my place. So things went on until the twenty-first of November, and at the time I was working as a bartender and I got a phone call from Theodore asking me if I would be willing to go overseas and bring in some narcotics—smuggle in some narcotics. So we arranged a meeting the following morning in my trailer, and with him he brought an Alexander Kulik, whom I had never seen before, and they explained to me that this was hash oil, which was new to me, and they said they would pay for my expenses, which was the air fare over there, plus my living expenses.

"I was supposed to go to Kabul, Afghanistan. We would be over there about two weeks, and they wanted to smuggle back one gallon of oil of hashish, and I asked them what the value was, and they said it was around a hundred thousand dollars. So I asked them what my pay would be and they said they would pay me $2,000 cash, plus my expenses, but as soon as that happened, then I could start doing it on a twice-a-month basis and my fee would be greater. So then I asked them, 'What happens if I get ripped off over there? Arrested by a foreign government?' You know. And they said, 'Don't worry, the brotherhood will take care of you; you are working for us now.' I said okay, I'd do it.

"So the next day I went to the district attorney's office and related what had happened, and they introduced me to an officer who, in turn, brought up Sergeant Purcell from Laguna Beach and several of the state narcotics officers, and I told them the story and said I wanted to cooperate. Well, they checked with the feds, and the feds said I couldn't do it because they couldn't protect me in Afghanistan. And I told them, 'Well, I've put a lot of time in on this and I'm not going to give it up now.' So they said, 'Well, if you want to go as a private citizen, okay.' Then I went back to Theodore and this Kulik, and we talked about how it was going to be done. They were going to take my measurements for a vest and make a plastic vest with pockets in it to put this oil of hashish in and I would be able to carry a gallon of this oil. I said, 'I'm an old guy, and I have no dealings with narcotics. Why me?' And they said that an older man dressed as a businessman was not followed by Customs; it was the long-haired types who got the skin searches.

"So Kulik and I went over; Theodore stayed behind. We stayed apart on the plane because we'd stay apart when we got there, too, because he was definitely a dirty hippie-type person and would draw attention to me, who was a businessman. When we got to Kabul, he was going to go to my hotel and check in under my right name and he would contact me. We stopped over in Frankfurt and we stayed at a hotel near the airport, and I saw him there. Well, he had taken some patties of pressed hashish with him to smoke en route. So, when we were in the hotel that night, he smoked almost continuously the hashish. We finally arrived in Kabul after seven stops. On the second day there, or about on the fourth of December, Kulik stopped by and said everything was going fine, that his friend had procured a hundred gallons of alcohol to manufacture the hashish, and he was going out to buy some other little home pressure cookers, trying to speed up the production. Then on the seventh he came by and reeked of hashish powder. In fact, he had borrowed some long woolen underwear that I had, and he was coming in to take a shower and to change underwear, and even the underwear was impregnated with this pure hashish. He withdrew from his pocket a wooden matchbook like you would get in a hotel or something, but it was filled with hashish in its original form. On the eleventh of December Kulik and I drove to a little town to buy the hashish, and he got it from some rug dealer. He had a minibus, with a driver furnished, and it's on the Russian border, north on the Russian border. So we went up there, and I entered into the store with him and saw him buy ten pounds of hashish. This was just for local use.

"We went back to Kabul, and after about a week Kulik came up to the hotel carrying this overnight bag and it contained a vest—not a plastic vest. I asked him what happened to the plastic vest. Well, the large suitcase that he had tried to bring on the plane was too heavy, and it would have cost him an additional $700 just to ship it over. There were a lot of health foods in there plus the plastic vest. Theodore was supposed to ship it over the next day, but evidently he never did. So Kulik had to improvise. What he had done was taken a piece of sheeting, kind of a pullover sweater, but with the sides open. It was like a serape you pull over your head, and then they had taken fourteen baggies and put this gallon of oil in the fourteen baggies. He sealed it and then had gotten some epoxy glue and glued on the corners, on the front and back, to this so-called vest. Well, the minute he walked into my room with this package, it reeked so strong it almost turned your stomach. It reeked with hashish. I said to him, "There's no way I could get this through any Customs place.' And he said, 'Don't worry about it, everything's taken care of, it's cool.' I said, 'All right, I'm not going to argue.' He said, 'You've got to get ahold of some bandage or some elastic thing,' and he had me take my shirt off and put it over my head and let it hang there. Two of the bags were leaking. Grease was leaking out, and it was a wonderful situation. I said, 'Why don't you leave the stuff here and go on and come back about two this afternoon, and I'll go out and get the elastic bandage, wrap me in it, and I'll put on a shirt and overcoat and make sure it's not too bulky.' So he left, and as soon as he got away I figured I was clear and took a cab and went down to the American Embassy and asked for a Customs man. So I laid out the whole story—what I had done, what happened back here, and what was happening. So the agent managed to get surveillance on my room, and we agreed that, when Kulik got into the room, I would close the drapes.

"So, on scheduled arrival, Kulik entered, and as he entered, I said, 'I'll pull the drapes so nobody can see us.' And he said, 'No, stand in the window so I can see what I'm doing.' So I stood in the window, and he was wrapping me with these baggies of the oil and the agent was over there and saw it all. We were ready to depart the morning after the fitting of the vest. The Customs guy called me that night and told me we had to get the bust in Kabul because the first point of landing after Kabul was Teheran, Iran. If you are caught smuggling through there, they take the man or whoever it is to the police station, and your pockets are emptied out. Your next of kin's address and phone numbers are taken, and you are taken in the back and shot. There's no trial. They listed seventeen Americans that had been executed in the month of

November. They don't have a drug problem there. So the next morning, rather than put the vest on, I took the vest and put it in Kulik's little handbag and bundled myself up like there was a bulk, like I had the vest on under my coat. Now I had Kulik's bag with the oil in it. After about twenty minutes this Kulik entered. There was a long line. The airport was crowded. This is the time they [the Indians] were bombing West Pakistan, which was only a matter of a few hours' drive away, and there were many, many refugees crowding into the airport. Finally, as he approached the ticket counter, I walked up behind him. It was easy to do with the crowd. I noticed the agent on the side. As Kulik reached the counter and surrendered his passport, I tapped him on the shoulder and said, 'Alex, it's too hot for me to carry,' and I put the bag with the hash oil in it down beside him. Then I walked into the passenger loading area. Kulik looked at the bag and didn't say anything, he didn't pick it up. Then the agent said, 'Your bag, sir,' and Kulik picked it up, and the minute he picked it up they arrested him for holding a gallon of hash oil."

If Owen Caldwell, that cagey old flim-flam man, was worried, he had no reason to be. Standing behind him in the passenger loading zone was the federal agent who had been assigned to track the Brotherhood of Love in Afghanistan. Agent Terence Burke, who spoke fluent Pushtun and Farse, was a veteran of twelve years in the Central Intelligence Agency, most of those years in Vietnam, specializing in counterinsurgency and tactical intelligence.

Most of Afghanistan's top-quality hashish crop grows near the Afghan-Pakistani border. It is a no-man's-land without the legal jurisdiction of either government and where tribesmen are left to govern themselves. Neither Afghan nor Pak police enter because too many macheted corpses have been sent back to police stations, their mouths bulging with genitals. A lot of hippies go there seeking their cheap highs, and a lot of them never return. In January of 1972 four French hippies were decapitated. Two desert tribesmen had invited them into their homes and figured they could become heroes of Islam by butchering four infidels; they mutilated the hippies with gleaming swords. It was this no-man's-land at which agent Terence Burke arrived while investigating the Brotherhood of Eternal Love. "We find bodies of Western kids in the desert all the time," he said, "and nobody ever knows who killed them and no one knows about it. The bodies just rot in the sun."

Terence Burke's Federal Bureau of Narcotics and Dangerous Drugs identification card number is 107, which puts him a single digit away from James Bond. Suave and swashbuckling, he once served as an undercover courier smuggling hashish from India to the United States and then joined with German Interpol to bust the smugglers. Agent Burke identified the "overlords" of the no-man's-land hashish fields as those two mysterious Kabul brothers, Hyatullah and Amanullah Tokhi.

Hyatullah ran a hotel and rug shop in Kabul; Amanullah worked for six years as the maintenance supervisor of the American Embassy. He quit the job in October of 1971 when, agent Burke said, "he started disappearing from work and then showed up with gold rings and expensive suits rather than in his very simple Afghan clothes." According to Terence Burke, the Tokhis were two of the biggest dealers of hashish in the Middle East, yet he would admit later that he had never even visited their rug shop "where all the deals were made." Why not? "Because I didn't think it was important."

The brothers were dealing in hash oil, Burke said, "now the hottest new commodity on the international market." "It is a distillation of hash in which they use 180-proof alcohol in boiling it down and then come up with what they refer to as the essence of hashish. Your normal hashish has a THC [tetrahydrocannabinol]—which is the basic ingredient of the marijuana plant—content of between eight and twelve percent, and the liquid hashish oil has a THC count of fifty-eight percent. A tiny drop onto a regular filter cigarette can knock you out."

The factories where the oil was distilled, Burke said, were also run by Hyatullah and Amanullah Tokhi. "The main cooker is a house behind a place called the Arina Hotel in Kabul. On one occasion I was watching this house—it is surrounded by a fifteen-foot-high wall—and I was on top of the wall one night, just outside one of the rooms, and I practically got knocked off the wall from the smoke coming out of the window. I finally convinced the Afghan police that we should go in there, and there were some Americans in there I had been informed were members of the brotherhood. It was a large house and a very fine house, by Afghan standards, and was very well furnished by expensive carpets—no other furniture, just carpets and pillows. Upstairs it was divided into several bedrooms, and in the first bedroom that was searched a fairly large quantity of hashish was found, both in bulk and in pollen form.

"There was one room, which was locked, and in this room, after the door was removed, we found what was—what looked like—a still, an old Kentucky still. There was a large container that had twenty-five gallons of liquid hash. There were two twenty-five-gallon Sears pressure cookers, and they were connected by tubes with heating implements. The whole operation was run by the Tokhi brothers. After they got the stuff out of the factory, then whoever wanted to take the stuff back to the United States would leave their vehicle with Hyatullah. The most popular vehicles are the Volkswagen vans. There are also some Mercedes vans, and then in a few cases we have just seen normal sedan-type vehicles. The vehicle is left with Hyatullah, and he sees to it the placement of either the traps or the loads and sealing of the hash [*sic*]. The business had been so good for Hyatullah that, when you take your vehicle to him and leave it with him, you might have to wait several days because there is a long backlog of vans waiting to be serviced."

Working with German members of Interpol assigned to monitor Afghan hash heading for Hamburg. Burke convinced the Afghan police, who like to ignore hashish smuggling, to bust Hyatullah Tokhi. "Well, we got him arrested, and it was because of these German police advisers. His hashish dealings were getting so flagrant, and on the basis of this he was arrested. His Mercedes 280 was seized, as well as a large supply of hashish. However, he was released about three hours later. Now the Afghan police director general doesn't know if he is going to be director very long, all evidence has disappeared, and the charges have been dropped."

If Agent 107, the CIA counterinsurgency expert, couldn't get Hyatullah Tokhi arrested, Laguna Beach's Neal Purcell still wanted to give it a try.

The Tokhi brothers took a trip and left their no-man's-land friends. They came to Orange County, to Disneyland, and to Lion Country Safari, where the Brotherhood of Eternal Love's alleged Mr. Big, Fat Bobby Andrist, showed them the sights of Frontier and Fantasyland.

Hovering high over Disneyland, directly above a place filled with funhouse mirrors and plastic goblins, was a Huey-model police helicopter that made a lot of noise. Narcotics agents from Laguna Beach, the Bureau of Narcotics Enforcement, and the Federal Bureau of Narcotics and Dangerous Drugs rode merry-go-rounds armed with miniature cameras, videotape machines, and Japanese listening devices. The Tokhi brothers, foreign tourists to Walt Disney's wonderland, were surrounded by narks.

On their way to Orange County, Hyatullah and Amanullah Tokhi stopped in Hawaii, delivering rugs to a place called Far Out Imports, which police concluded was a brotherhood front. They were greeted at the airport by Customs agent Jerry Snyder. "They said they were major suppliers of rugs and were there to give a guy hints and went there to assist him in selling the rugs at a better price. They said they were bringing about ninety meters of rugs, or sixty rugs, on consignment to this Far Out Imports. They were very friendly and acted like nothing was up. They said they were going on to Los Angeles to see Disneyland."

When Sergeant Neal Purcell heard the notorious Tokhis were headed for Disneyland, he coordinated his forces with the Bureau of Narcotics Enforcement, and a BNE agent watched as Fat Bobby Andrist drove them from the airport to the Holiday Inn in Anaheim. "At approximately eleven:twenty," BNE agent Kenneth Newton said, "I noticed Bobby Andrist talking to Hyatullah and Amanullah Tokhi. Ten minutes after this they got into a station wagon and drove to the Disneyland Hotel. They went to the desk, where Andrist registered these Tokhi brothers. We took pictures of them there. After the registration process was completed, they entered the elevator and went up to the rooms.

"There was a guy with them we didn't know, and, when this guy left, we had an Anaheim policeman pull him over on a routine traffic stop. The policeman looked at this guy's driver's license, and in this way we were able to ascertain that this guy was also reputed to be a member of the brotherhood. The next day these Tokhi brothers took the tramway and went into Disneyland. They walked all over Disneyland, inspecting everything and laughing a lot. These Tokhis seemed to be in a very happy mood. Andrist seemed to be very happy, too, because he was laughing right along with them. We were not able to ascertain the cause of this laughter."

The next day, the BNE agent said, the Tokhi brothers and Fat Bobby Andrist went for another drive—this time through Lion Country Safari. Massive police surveillance was once again summoned. The police helicopter fluttered above their car and the lions that prowl the grounds.

BNE agent David Genens, who was following them, later told the Orange County Grand Jury what happened.

Genens: Well, Andrist had stopped. He had stopped his vehicle. He stopped it several times in the middle of the road. He made U-turns. One time he made a U-turn, and as he was coming back toward me—

Q: He looked at you?

A: He looked at me.

Q: And what did he do?

A: He raised the middle finger of one of his hands at me.

Q: Pointed it at you in an upward motion?

A: Yes, in an upward motion.

Q: You concluded he realized he was being watched?

A: Yes.

The brothers Tokhi, who had seen the splendors of Disneyland, had eaten their share of hot dogs, and had been accompanied everywhere by the clatter of a police helicopter, went back to Afghanistan the next day.

Early in 1972 Neal Purcell asked the cooperating agencies for a "summit meeting" to "coordinate intelligence." Purcell asked that the meeting be held at a secret location, preferably away from Southern California. "The brotherhood has a whole spy network," Purcell said, "and has men on patrol outside the police station. Whenever we go somewhere, brotherhood members follow us."

The meeting was held at a San Francisco hotel. Participating were local agents from Laguna Beach, Newport Beach, and Santa Ana, and there were state and federal agents from all over California, Customs agents from San Pedro and San Francisco, and sheriff's deputies from Oregon. Among the participants were Bob Ramsey, who would later link his brother-in-law to the brotherhood in front of the Orange County Grand Jury, and Bay Area BNE agent Robert Luca, an instrumental witness in the controversial case against attorney Michael Metzger, busted after he criticized BNE tactics.

The "summit meeting" was tape-recorded and a typed summary of the "intelligence" sent to the participants, "so you'll have notes of the date." A Josephine County sheriff's secretary was assigned to type the summary and told to "keep a good eye on it because, if it gets into the wrong hands, they'll know what our information is." Agents were told "to keep the summary in a safe when you get it."

The summary runs twenty-eight single-spaced pages and will be referred to here as the "Nark Papers." These are its highlights (certain names, of persons not indicted, have been changed):

"The meeting started by Neal Purcell filling the group in on the past history of the Brotherhood of Eternal Love. The brotherhood was started [in] approximately 1963 under the guidance of Timothy Leary in New York. Leary was run out of New York . . . . During 1968 police agencies learned that the group acting under Leary were able to dispose of approximately 500 keys of grass or hash within less than an hour's time. Their attorney, right from the outset in Laguna, has been George Chula, who apparently is the attorney for the group no matter where they are arrested. A special point was made indicating that Chula was on such tight retainer with the group that quite often he beat the arresting officers to the jail on arrest of these subjects.

"There appears to be a new group of people forming there that claim to be the brotherhood. This is a phony group, and as far as intelligence has been able to establish, they are not the real members of the Brotherhood of Eternal Love. The members of the meeting feel that the old Brotherhood of Eternal Love, as we know it, does still exist and is still being controlled by the people that we have been naming, with some new faces, but this is not the young-age group that is calling themselves 'Brotherhood' at this time.

"From Newport Beach PD comes information that in 1968 a person by the name of Robert Mapes was a financier for the group. He was based out of Newport Beach. Mapes is an A K A; his true name is Jack Pope. Pope is a con man from the area of Arizona and Las Vegas. He was associating very heavily with the brotherhood people. It appears that the brotherhood likes to use Oregon, Nevada, and Utah identification. It has come up quite often in the past. During a bust in Laguna for hash oil, they found large stacks of blank birth certificates, driver's licenses, in fact one of them dated back to 1898.

"At this time Mike Barnes of the BNE has put an organizational chart of the brotherhood, a flow chart, on the blackboard, which more or less describes the type of action, and the known people involved, along with their placement as to importance on the chart. This chart is

135

now being discussed. The discussion of the chart has included several names that were not on the chart at all, and has also caused replacement of other names. The chart has actually been in construction since June 1971 by Mike Barnes, acting with the Laguna people. The chart reflects an M.O. profile that will be distributed. They have more contacts and involvement. It is Barnes's opinion that for every man on this chart, there are probably at least five men on the street that are not known. The higher the names appear on the chart, the dirtier the people appear. The name Commodore Hodge has come up and it appears he is a brotherhood fellow-traveler.

"Herman Donaldson, the father of one of the brotherhood members, is now the object of discussion. Donaldson has been an owner of motels in the Anaheim and Disneyland area. He has been connected with running girls in the past. He is suspected of having connections with the Mafia, and also of providing money to the brotherhood. His attorney goes by the name Luis and is listed as a probable Mafia member.

"A lot of the money for the group comes from girls whose parents just don't want to see them anymore. They pay them large sums of money to stay away from home. The girls, although they supply a lot of money, do not appear on the charts and are seldom mentioned in the brotherhood circles.

"Now information comes from Ramsey about George Chula, the brotherhood attorney. Ramsey made special note of the fact that while he was in Chula's office to meet a brotherhood member, the secretaries in the office did not recognize the member by name. Ramsey overheard them conversing, and one of the secretaries mentioned to the other that had Ramsey referred to the member as Number Four, she would have known what he was talking about. The indication was that members of the brotherhood were listed by numerical files rather than by names in Chula's office and that when they contacted Chula, all they had to do was give him a number and Chula would know who he was talking to. Ramsey described Chula as 'a gangster type.'

"Then the discussion turned to brotherhood front organizations. Business cards are turning up for the Rainbow Surf Shop in Laguna Beach with most members of the brotherhood now and anytime they turn up, consideration should be given to adding the holder to the brotherhood file.

"Information is offered about Al Phillips. It is undetermined at this time whether or not there is a link to the brotherhood with this man, who is an attorney in Van Nuys. However, this attorney was a member of the Owsley defense team. He is described as being an ultraliberal with leftist tendencies.

"The discussion turned to the M.O. of the brotherhood in pulling their scams. The method of concealing drugs in radiators and under-carriages of vehicles, and the fact that when they are doing business, they get clean-shaven, generally rent expensive cars, dress well, leaving no indication that they normally live scroungy lives. At one point it was mentioned that at a party involving members of the brotherhood, a bust was about to take place and there was $1,700 on hand from in the residence. Rather than get caught with it, they flushed it down the toilet. This is further indication of how little money means to them.

"Ramsey is filling the group in on the fact that they do not go get a load and then come back and try to sell it. They have all the arrangements made prior to their return, and when they come in, they dump it immediately. There is no waiting around. He has also been queried about connections to the Mafia. He stated that at one time there was a group called the Businessman of L.A., that's the way they were referred to, and that brotherhood members did not like running for these people because they were too sensitive and too rough with their money. They didn't mind if you lost a load but if you lost, somebody would have to pay.

"Information was put out that Fat Bobby is a homosexual. As confirmation of Andrist being a fruit, the information was put out that he has made it with another brotherhood member several times.

"At this point Mike Barnes seemed quite concerned that hash oil could be used in making pumpkin pie. It is felt that Mike will be checking all pumpkin pies in the next few months.

"Information is being put out now from Southern California authorities that one of the most consistent signs that go along with dopers is that they are non-meat eaters, vegetarians, and when you enter a house they almost without doubt will have a Buddha sitting around someplace. Pictures of India, this sort of thing. The Buddha will often have, in the cupped hands, an offering of grass or hash, or some of them will even lay their hash pipes there.

"Southern California is giving information on canning factories in which they are using tomato cans, sizes up to four-pound cans, to pack their hash. They actually have canning factories. Bobby Andrist appears to be involved in this. They indicate that some of the cans will have just the flowering tops of cans in them, this sort of thing. They wil just have masking-tape labels, indicating they are squash, green beans, vegetables, or peas. This is used to throw the authorities off the track. A large part of the packaging labels will just indicate organic food of one type or another.

"Many of the people coming back from overseas are bringing back Afghan carpets, and although no known method has been discovered for them to use rugs in the transportation of hash oil, it is possible that they have come up with a method.

"Advice is given that all surfboards coming in from Hawaii should be broken. The indications have been that they do contain hash. However, there are so many surfboards coming into the United States that it is impossible to break them all. Conjecture is prevalent at this time about the fin set up on surfboards. About the skags on these surf-boards—whether hash could be fitted into them and look like skags. There are grooves in the rear of the surfboard for the skags, and it is possible that hash could be molded to fit these grooves.

"Advice is now given about steps to take with the brotherhood. These steps are not known to the public and every effort should be made to keep them secret. U.S. Customs is saying in this regard that one of the ways they could be of assistance to all agencies is that, if we have information that a subject is out of the country and due to arrive on the West Coast, if the officer will call Customs and put out a request, Customs will activate their computer system. When the subject comes through Customs, he will be searched and his papers can be taken out, and all the papers photographed for intelligence informations. Further information along this line: If you find a subject that you have reason to believe is involved in narcotics activity, and he has a passport on him, take the passport number and call it into Customs. They can include that in their Soundex System, and any time he leaves the country he will be given special consideration.

"Federal narcotics, that is BNDD, comes forth with the information that they are meeting with some success in working with the IRS's new Narcotics Task Force, which is aimed at hitting drug trafficers [sic] financially. They are building case files on these individuals. Repeated attention is called to the fact that any and all available documents, slips of paper of any type that are seized, or available on arrests of any of these people, should be confiscated or copies, or at least the information obtained off them."

One of the secret "Nark Papers' " most remarkable conclusions was this: "At this time Leary is *not* presently really involved in the upper echelon and not realizing any profit from this group." Remarkable because, when the indictments were announced, District Attorney Cecil Hicks said Leary was the "brains" or "god" behind the Hippie Mafia, able to travel and live comfortably on smuggling profits.

District Attorney Cecil Hicks and his assistant, Ed Freeman, seeking their headlined conspiracy indictments against the Hippie Mafia, had to convince the Orange County Grand Jury of two things: the existence of the Brotherhood of Eternal Love and its conspiratorially felonious intent.

They trotted out various pieces of evidence, some of which, to other observers, bordered on the ridiculous. There was a brotherhood because the state of California incorporation papers said there was. There was a brotherhood because there was evidence many of the longhairs referred to each other as "brother." Because a man arrested for possession of marijuana had a letter in his pocket that began, "Dear Brother Fred." Because, during the Christmas Fest in Laguna Beach, posters were seen signed by "The Brotherhood of Eternal Love." Because, at that same fest, hundreds of cards were found with the words, "May the sun shine on your fields and the river flow and the Great Spirit watch over you." Because many of the letters confiscated were decorated with the Om Tao, "a known brotherhood symbol." Because almost all the letters between "known brotherhood members" were signed "love and peace," which an informer said was "the brotherhood salutation."

There was a brotherhood, finally, because the informers, like the ex-sheriff who attended the nark summit, Bob Ramsey, said there was a brotherhood, and because several witnesses saw all these longhairs hanging around together, going to the same houses, headshops, and health-food bars.

Mrs. Jane Davis's testimony, for instance, was crucial. Mrs. Davis is a Laguna Beach housewife who lives on a hill overlooking a house on Monterey Drive. The house was rented by two persons whom informers identified as "known brotherhood members." Mrs. Davis watched dozens of cars come to this house each night. She was curious and annoyed. The cars made a lot of noise—"One night I was awakened and there were five cars tearing down that street, one right after the other. I thought, 'There's something going on down there.'" Mrs. Davis bought a pair of binoculars, and each time a car pulled into that driveway she used them. She wrote all the license plates down and, after two months, presented the Laguna Beach police with her list of numbers.

Sergeant Neal Purcell raided the home and found quantities of hash oil, hashish, and LSD, and, on the "intelligence" provided by his informers, he concluded the house was a "brotherhood drop-off spot."

The district attorney's office took Mrs. Davis's license numbers, traced them, and had a list of names. Then, in front of the Orange County Grand Jury, the district attorney read the names to Sergeant Neal Purcell.

Sergeant Purcell established at the start that Bobby Andrist was "a known brotherhood member" through information provided by Glenn Lynd's brother-in-law, Bob Ramsey. Bobby Andrist used marijuana, smoked it openly in the streets, even tried to convince Sergeant Purcell of its benefits. As a matter of fact, Sergeant Purcell once arrested Bobby Andrist for possession of marijuana, but the case was thrown out of court.

Once he established to the grand jury's satisfaction that Bobby Andrist was a member of the brotherhood and a dope-smoker, he moved on to other names, many of them acquired through the efforts of that curious housewife Mrs. Davis. What followed was almost comic, a master list of guilt by association.

"I have seen Bobby Andrist in the Woodland Drive area from the first day I was there," Purcell said. "I have seen Mr. Andrist with Rick Bevan. I have seen them in and around the area of 237 and 250 Woodland Drive, and I have also seen them in the Mystic Arts together. I have seen them with John Gale. I have seen them with James Crittenden in the area of the Mystic Arts and Woodland Drive. I have seen him with Jeffrey Lange. Also, I have seen him with Ellis Wesley Scott. I have seen Glenn Lynd and Andrist together. This was at the Mystic Arts.

"I recall having numerous conversations with, like, Andrist and Gale together, and these individuals were talking about their trip and their philosophies and, you know, why can't we swing their way, where they just openly said dope was their way of life. I have had many discussions with Andrist and Gale, in particular, due to the arrest I made of Dr.

Leary, and he was looked up to by them, according to their statements, as their high priest.

"I have discussed the brotherhood with Andrist and Gale, where they would not come out and say there is actually a brotherhood, but they would say, 'Well, you know, we're all brothers.'"

"I have seen Andrist with Brian McAdams. I have seen Jimmy Otto and Andrist together. I have seen Andrist and Timothy Leary together. I have seen Gerald Padilla and Andrist together. I have seen him with Mark Stanton and James Clay, with Travis Ashbrook and Gary Allen, with John and Rosemary Leary, with Michael Pooley, with Robert Tierney, with Price Lock, with Michael Randall." The list went on and on.

The district attorney concluded, "I think the evidence shows that under Timothy Leary's leadership it has developed into a very sophisticated organization in terms of smuggling." He referred to a movie: "If you have seen *The French Connection*," he said, "you are aware of these things."

The grand jury handed down its indictments on the people Purcell named. Neal Purcell, the man who had busted Leary and started the investigation on his own, now provided the link between the members.

Everything was ready for the headlines and the bust, a coordinated assault to be launched at six o'clock on the morning of August 5, a time chosen because "most of these people use a lot of dope and late at night and that early they won't be able to resist."

It was a geometrically triangular operation, with its focal points being the Idylwild ranch, Laguna Beach, and the island of Maui in Hawaii, where Fat Bobby Andrist was reported to be running a hashish canning factory.

The Ranch Bust was led by BNE agent James Smith: "We met at Lake Hemet at four o'clock in the morning," he said, "and, after briefing and assigning agents to particular buildings, we proceeded about five o'clock to the ranch. There were about twenty-five officers. We had two large vans, a regular four-door sedan, and we drove up the dirt road. There were two closed fences, both of which fences were passed through. The fences were locked, but the keys were placed nearby. There is a key required by the U.S. Forestry Service to be placed nearby; so we used their key to get in. We broke off into predetermined teams, each taking the house or houses assigned to them. We thought we'd find a lot of people, but, when we got to the ranch, we found, well, four children and nine adults.

"I was in the main ranch house itself. Agent Newton announced his purpose and authority, and we made entrance into the house. There was nobody moving. The reason there wasn't anybody moving was because everybody was naked in bed. In a bathroom near the bedroom we found an Ohaus triple beam scale, which is used in the weighing of narcotics prior to sale. We confiscated the scale. Then we found a letter. The letter talked about an individual using marijuana. Then we found a letter which talked about not using tinfoil for dope at the airports. That's because tinfoil will react with the magnetometer, like guns, and it will set off an alarm, and that person will be searched for weapons. Hippies, whether they tip off a magnetometer or not, are usually searched pretty extensively on flights. Then we went up to a small, single-story frame house, and in that dwelling were two individuals we arrested for possession of LSD for sale. Then we arrested two people for possession of a small quantity of marijuana and found the caretaker, and we arrested him for possession of LSD. In his dresser was a glass jar containing a number of gelatin capsules. But the gelatin capsules were nonnarcotic; they were not LSD. However, we also found a roach clip containing marijuana residue; so we didn't have to release him."

While the Idylwild ranch bust was netting naked bodies and roach clips, Laguna Beach Detective Bob Romaine, Neal Purcell's partner ("He's my type of guy," Purcell says), was having even greater problems in Hawaii. Officials in Maui wouldn't give Bob Romaine a search warrant. Leading the Hawaiian prong of the brotherhood bust, Romaine selected six addresses, "known brotherhood hangouts," and asked the Maui district prosecutor for search warrants, claiming the brotherhood was running canning factories and growing a form of grass called "Maui Wowee."

The prosecutor turned him down flat. So Bob Romaine, wanting to fulfill his part of the coordinated nark effort, went to those houses anyway on the morning of August 5. He went to each house and knocked on the door. He said he was looking for a Mr. Robert Andrist. Some of the people in the houses were very polite, asked Bob Romaine inside, but didn't know anything about Bobby Andrist. In the next four days, thanks to the efforts of a Hawaiian narcotics detective in some high-pressured string-pulling in California, Bob Romaine got his search warrant. He knew which was Bobby Andrist's house, went there, knocked, found no one home, and broke in.

He found: a cocaine testing kit legally available from mail-order houses for $100; a Pyrex labware book—"they haul their hash oil in Pyrex bottles"; a map of Afghanistan; a canning device; a Christmas card saying, "Christmas greetings, wish I could be with you. Om Tao"; a letter that said, "There's a destiny that makes us brothers. None goes his way alone. All that we send into the lives of others comes back into our own." He also found a small bottle of hash oil and a box of Kodak slides, slides that would be dramatically shown to the Orange County Grand Jury, slides showing the smiling faces of Hyatullah and Amanullah Tokhi. But that's all he found, going back to Laguna Beach without Fat Bobby Andrist—the Mr. Big, as Cecil Hicks would call him, of the brotherhood.

When he appeared before the Orange County Grand Jury, Bob Romaine had to hang his head in shame.

"Now you're going to get Andrist within a week?" the district attorney said.

"I wish I could say that," Romaine said.

"What promises are you going to make to us? We have taken a lot of time here."

"In the movies," the district attorney said, "this gets done all the time. The police always get their man."

On August 5 Sergeant Purcell led the Laguna Beach arm of this global bust and went after Jimmy Otto, the owner of Laguna's Sound Spectrum record shop. At the nark summit meeting in San Francisco agents described the Sound Spectrum as "a brotherhood front" and said, "The first thing that Bobby Andrist does when he gets into town is call Jimmy Otto."

Purcell went to Otto's house at six o'clock in the morning, and Otto, a laid-back sort, came groggily to the door and asked, "Who is it?"

"Jimmy Otto?" Purcell asked.

"Yeah, but it's too early."

Purcell identified himself and said he was carrying a grand jury indictment and demanded entrance. "I then heard movement," Purcell said, "that led me to think it was going away from the door instead of to the door. I tried the door, which was open, and saw Otto head toward the bathroom. At this time I noticed there was a female near the bathroom.

"I saw Otto extend his right hand out toward the bowl of the toilet, and at this time I observed several cigarettes land in the toilet and outside the bowl, and at this time I observed Otto grab the handle of the toilet as though he was going to flush it. I was struggling to keep him from flushing the toilet, and it became necessary to place standard holds on him. At this point the female reached for the toilet bowl, and I told her to put her hands on the wall."

Neal Purcell reached inside that toilet bowl and told Jimmy Otto he was under arrest. It was the climax of his personal drama, the fruit of the effort he had started on his own time four years earlier. It had begun with Timothy Leary and two marijuana cigarettes, and it ended with Neal Purcell reaching inside a toilet bowl. He put his hands into that urine-filled water and retrieved five marijuana cigarettes, and the next day he made the front page of the *New York Times*.

On South Broadway Avenue in Santa Ana, a twenty-minute drive from Laguna Beach, just down the street from the Schmitz for President headquarters, George Chula, forty-eight, who moved to California from Akron, Ohio, sits with one of his law partners. His partner is an old man with white hair, weathered elfin eyes, and the stance of a bantam rooster. The old man is Russell Parsons, who defended Sirhan Sirhan, the man who assassinated Robert F. Kennedy. George Chula is the man who defended Timothy Leary and now represents many alleged members of the Brotherhood of Eternal Love. He was described, at that summit meeting of narks in San Francisco, as "a gangster type." He is a distinguished, graying man whose hair is over his ears and who dresses with dignified flair. In Orange County's legal circles he is respected as a tough criminal lawyer who goes all out to win and usually does. He knows Neal Purcell, and he goes to parties with Cecil Hicks, and in his den above his desk there are two pictures. One is of Timothy Leary, the other of Cecil Hicks. "You've got to protect yourself," he says; "that way I figure I take care of both sides."

The day before, a federal narcotics officer named Strange described George Chula as "a brotherhood stooge," and Chula says there are days when he is worried, when he hears from one or another of his friends that some narcotics agent has said, "We're gonna get Chula."

"What you have here," George Chula says about the great brotherhood conspiracy, "is politics, pure and simple politics. Cecil Hicks gets a chance to hold a press conference and goes on TV and gets on the front page so he can get more votes when he runs for attorney general. Sergeant Purcell gets a chance to justify his own existence, to convince people there is a paramount need for his services and his salary. He'll get promoted, and maybe he can get to be a police chief somewhere someday. And all these other agencies, all these guys who get their rocks off busting longhairs—well, now they have this great chance. They can work on the public consciousness and establish a link between long-haired kids and the killers in the Cosa Nostra. They can use the word 'Mafia.' They can reinforce a lot of public prejudices and get Mr. Taxpayer to launch future witch-hunts against longhairs. Meanwhile, heroin use is on the rise all over California, and you have all of these agencies, all this manpower working day and night against hash oil and grass.

"They can bring Leary's name into it again, of course, and guarantee themselves sure-fire publicity. Politically, Tim Leary is the best thing that ever happened to these guys. They should get down on their knees and thank God Tim Leary ever stepped into Orange County. How they can talk about Tim Leary running this international syndicate as if he were Lucky Luciano or something. Shit, Leary is no smuggler; he doesn't know anything about profit-oriented criminal activity. The guy is an intellectual. At worst, some people could call him some kind of crackpot, but to make him look like the Godfather is just too much.

"Then you've got Bobby Andrist, old Fat Bobby, this Mr. Big. They not only call him Mr. Big, they even malign his masculinity and call him a homosexual. I happen to know that, when Bobby Andrist was on Maui, he was living with a very beautiful lady. But these guys feel better if they can convince themselves he's a homosexual. It would really be perfect if they could nail him as a card-carrying member of the Communist Party. "Well, let me explain some things about old Fat Bobby. Bobby is one of the world's real characters. I mean, Bobby actually used to walk the God-damn Laguna streets, just about the point they were ready to declare martial law over there, smoking these big fat joints. He was no Mr. Big. He was some crazy Christ figure trying to redeem the world with grass and trying to convert Purcell even, convert everybody. How would this big shrewd smuggler act like that? Would he go around town being a walking piece of marijuana half the time? Of course, Purcell watched him for a while and finally busted him for grass. Then Purcell really got pissed off because, as he was arresting Bobby, some kids who were there stepped on Purcell's hands. Then, if that wasn't enough, the case gets thrown out and Purcell had his hands stepped on for nothing.

"And then you've got me. I'm supposed to be on this $100,000 retainer, getting to be a millionaire on all this brotherhood dope loot. Well, there are several of these guys I'm representing who don't have any money and can't pay me. After they made their big bust, my biggest battle was to get the bail down. They had colossal bail on them, and they would have rotted in jail; they didn't have any big money. Now, if they're a big Mafia, would they have to worry about money?

"I represent them for two reasons: One, these guys are good guys. They don't hurt anybody. They don't believe in violence. In all of Purcell's busts I don't think he has found a single firearm. Sure, a lot of these guys believe in dope, but a lot of people all over America believe in smoking dope these days. Two, I don't like to see people get screwed. Now a lot of these guys love Laguna Beach. It's their home—like they say, 'The surf is their turf.' So suddenly they are being busted all the time, beaten up, and now they're a part of the Mafia. I just don't like seeing people get shit on.

"Now I'm supposed to have this boat I got from the brotherhood. It's been described as a yacht by certain people in the D.A.'s office. Let me tell you about my yacht. First of all, it's a little boat that I had for several years, and it finally got so beat up that I couldn't keep it in the water because the God-damned thing would sink. So I brought it to this parking lot behind my office and left it there. It got rained on and looked like a piece of garbage.

"Well, Bobby and some of the guys were in here one day, and they spotted the boat. Their eyes lit up. I could see they loved it. They didn't have any money to buy a boat of their own. So I said, 'Take the God-damn boat, fix the holes in it, take care of it, play pirates with it, and I'll use it every now and then. So they fixed it up and used it and had a lot of fun in it—and now I see it's some $100,000 yacht I got from the Hippie Mafia.

"I got tied up with Tim Leary when he got busted. He asked around to see who was a good lawyer, and somebody recommended me to him, and we got to be good friends. He's one of the most dynamic guys I ever met. I met some of his friends in Laguna, and, when they got busted, they came to me. They were always getting into trouble because Purcell was always busting them.

"Purcell has this great ploy. Back in the beginning when he started busting people, he was crude and sloppy. There were search-warrant violations and excesses. We had hundreds, literally hundreds, of his cases thrown out. But then he figured out his new trick. He sees these long-haired kids hanging around at places like the Mystic Arts and knows who his targets are. So he waits. Then, if they get arrested for speeding and don't show, or if their dogs bark too much, or if their house looks a little messy, Purcell makes sure he serves the warrant. Now the trick is this; he makes sure to serve these warrants and citations and warnings late at night. He figures that if you're gonna smoke some dope, you'll probably be smoking it around eleven o'clock or midnight. So there he is, with some traffic beef, at midnight. Then he either sees some grass 'in plain view' or he smells it and searches the place.

"You have to understand you're talking about a man who got his reputation busting Tim Leary. He was a nothing cop when he did that; now he virtually runs that department. He got a big reputation. The nark business is like that: You get your scalps and you wear them. Now he claims he's got the long-haired Mafia or whatever, and he's going to be the Elliot Ness of the nark world. It's not a bad gimmick.

"There is only one basic thing wrong with this whole brotherhood business. There is no brotherhood. Sure, there used to be the group that was incorporated in 1966, but, when Farmer John died, that was it. What happened is that a whole aura developed around the brotherhood. Its vibe was perfect—a lot of kids in Laguna kept its image alive by saying they were 'brothers' and holding that Christmas thing. Now if you're running this international conspiracy, are you going to bring 30,000 of your friends into town and have every cop within a hundred miles there, getting pissed off at you? The brotherhood is a concept that appeals to young people. That's all that happened.

"There was another way the whole brotherhood business developed. Whenever Purcell and his guys made some bust, they'd ask the guy what he knew about the brotherhood. The guy knew what the score was: If he cooperated with them, they'd go easy on him. The guys knew damn well there was no brotherhood. But what the hell? They were put into a position where they had to invent to save their own skins. So they invented their heads off, used real imagination. That's where all this stuff about the Spy School and the Board of Directors comes from.

"The kids on the beach heard all this brotherhood talk, and it got to be a game. Kids started hearing about this mystical brotherhood, and they were going around showing off and saying they were members. They could claim to belong to something that had allure and romance. It was like being in a hip fraternity. The narks took it from there: all that stuff about kids calling each other 'brother' proving there was an organization. Well, how many young people go around giving each other the power shake, calling each other 'brother,' and signing 'Love and Peace' on their letters?

"I'm going to be very honest about this whole bullshit. There were some guys here, and some of them are my clients, who were involved in various dope scams. But they worked independently on their own. Separately, by themselves, none of these scams amount to anything. There are no headlines, separately, in these scams. But you lump them together and put a Mafia behind it, and it goes out all over the country.

"The narks and the D.A. did a very devious thing. They took a lot of busts, many of which were done a long time ago, many of which had already gone to court, and they resurrected them now by calling it a conspiracy. This way they could say they recovered all this dope and make it look like it came off one bust, instead of about thirty over a period of a year. Let me give you an example: They got a guy who tried to bring some hash in from Canada in a camper. The bust is made about a year ago and the case goes to court. Now, suddenly, that bust is a part of the brotherhood conspiracy, and Cecil Hicks, a year after that bust, can talk about it in his press conference. Now why in hell, if there's a great conspiracy, didn't they bring it up at the guy's trial originally?

"To make a great case of the brotherhood is kind of like taking a lot of black crimes and a lot of crimes, say, committed by Catholics, and saying the whole thing is a black and Catholic conspiracy organized by the ghost of Dr. Martin Luther King and by Pope Paul VI, working in league with the Knights of Columbus. They did the same thing here, except that they got a lot of longhairs and put Tim Leary in the Pope's place and had a board of directors acting as the Vatican."

George Chula laughs: "Ahh," he says, "life in Orange County!"

Russell Parsons, who hasn't said much all this time, growls: "I've defended a lot of clients in my time, Communists and policemen and labor officials and company presidents, and I represented Sirhan, who killed the man who probably would have been the President of the United States."

Russell Parsons is silent a moment, flicking through the memorized scrapbook of his seventy years, and then he says, "I represented Sirhan

Sirhan, but there is no way, not on the pain of eternal damnation, that I would represent these, these"—he spits the word—"narks."

Love Animals, Don't Eat Them is a health-food bar on the Coast Highway, one of the places the nark summit meeting referred to when it talked about dopers being vegetarians. These particular vegetarians were militant vegetarians who wanted to say something to the people of Laguna Beach about the practice of eating animals.

They got a camel and a rooster. They called the camel Boney Banana and the rooster Colonel Sanders. One fine morning they put Boney Banana and Colonel Sanders into a Cadillac limousine driven by a chauffeur and had him drive Boney and Colonel to the place called Love Animals, Don't Eat Them.

They were fed nut butter and raisins and banana sandwiches, which they munched with relish. The cops came. Everybody got busted. The health department said it is illegal to serve a camel and a rooster unless you are serving camel and rooster cooked. Boney and Colonel Sanders were led away, as was the guy who fed them the sandwiches.

The next day Sergeant Purcell informed his police chief, the former Marine Corps provost marshal, that Love Animals was a "known brotherhood front." Boney Banana and Colonel Sanders had made their appearances just to drum up some dope business. The business was the sale of hashish oil. The oil was hidden in the banana sandwiches.

For the next week a police intern wearing a shoulder-length wig toured Laguna's health bars buying banana sandwiches. The sandwiches were taken back to the police stations, chopped up into little pieces, and chemically tested.

Alas, no hash oil was found.

October 1, 1972

[AUTHOR'S NOTE]

Almost two years after the scare headlines and civic hoop-de-doo over the "Hippie Mafia," Orange County still has not made its global conspiracy case. Nor is it likely the case will ever be prosecuted. Many of those named in the massive indictment have copped lesser pleas—indeed, much lesser pleas: like possession of marijuana.

"It's obvious now legally," says attorney George Chula, "that they just lumped a bunch of minor busts together for the sake of all that beautiful publicity. I expect we'll hear no more about it and then, maybe a year or so from now, they'll come up with something as outlandish as this and they'll get their headlines all over again. Then, a few years after that . . . it'll just go on and on."

The group's alleged Godfather, Timothy Leary, was captured by federal agents in Afghanistan on January 13, 1973, and extradited to the United States. He is now serving time on the original Purcell bust, the marijuana charge.

Tim Leary and his new girl friend, Joanna Harcourt-Smith, had just arrived in Kabul from Switzerland and were greeted at the airport by an American Embassy official—a little man with a Charlie Chaplin mustache.

According to Leary, the little man "quickly droned a legal incantation, purporting to revoke my passport from my hand, and executed an inelegant but speedy withdrawal." They were under house arrest in Kabul for three days while Leary tried to get the king to intervene and save him. Unfortunately, the king was in "religious retreat," and they were soon hustled aboard a Boeing 747 bound for Los Angeles.

The man who met them at the plane was James Bondian nark Terence Burke.

"Burke!" the unflappable Leary cried. "Burke! You're famous! I read about you in Rolling Stone!"

Leary just laughs these days when one of his jailhouse visitors brings up the Brotherhood of Eternal Love. His lawyers are confident "Orange County won't be zany enough to bring up that Godfather stuff in a real courtroom."

Brotherhood of Eternal Love posters can still be seen around Laguna Beach. They wish one and all Happy Holidays! Happy New Year! Happy Life!

Neal Purcell is still a respected agent of the Laguna Beach police department (why not?), and the department still militantly arrests and captures criminal skateboarders. The high crime rate, they say, is going down.

3. Death in the Wilderness

Stretching from the fog-shrouded Mendocino coastline toward the cragged Oregon border, California's Humboldt County is a wilderness of skyscraping redwoods, richgreen and russet foliage, and rockstrata stark and magnificent. Sheep wander the sun-stabbed hills, and, except for Highway 101, the roads are knife-thin, venous, and steep. Parenthesized by mountains, the emerald countryside seems velvetlike and soothing. It is easy to be charmed here, to conclude that this dazzling polychrome beauty exudes a serenity; a nimbus of peace that hovers motheringly over the treetops. But there is little harmony in Humboldt; its splendor is a cruel mirage. Acres of redwoods have fallen victim to the corporate cash register, to conglomerates like Pacific Lumber in Scotia and its arsenals of uglifying chainsaws; so there are hundred-acre hillsides which form sad and gutted bleakscapes of stumps. The stumps are profound and eloquent testament; it is as though the inexorable savagement of the big trees has exacted a bloodred penance ... as though the sound of sawtoothed metal screaming into wood has been echoed by the screams of dying men and their killers' weapons.

They were asleep in their cabin, at the edge of a woodline of sequoia and madrone, tucked safely into that vastitude of green darkness. She awoke to find him trembling.

He told her:

.... They were coming for him in an execution squad: shotguns in their hands, with hair as long as his own, wearing jeans, Army jackets, holstered .38s on their hips. They shouldered the cabin door, ripped it from its hinges, and kicked at the dogs with steel-toed combat boots.

151

They saw him and stopped. He was on the back porch, frozen by panic, and couldn't move. They said nothing. Their faces were blank and waxy. They aimed and fired. He heard the gunshots and saw the glop of his own blood. He sucked at the air. He was dying. . . .

"Oh, Dirk," she said and held and shushed him, and, together, they sought the familiar reassurances of their pitchblack nights: susurrus of coastal wind, the languid whoosh of redwoods, the thud and patter of the Saint Bernards' paws, the moon's gentle white eye.

She thinks about the dream when she visits him these days. Judy Arnold looks at Dirk Dickenson's grave, on a plot of tacky suburban land far from his rugged pristine mountains, and remembers how she calmed him.

You aren't going to die, babe, it's just a dream, a lousy, rotten, silly dream.

On the evening of February 26, 1860, a delegation of Humboldt sourdoughs, white settlers, visited a tribal celebration of Mad River and Yurok Indians. A young newspaperman named Bret Harte recorded their visit in the Arcata *Northern Californian*: "A report was brought from Eureka during the night that nearly all the Indians were killed by persons unknown. A few loaded canoes bringing the dead bodies to Mad River confirmed the report. A more shocking and revolting spectacle never was exhibited to the eyes of a civilized people. Old women lay weltering in blood, infants scarce a span long with their faces cloven with hatchets and their bodies ghastly with wounds." Two hundred Indians died—massacred, a local historian wrote, because they were Indians.

Twenty-five years later another posse of sourdoughs collected 480 "Mongolian Highbinders," as guilty as the Indians—of being Chinese. The yellow men were accused of practicing amoralism and of smoking heathen opium. They were herded into a warehouse on the Eureka waterfront and then banished to San Francisco aboard two barely chugging steamboats. The Eureka City Council passed a statute that legalized: "1. Expelling all Chinamen from the city and that none be allowed to return; 2. Appointing a committee to act for one year whose duty it shall be to warn all Chinamen who may attempt to come to this place to live and to use all reasonable means to prevent their remaining;

3. Issuing a notice to all property owners through the daily papers asking them not to lease or rent property to Chinese." No Chinese infected the city until 1945, and in 1937, the international year of the swastika, Eureka's Chamber of Commerce still pointed with pride to the success of its program: "Eureka is the only community in the country in which there are no oriental colonies."

Says another newspaperman, Dan Walters, the managing editor of Eureka's daily *Times-Standard*, a man with tublike shape, moony face, and spontaneous warmth: "Until about ten years ago, when 101 was built through here, Eureka and much of Humboldt was a very insular place. Understandably. Not many people ventured through. We had two-lane roads often blocked by mudslides. Lumber trucks would barrel and rocket up and down and some people would suddenly find themselves sandwiched in some tiny car between tons of wood and steel. The world stayed away from Humboldt. The ideas and, I suppose, the prejudices folks had suckled since the days of their grandpappies were allowed to stand unchallenged. Then they built the super-highway and the world rushed in full chisel. Tourists, money, crime, thousands of students to Humboldt State University, and, worst of all, hippies. It was future shock pure and simple, the greatest trauma to hit the county . . . since the whores were forced out of Old Town in Eureka and moved to Rio Dell, where they changed the name of the place to Wildwood and set up probably the only official Whore City in America."

The hippies came in the fall of 1969, fleeing smogsets and draft boards, looking like furtive refugees, autobumming their way up the Coastal Highway from Marin and Mendocino into Humboldt, ragged out and piss-elegant in their sweat-patched surplus-store finery, some of them so thin and wasted the lumberjacks claimed they could smell the shit right through them. They were the aging kids who'd left the ghettoized acid holes of the cities and, seeking transcendental salvation, satori, and quiet, carrying joints and snorebags and little else, they came now to the high deep parts of the wilderness, to rough raw places like Garberville and Alderpoint and Whitethorn, so tiny you could just about piss from one end of town to the other. Adventurous freak pioneers, the survivors of other trips, they came to grub for survival. Seduced by the meretricious charms of the land, they came joyously to settle and discovered themselves despised and unwanted aliens . . . the Mongolian Highbinders reincarnate . . . furry-faced *redniks* among redwoods rednecks . . . shitferbrains no-accounts leaving their pecker-marks all over the do-right folks' tidy acres.

The new pioneers picked their shady spots and tumbledown cabins, paid their few city-earned dollars, and moved in, befouling the raddled countryside with packs of yelping unleashed dogs and caftaned, birdlike tomgirls, the child-eyed, haybag nymphets they ruefully called old ladies. They made crowbait homes like one inspected by Eureka architect William Van Fleet: "The place we saw was a pleasant area carved out in the madrone trees, remotely situated on an old dirt road, with little more than a lean-to for inclement weather. Though they had to carry water a mile from the nearest river, their sanitation facilities seemed quite adequate. They had no electricity, but they were well-stocked with candles." Many settled in southern Humboldt, around Garberville and Alderpoint, and the sourdoughs, creatures of routine and certitudes, responded predictably. Skittery storeowners claimed they were being "stolen blind" and filed insurance claims; Garberville Chamber of Commerce members said they were "scared to death"; a real-estate agent said: "The county would be better off if they'd never started coming here. A couple of hard winters ought to be enough to phase them out." But the new pioneers had an old-fashioned settler's stiff-neckedness that wouldn't countenance "phasing out." More and more of them arrived, some of them apostatized and solipsistic dopers who craved the sanctum of the woods; others banded together in free-flowing communes where, the sourdoughs were sure, the dope addicts humped like rattlesnakes, fed their women at both ends, and group-pissed ceremoniously on the American flag.

While a lonely county official defended the "invaders"—"They are young, college-educated and pessimistic. They are trying to live their own lives. They feel misunderstood"—other residents saw whorls and splotches of blood. Their sheep were being cannibalized: Packs of wild, starved, hippie dogs stalked their ranches like mountain cats, feasting on their livelihood . . . their dollars. On February 26, 1971, a ramshackle farmhouse in Whitmore Valley burned to the ground. It was the home of a Christ-bitten freak commune. On March 18 near Maple Hill, down the road from Alderpoint, another house burned. Occupants: a long-haired family. March 19, a farmhouse between Briceland and Etters-burg; occupants: a black man and three pitchfork-breasted white women. March 22, two fires in Briceland: a garage occupied by a bearded poet and a house that the Division of Forestry termed "a hippie domicile." The freak pioneers were being torched out. There were more fires: on April 5, April 12, April 19, April 20. On May 24 three houses burned at the same time. All the fires were the result of "suspected" arson. No one was arrested. A Division of Forestry spokesman said: "No, we never discovered who set the fires. The woods are very dry that time of year."

On June 22 near Garberville three freaks hitch-hiking at dusk along a hinterland road were met by a hog-assed pickup truck. The truck carried six men, several of them wearing black cowboy hats, all of them armed and snot-flinging drunk. The freaks were pistol-whipped and left semiconscious in the middle of the road, convenient fleshbag targets for cars barreling around the blind curves. The cowboys reeled on into the black night.

But the new settlers found one unlikely friend, the Garberville justice of the peace, a man the sourdoughs called the Just-Ass, Charles Thomas, a former sawmill operator, who watched the influx and said: "In the past, when I was working in the woods here, this area was filled with drunks, parole violators, and pranksters. I think these longhairs have upgraded the place." A recall drive was initiated, spearheaded by a rancher named Archie Brunkel, and, interestingly, a Humboldt County sheriff's deputy. The Just-Ass was accused of not knowing his testicles from teabags, of letting hippie dogs ravage the hillsides, of "constantly rendering decisions that in the opinion of the large segment of the community tend to favor the lawbreakers." Archie Brunkel, as florid as his television namesake, put it more bluntly. "The judge is soft on hippies," he said. "It's no good for our deputies to make an arrest," a rancher added, "because everything is suspended—the fines, the sentences." The recall motion failed, but emotions grew more fevered. Loaded shotguns were racked into pickup trucks; freaks stockpiled their cabins with ammunition.

No more ravaged sheep, the sourdoughs said.

No more burnings and whiskey-rage beatings, the new settlers responded.

Guns counter-pointed both ultimatums.

Into this setting, into this landscape of soaring beauty, charred wood, and the pastime of shed blood, came one more settler in the fall of 1971. He sought anonymity and peace; in another year his name would be a

155

woods legend. Dirk Dickenson, twenty-four years old, auburn-red hair poured to the middle of his back, came with his lovely sloe-eyed lady. He and Judy Arnold, blond hair as soft as gossamer, wanted to get away from the gaseous mists of the city, from the hassles and fears and false-teeth smiles of making it in the urban streets. They wanted to sit on the back porch in the misty-gold sunset, sip Black Jack Daniel's, and live ... happily ... ever ... after.

✝

PATRICK BERTI
1948–1970

"WE DRINK HIPPIE BLOOD," the sign read in majuscule letters at a place called the Ivanhoe Bar in Ferndale, a few miles south of Eureka. Backpacking caravans of barefooted freaks—woolly-haired, their belly hairs showing—trudged through town in the summer of 1970, and the mudbathed hordes were contagious with crotch rot, sloth, and inner decay.... During commencement ceremonies at the local high school the senior class had the brazenness to castigate its own administration.... At College of the Redwoods four students showed up for their graduation carrying a coffin with a placard that said: "College of the Redwoods, Business as Usual." An enraged off-duty Ferndale policeman hastily performed a citizen's arrest and took the pallbearers to the pokey. The local paper urged citizens to show some dog-sense and defend themselves against the plague: "For years we have been warning children not to accept rides from strangers. In today's world we must also tell them not to accept anything from strangers. Dispensers of drugs seem to not only frequent the big cities or some place miles from here, but have been known to recently approach local students with the idea of selling to them."

On Sunday, October 4, 1970, a young and ambitious Humboldt County sheriff's deputy sat on a dope stakeout in the deadfall on the banks of the Eel River near Ferndale. Two four-foot-high marijuana plants bloomed there, in violation of the state of California's criminal code. Hawkeyeing the plants all week was Sheriff's Inspector Mel Ames, a hardnosed fifteen-year veteran of the department. Ames asked Deputy Larry Lema to watch the plants while he rested his strained eyes and took the weekend off.

156

Two young men came to the riverbank that Sunday afternoon and scrutinized the plants in obvious merriment. One of them was Pat Berti, twenty-two years old, born and raised in Ferndale, a graduate of Chico State College, a member of Tau Gamma Theta fraternity, about to enter San Diego Law School.

Deputy Sheriff Larry Lema saw Pat Berti, a lifelong acquaintance of his, holding a twig of marijuana.

Deputy Sheriff Lema thought the twig was a gun, a deadly weapon in the hands of a dope grower. He drew his revolver and fired once. Pat Berti, blood oozing from his chest, gasped, "Christ, Larry, you've shot me," and died.

Humboldt County District Attorney William Ferroggiaro, formerly a public defender, elected to office in 1967, took the case to the grand jury. The Humboldt County Grand Jury ruled the shooting "justifiable homicide."

Deputy Sheriff Lema was transferred off patrol to guard duty at the crumbling Humboldt County jail; a griefstricken young man confessed to cultivating the two plants; Pat Berti, who'd visited the riverbank because he couldn't imagine marijuana growing beanstalk-high, paid the price of his natural curiosity—and was buried.

Their cabin was perched on the eastern slope of Pratt Mountain, where albino eagles nested, thirteen miles from Garberville on the road to Alderpoint, at the heart of the area scorched by the house-burnings. They chose it for its vista-point view: the back porch commanded a panoramic expanse of pigweeded mesa, woodline, and mountain. They used a wood stove for heat, piped water from a hilltop rancheria nearly a thousand yards away, and had no electricity.

When Dirk Dickenson, six feet tall, 165 pounds, with a firm but bemused presence, moved into the cabin with Judy Arnold, they faced immediate problems. To get to their forty acres from the road, they had to drive a snaking gravel path through the property of the rancher who had supplied water and electricity to their cabin's previous tenants. The rancher disliked longhairs and welcomed his new carny-haired neighbors by disconnecting the water and electricity. They answered him by making do. They built their own pipeline and didn't really need electricity. "After that," Judy Arnold says, "he let us alone."

They furnished their place as best they could. They lugged in a seven-foot redwood table and built a crude addition they called a living room. A bathroom was their next project. They already had a tub, but it was still out on the back porch. Until the new bathroom was ready, the living room would serve as a Saturday night bathing spa.

They missed the creature comforts of the apartment they'd rented in Hayward, a neon Bay Area suburb filled with taco stands and billboards, but the sacrifice was worth it. They were happy. Dirk was looking into the burgeoning burl industry and had collected the pieces of his fragmented existence. He knew his way around drugs, and, for a while in Hayward, his earth-buddies were stuffing pillow covers with money made from dealing dope. He tired of that hyper-rat race and set to become a backwoodsman, a burlmaker. He badly wanted to live in the mountains; thanks to the burls, he could make good easy money and still open his eyes each morning to a lofty view.

The redwood burl business was booming in Humboldt. There was an increasing demand for burl tables in the city; tourist-trap galleries on Union Street and at Ghirardelli Square in San Francisco sold them for as much as $800 apiece. Crafting burls was a relatively simple process. You picked out a good burl tree, cut it up, smoothed the wood, and stood to make as much as $10,000 from that single tree. Or you could buy dry burls for $20 apiece, take them home, polish and smooth them for two or three days, and sell each burl for a minimum $200. You didn't need a pisspot full of money to live in the backwoods, and Dirk Dickenson figured he'd even have an additional income from the hundreds of Christmas trees crowded onto his forty acres.

While Dickenson scouted his burls, the San Francisco office of the U.S. Department of Justice's Bureau of Narcotics and Dangerous Drugs was tracking what its agents believed to be the largest PCP-producing operation in California. PCP, phencyclidine hydrochloride, is a hallucinogen, an animal tranquilizer that provides an acidlike high and, some doctors say, gradually eats away the brain. The feds' tracking led them to Hayward, and two months later to Dirk Dickenson's cabin.

An informer providing "hard intelligence" told the BNDD the "million-dollar" PCP operation was rigidly organized and dangerous. The informer warned that all members of this organization were armed and "would not hesitate to use guns." The informer said the ring's "master chemist" was Dirk Dickenson and his forty-acre cabin site was the location of a "giant lab." The giant lab supposedly was guarded by

Dickenson's Saint Bernards, Boogie and Vernon, "both trained to go for the throat."

BNDD agents got in touch with sheriff's authorities in Humboldt County, with, specifically, Undersheriff Bob Bollmann, fifty-eight years old, bluelipped and gritty-eyed, the number-two badge in the department, a hardline law-and-order man who made no secret of his belief that hippie-dopers were converting his county into a nightmarish cloacal scum pit.

Bollmann assigned one of his most trusted aides, Sheriff's Inspector Mel Ames, to coordinate the investigation with the feds. Mel Ames was his "dope expert," the super-dedicated cop who'd spent a full week hiding in the bushes with his eyes peeled on the two marijuana plants in the days before Deputy Sheriff Larry Lema shot and killed Pat Berti.

In February and March of 1972 Mel Ames scouted Dirk Dickenson's property three times, seeking a single glimpse of the "giant lab." He saw nothing but treetops and foliage. For reasons known only to Mel Ames, all the reconnaissance was done from an airplane 5,000 feet in the air; no surreptitious visits were paid to the property itself, though Dirk Dickenson made several trips away to see his parents near Sacramento.

It was Mel Ames who devised the ploy of using an "inside man" to help effect any future bust on the Dickenson property. The inside man was tailor-made for the job. He was the county dog catcher, squarefaced Bill Bushnell, who held office hours at the Garberville sheriff's substation, headquarters of the sourdoughs' recall campaign against Just-Ass of the Peace Charles Thomas.

Bushnell had more than just played pattycakes with sheriff's deputies in the past. The dog catcher knew the traps and secrets of the rugged terrain and often hiked miles to some laid-back hippie's isolated lean-to. He'd arrive sweating like a bull, armed with a gun in one hand and a complaint about an unleashed/untagged hippie dog in the other. He'd finagle his way inside the hippie's house, radar eyes zooming in on ashtrays, spot a few suspicious cigarette butts, and come back two hours later with Jeepfuls of high-booted sheriff's deputies. Some freaks around Humboldt claimed the crusading dog catcher was full-time undercover nark and part-time poundmaster.

Fate provided Bill Bushnell a further qualification for being the inside man on the Dickenson case. The BNDD informer said that Dickenson had those two go-for-the-jugular Saint Bernards. Bushnell was expert in "incapacitating" dangerous dogs.

As the coordinated fed / county investigation continued, Undersheriff Bollmann added another gothic wrinkle to the case. He neglected to tell the district attorney about it. In the undersheriff's opinion, William Ferroggiaro was a fuss-assed liberal, soft on law and order, a hoity-toity Hitalian egghead who talked as if he'd swallowed a dictionary and more often than not acted like a puregrade mule's ass. The Hitalian might somehow botch the whole investigation. What the D.A. didn't know wouldn't hurt anygoddamnbody ... not the sheriff's office, not the U.S. government.

The undersheriff saw no need, either, to concern the sheriff much with the Dickenson case. For all practical purposes, as the grand jury report of 1972 was to point out, Humboldt County was without a sheriff. Oh, yes, there was a man sitting in a courthouse office behind a fancy door that said "Sheriff" on it, but the poor guy looked eroded and sallow and had all-consuming problems of his own. Sheriff Gene Cox was drunk much of the time and spent a few weeks down in Napa now and then under clinical supervision ... drying out.

BUNKY FERRIS
1950–1971

On December 4, 1971, in a shitkicker Willow Creek bar near Hoopa in northern Humboldt, site of the largest Indian reservation in the state of California, a fist fight broke out between Indians and local sourdoughs.

One of the participants was Bunky Ferris, a twenty-one-year-old Indian, a student at UCLA, home on the reservation between semesters. Ferris was proud, militant, long-haired, and tough.

Robert Marmon, the jowly bartender, tried to "break up" the fight. Bunky Ferris and some of his friends disliked and distrusted him. Marmon, they said, hated Indians and liked to taunt them with racial slurs.

The bartender tried to break up the fight with a gun.

The gun "went off," and Bunky Ferris was dead.

Indian activists demanded District Attorney Ferroggiaro seek a murder indictment against Robert Marmon. The district attorney refused and took the case instead to the Humboldt County Grand Jury.

One of the witnesses on the bartender's behalf, Indian militants claimed, was so drunk she fell off a chair. The district attorney let the pratfallen woman's testimony stand.

The district attorney, an Indian leader alleged, did not present a strong case. "He played to the majority, and the majority around here still feel the only good Indian is a dead Indian." William Ferroggiaro said he had done the best he could.

The death of Bunky Ferris, the grand jury ruled, was "accidental."

"If it wouldn't have been for Undersheriff Bollmann's ego," says portly Dan Walters, managing editor of the Eureka *Times-Standard*, "chances are the world never would have found out about Dirk Dickenson. Chances are things might have been, you might say, *tidied up*."

On Friday, March 24, 1972, in McKinleyville, a tanktown outside Eureka, a crew-cut twenty-year-old named Allen Thornhill went shitfit berserk, barricaded himself in his house, and started shooting target practice at passersby with two pellet guns and a rifle.

All available sheriff's deputies surrounded the house and were pinned down by Thornhill's gunfire. It was a moment of high frontier drama, a carnival-like siege just like the ones produced periodically in Brooklyn, Chicago, and Detroit City. The whole town buzzed about the shootout, and reporters and photographers from the *Times-Standard* flitted grimly around the scene.

After several melodramatic hours Thornhill, as a deputy said, "came crawling out." *Times-Standard* photographers recorded his capture, and next day's front page was plastered with three- and four-column pictures of gun-toting lens-hog deputies leading the sniveling, owly-eyed sniper off to jail.

"Bollmann loved the publicity," said Dan Walters. "I mean, he thought it was the greatest thing to ever happen to the sheriff's department to get splashed like that all over the paper.

"Of course," Dan Walters added sardonically, "I thought they looked like a bunch of assholes."

The reason why Dan Walters, who likes policemen and types himself a political conservative, thought the deputies looked like assholes was directly attributable to Undersheriff Bollmann.

The undersheriff, more than anxious to command his forces in battle, never made it to the shootout. He didn't make it because, speeding to McKinleyville, he crashed a red light at Fifth and V streets in Eureka.

His patrol car glanced off one car, careened into another, then flipped like a jumping bean and tumbled fifty feet. Three Eurekans were rushed screaming to the emergency room, casualties in the war against crime. The *Times-Standard* ran a picture of Bollmann's belly-up sheriff-mobile with a headline that said: "The Undersheriff Didn't Make It."

On the night of April 3 Undersheriff Bollmann called Dan Walters and said he was giving him a good story, a story even better than the McKinleyville shootout. Undersheriff Bollmann was officially in charge of the department; Sheriff Cox had temporarily exiled himself to a rehabilitation center, by the name of Duffy's, in Calistoga.

Bollmann self-dramatically ordered the managing editor to assign a reporter to him the next day and make sure the man brought his camera. He couldn't say why, but, sonumabitch, it was Big!

Walters pressed for details. Bollmann said: "The sheriff's department is going to assist in the biggest narcotics bust in the history of Humboldt County! Maybe the biggest bust in the history of the state of California!"

The undersheriff didn't tell Dan Walters anything else, except that the bust would take place "up in the boonies."

On the morning of April 4, 1972, a bright and sunny day, Dirk Dickenson and Judy Arnold got up at nine o'clock and decided to visit their tree. It was a splendorous majestic burl stretching high into the cloudless alkaline sky. Perfect, Dirk thought, for eight to ten tables.

"It was so big we couldn't believe it," Judy Arnold says. "We stood there and looked up at it. Dirk was really jazzed, he was so excited."

They decided to buy it and inquired at a nearby ranch after the burl's owner. It belonged to Bill Bushnell, the dog catcher.

They drove to Garberville, looking for Bushnell, and found him at the sheriff's substation. Bushnell had time to talk to them; he was killing time. He was waiting to hook up with the fed / sheriff posse that would raid Dirk Dickenson's property with a warrant for his arrest less than three hours later.

The cagey dog catcher, however, said nothing to Dirk Dickenson about that. When Dickenson asked whether the tree was for sale, Bushnell said, "Sure, no problem. You wanna buy it, it's yours."

They agreed to conclude their deal "tomorrow."

They shook hands on it; the dog catcher smiled.

Dirk Dickenson and Judy Arnold climbed back into their blue Scout and drove down the street to a craft shop, listening studiously to the aged owner's doddering advice about smoothing their burls.

"Then we went home," Judy Arnold says. "We stopped at the liquor store, and Dirk bought me a real big bottle of Jack Daniel's. We were going home to celebrate our tree."

When Kenny Krusco, the pint-sized boss of the federal narcotics team, heard that this blundering hick, the undersheriff of Humboldt County, had actually invited three newsmen ... witnesses ... to accompany and film the mountain raiders, he was furious. The bust would be a high-tension commandolike operation; they were going after criminals their intelligence said were armed and dangerous; they would be exposing their throats to the fury of homicidal Saint Bernards. The newsmen would foul everything up; the witnesses would have to stay behind.

But Undersheriff Bollmann, his eyes trained on Sheriff Cox's wobbly job, the memory of those pretty Marysville headlines buoying his vanity, insisted the reporters go. There were some harsh words, and Kenny Krusco, perhaps not wanting to offend a cooperating agency, backed off. No sweat, Bollmann assured him, the reporters would take orders: They had promised to ask questions of no one except the two of them. There would be three reporters: two Eureka television newsphotographers, Ron Rose and Carol Olson, and Richard Harris, the sour ace of the *Times-Standard* staff, a former Vietnam public information officer, so straight he didn't even drink, a young man with an old man's love of the golf course.

Krusco would huncho the Bust. The raid would be composed of two assault teams, a total of nineteen men: five BNDD narks, two federal chemists, nine sheriff's deputies, and an IRS agent whom one of the reporters would describe as "a gray-haired Dustin Hoffman." Plus Bushnell, the dog catcher. They would all be armed with shotguns, revolvers, and rifles; fed narks would be camouflaged in long hair, Levi's, and tie-dyed T-shirts.

Two platoons were needed because of the tactical importance of the element of surprise. No one knew how many crazed bigtime dopers would be holed up in the cabin. Gunplay, their intelligence said, was a probability since the members of the "Dickenson Ring" were thought to be armed. One nark team would drive to the cabin, lurk in the trees, and strike as grunts from the road. The other would be airlifted in a Huey helicopter borrowed from the U.S. Army. When the chopper touched down in a clearing near the cabin, both teams would run for the cabin door. The Saint Bernards, it was clear, might have to be shot. The killing of the dogs was the dog catcher's special responsibility. The agents were certain the raid would uncover the "million-dollar . . . giant lab." The three reporters would stay the hell out of the way and under no circumstances would take pictures that showed any of the agents' faces.

If there were any problems, Kenny Krusco would bark all the signals. Krusco was an experienced federal narcotics agent, the little-big man of the BNDD's San Francisco office, a legend among his nark colleagues: the man who had put the cuffs on the Acid King himself, Owsley Stanley. He had also participated in the Kafkaesque 1970 arrest of Bay Area attorney Michael Metzger.

On this sun-flecked day in the mountain town of Alderpoint, as the three reporters waited for the land/air assault to be launched, they kept hearing federal agents refer to the suspects they'd find in Dirk Dickenson's cabin. The agents kept describing these suspects with a hissed single word: "Creeps."

Richard Harris, the golf-loving reporter, had an unnerving flash of *déjà-vu*. It was Vietnam all over again. They were going to take a remote hooch with a kind of helicopter strike; this time instead of gooks they were hunting creeps.

✝

DIRK DICKENSON
1948–1972

When they got back to their cabin, Jack Daniel's No. 7 Tennessee sour mash in hand, Dirk Dickenson and Judy Arnold stretched out on the back porch, broke off the seal on the new bottle, and toasted the burl tree that would make them rich. The bathtub was sitting out there, too, incongruous and absurd in the noonday sun, and they decided to devote a lazy afternoon building a room for it.

But the gunmen were coming for them. While Undersheriff Bollmann, Inspector Mel Ames, and seven federal agents were airborne in the Huey, cameraman Ron Rose was near the rear of an elaborate nark caravan. "A blue Ford pickup with Bushnell, the animal control officer, was leading us," says Ron Rose; "the bed of the pickup had regular facilities for carrying animals. Then there were two sheriff's cars and a green Ford van plastered with tourist stickers that had two federal agents in it, followed by a Scientific Ident man's station wagon. Then us—Carol Olson, Rich Harris, and I.

"We stopped twice, once half a mile from the cabin. The deputies were trying to make radio contact with the chopper. The chopper was about ten minutes out. We sat there for two or three minutes, and then the caravan moved on to another clearing. There was a house on the right. People were out mowing their front lawn. This clearing came back to a point. At the end of that, a dirt road went on through the trees. We stopped the cars there. We still couldn't see the house. We got out of the cars and started walking. This was a heavily wooded area. We went from the roadway onto a hillside, and we kept concealed in the trees, waiting for the helicopter."

Judy Arnold says: "We were clearing the bathtub out, and we were going to bring it inside, trying to figure out where to put it, and that's when we heard the helicopter."

Aboard the Huey, federal narcotics agent William Filben, gangling and carotene, looked down and saw armed longhairs hanging like apes out of the trees surrounding the cabin. Kenny Krusco's briefing had been less than complete, and Filben got nervous: he thought the longhairs were creeps. "I really didn't think the whole time in the air we'd find anybody in the place at all," he'd say later. "But when I saw the bunch in the trees, I thought, 'Oh, boy, we really walked into it.' It wasn't until we got down and I saw the TV cameras that I realized they weren't hostile."

"We heard the helicopter," Judy Arnold says, "and we'd just come inside. So we went out on the back porch again. We had our two dogs, Boogie and Vernon, with us. We weren't afraid. Dirk wanted to show the dogs, they'd never seen a helicopter before. He said, 'Come on, you guys, wanna see a helicopter?'

"The copter was coming toward the house. It was a long, green, unmarked copter. The door opened. It got right over the cabin, and they looked down and smiled and waved at us. We smiled and waved back. They didn't look like police people at all. They all had fairly long hair, and most of them had mustaches, and they looked happy. They looked like they were having fun.

"Dirk said, 'It looks like it's gonna land.' It was over the house, and it was really low. We left the back door open and came back inside the cabin. Boogie and Vernon weren't barking. They were calm. Our front door was open, and the copter was starting to land. Dust and dirt were coming into the cabin. Dirk walked over and closed the front door. Most of the door was glass. We stood at the corner of the big redwood table in the kitchen facing out the front door. We could see out the door. The copter set down, and the men jumped off."

Landing the big Huey in the clearing next to the cabin wasn't easy; Mel Ames's skybound surveillance had miscalculated the length of their chaparral landing zone. When the chopper finally touched ground, the grunt assault team raced from the trees toward the cabin. So did the nine gunmen who scrambled out of the Huey. It was a distance of sixty to ninety feet; a two-to-five-second dash. The noise was deafening; agents couldn't hear each other from the shrill kuh-chook-chook-chook whirring of the blades. At the crest of the hill overlooking the cabin a logger named Ronnie Robertson observed the figures scurrying below and thought: "It's like some stupid rabbit hunt, all those people running around like crazy men this way and that." *Times-Standard* reporter Richard Harris watched the attack and jotted a nervously scribbled sentence into his notebook: "Looks like an assault on an enemy prison camp in Vietnam."

Both film photographers, Ron Rose and Carol Olson, saw the Huey land and the men running, but both failed to catch the full sequence of the action with their cameras. The gust from the force of the chopper blades knocked Carol Olson to the ground. Her pictures blurred. "Just as the helicopter touched down," Ron Rose says, "something happened. It was the wind. It blew a large branch off a tree, and it started showering down on me. So I turned my back and shut my camera off momentarily. And then I turned back around and started filming."

Judy Arnold says: "I didn't have anything to be afraid of until I saw the guns, and I got petrified then. The guns were drawn—shotguns and rifles and everything. I thought it was some kind of ripoff."

As the commandos vaulted from the Huey toward the cabin door, agent William Filben allegedly stumbled and fell. "I did a bellyflop," he'd say later. "I just outran my feet."

Three men are alleged to have seen Filben fall—agents Krusco and

Lloyd Clifton, a beefy thirty-year-old former Berkeley policeman with a drooping mustache and long hair stickily layered with hair spray, and Undersheriff Bollman. No one else purportedly saw Filben's fall; neither camera recorded it.

Bollmann, who declared he had to step over Filben, said he didn't think Filben was hurt.

But Lloyd Clifton, as he was to testify, thought Filben had been shot by a sniper in the cabin.

Kenny Krusco corroborated his testimony and said he, too, thought Filben had been hit.

Judy Arnold says: "I saw a foot come through the door, the foot and then the door was pushed open. It was busted open. And at that time Dirk turned and ran, and he told me to run."

The man who broke the door down, shattering its plywood paneling and cracking the jamb, was Lloyd Clifton. Right behind him were Krusco, Bollmann, and federal agent Ed McReedy, thirty-seven years old, a former Arizona highway patrolman, bearded, frizzy-haired, and looking a dozen years younger.

"Before I could do anything," Judy Arnold says, "they had me. Dirk jumped off the back porch and ran. There's a terrace back there and a slope toward the woodline. They told me to freeze. There were at least ten of them inside by now. The one who broke the door down, Clifton, ran through the house after Dirk. He wore a pair of Levi's, a T-shirt, a corduroy jacket, and hair down to his chin. His size struck me. He was big, really big.

"It was terrifying. I was shaking. It was like some terrible storm had crashed down out of the sky at us. They held me. The dogs got excited, and they were barking. There was mad confusion in the place."

Lloyd Clifton was standing on the back porch.

He saw Dickenson running for the treeline.

He raised his snubnosed .38 revolver.

He aimed it at Dickenson's back.

He yelled, "Stop, or I'll fire!"

He fired one shot.

Kenny Krusco, standing next to Clifton on the porch, had his shotgun trained on Dickenson's back but didn't pull the trigger.

The roaring kuh-chook-chook-chook of the helicopter had muffled the gunshot and, some said later, Clifton's command to stop. "I heard a crack," Carol Olson says, "which at the time in the rush I interpreted as a tree breaking. Agents were running around. Then I saw somebody down on the ground. It didn't occur to me that it could have been the sound of a shot until I actually saw somebody down on the ground."

"I heard somebody say, 'He's been hit!'" Judy Arnold says. "I didn't hear the shot. The copter was taking off again and making this insane noise, and the dogs were really barking. It was chaos."

Dickenson was shot in the back at a distance of forty yards from a position forty feet higher in elevation. He dropped twenty-five yards short of a steel and wire fence at the wood line, face down, and crawled forward a few inches. He wore a pair of Levi's, work boots, and a brown T-shirt. The bullet entered his back three inches above the waist next to the spinal cord, sliced down at a sixty-degree angle, and exited through a small bloodless hole in the groin.

Undersheriff Bollmann, gun in hand, ran toward the body, "sure I'd find some sort of weapon." He found nothing. Incredulous, he got down on his hands and knees and searched the entire area. Still nothing. Bollmann, a newsman noted, looked flour-faced.

Dirk Dickenson was still writhing on the ground, barely alive. "I was shooting film at close range," Ron Rose says. "Rich Harris and I were both asked to help hold his head. I heard Dickenson say, 'I can't breathe, it's hard to breathe.' A deputy said, 'He's already urinated his pants; he's in bad shape.' The deputy said, 'Get the God-damn first aid kit and stretcher down here fast.' He was yelling. Another deputy said, 'There's a stretcher in my car,' and threw the key to someone else, and this guy started running up the embankment to where the cars were parked."

Dickenson needed a doctor immediately; none was available. He couldn't be rushed to a hospital; the Huey had taken off again and had to be summoned back by radio.

Inside the cabin Judy Arnold couldn't comprehend what was happening. "I heard he was out there and he'd been hit, and I asked if I could go out there and see him. They said no. I said, 'Well, can I at least go out on the back porch and see how he is? So they held me and took me to the back porch. I looked off, and I could see him. I saw him move his leg. It was spasmodic, like a twitch. They said, 'Oh, it's okay. He's gonna be all right.' Clifton was leaning over him, saying something—I don't know what. He was too far away.

"They took me back to the cabin. They still hadn't identified themselves. I finally saw a badge on the inside of this guy McReedy's coat, but they still hadn't said who they were. So McReedy goes, 'I'm gonna take you outside, ask you a few questions.' There were a couple more of them leaning in the door, and they asked me if I was the only one there. As they were taking me out, I asked, 'How's Dirk?' They wouldn't tell me how he was, wouldn't say anything. So they took me outside. There was an orange truck out there, Dirk's, with a broken head. They put me in the orange truck, and I said again, 'Well, who are you?' That's the first time they officially told me who they were."

The three reporters, critically important eyewitnesses at the scene of a killing, were behaving less than authoritatively. They asked no questions. "I didn't ask anyone about the shot," Ron Rose says. "I didn't know who was who. I didn't know whether I'd be talking to an agent or a suspect. And we were told not to question anyone except Undersheriff Bollmann and agent Krusco."

"The narks were treating me all right," Judy Arnold says. "They said, 'If you promise not to run, we won't handcuff you.' So I told them okay, I wouldn't run. The guy said, 'We're federal narcotics agents looking for a PCP lab.' And I just laughed. I just laughed in his face, and I said, 'Well, you blew it this time. There's no lab here.' And he goes, 'Well, we know there is.' And I said, 'There isn't; there's no lab.' So they took me out of the truck to the other side of the cabin."

Ron Rose says, "I started working myself down the hillside and onto the flat portion where there were some rabbit hutches and a chicken coop. They were going into the chicken coop and around it and into the woods. I presumed they were looking for something other than eggs."

"Then this agent, McReedy," says Judy Arnold, "starts talking to me about the land, how much he liked the land—wasn't this beautiful country—how much he'd like to live here. He was trying to act super nice. He started telling me where he was from, his experiences in Arizona and all this. It was a big sick game. He was supposed to charm me into giving them information while they took my old man's body away. I kept asking how Dirk was, and they wouldn't tell me. The copter was back and they were taking Dirk away, and I said, 'Can I go with him in the copter?' They said, 'No, you'd just be in the way.' One of the dogs, Boogie, was out there running around Dirk's body. They were carrying Dirk on the copter, and Boogie was crying. I guess he wanted to go along. The copter took off, and Boogie stood underneath it, looking up. The roar wasn't scaring him at all now, and he was howling."

As the agents continued interrogating Judy Arnold, Dirk Dickenson—who had to wait twenty minutes before the Huey came back—was dying. The bullet did not strike any bones or vital organs but had punctured major blood vessels in the abdomen, causing massive internal bleeding. When the chopper touched down in Eureka, Dickenson was dead. ("There was absolutely no chance of saving him," the coroner, Ed Nielson, would say. "He would have died if he'd been shot in downtown Eureka.")

Kenny Krusco, meanwhile, ordered the three reporters off the property. "The cameras bothered the feds," reporter Richard Harris would write, "and a half hour after we got there we were told to leave the cabin area." Ron Rose says: "We were asked by Krusco, through Bollmann, to leave the area so that 'they could go about their work.' We went back to the feds' van. We got into it because it was cold. The wind had come up, and there was some cloud cover. We waited there quite a length of time."

"The copter took off," says Judy Arnold, "and they took me back to the other side of the cabin and took me back in the truck, and a guy said, 'I wanna ask you a few more questions.' Vernon, the other dog, was superprotective of me, and he wanted to get in the truck with me. So they let Vernon in with me, and the agent [McReedy] had the door open and he was talking to me about the dogs and everything. At one point I got really mad—I don't remember about what—and the dog could feel my vibes, and he tried to bite him. And so the agent slammed the door of the truck, and he goes, 'If you don't take care of the dog, I will. I'll have to shoot him.'

"So McReedy goes, 'Well, we better take you out of the truck. I can't talk to you with your dog snapping at me in there.' They locked Vernon in the truck and took me back to the cabin again. Then they left me by a tree while they searched the cabin. I was standing by that big tree looking up into the sun and starting to cry. I just kept thinking about Dirk, you know, wondering how he was, being scared, trying to feel myself together with him."

Ron Rose says: "We were sitting in the feds' van, and then Undersheriff Bollmann came out and gave us a very minor briefing. Then Kenny Krusco came out, and at that time we were allowed to ask any questions we had. We asked what the weapon was. We wanted to make sure of our own hearing. We asked how many shots were fired. We did not ask who did the shooting. I think we all had enough common sense

170

about us to know we would not get an answer. We were more interested, at this point, in whether they'd found the lab or not." Carol Olson adds: "I don't think we asked who did the shooting or why. Maybe we should have."

"We were asked at the scene," Rose says, "to have our film processed and before it was shown to take it over to the sheriff's office so that Krusco and Bollmann could look at it and—more or less—not censor it, but point out where we might inadvertently have gotten an agent's face into the picture. We agreed to this request."

"They took me to the county jail in Eureka," says Judy Arnold, "and after a while—I'm not sure how long because I lost track of the time—they called me out and told me he was dead. Just like that. No beating around the bush. No softening it. 'He's dead.' Almost like—'By the way, you know that guy you were with, well, he's dead.' I never felt that bad before in my life. The hurt was so bad I couldn't believe it. I got sick. I was in a trance. I was a puppet, and they had to guide me everywhere."

The fed / county raiders had a serious public relations problem. They had one dead body, and they had no PCP lab. Their "master chemist" had been shot in the back as he ran unarmed. An extensive search of the area netted only a penny-ante stash. The contents of the "master chemist's" stash were neatly catalogued and listed in a summary that some of Dirk Dickenson's friends would view as a grotesque requiem.

#1—One hand-rolled cigarette, suspected marijuana.

#2—Excedrin bottle containing one partially smoked cigarette, suspected marijuana.

#3—Plastic bag containing suspected marijuana.

#4—Plastic bag containing suspected marijuana.

#5—Bottle containing suspected marijuana.

#6—Bottle containing suspected peyote buttons.

#7—Bottle containing two suspected LSD tablets.

#8—Tin can containing five suspected peyote buttons.

#9—Brown jacket containing plastic bag, suspected marijuana.

#10—Bottle containing partially smoked cigarette, suspected marijuana.

In Lincoln, California, that day, twenty-five miles north of Sacramento, Mrs. Mittie Dickenson, the wife of a Chrysler Corporation manufacturer's representative, got a phone call from a friend. Her friend was listening to the radio and humming along with the music, and, as was her custom, she listened only half-heartedly when the news came on. That's how she found out, between jingles and commercials, that Mittie's son was dead. She called only to tell Mittie how sorry she was. Mittie Dickenson gasped. She wasn't expecting condolences. No one had bothered to notify her.

While they had a bullet-holed corpse and no historic PCP lab, the feds made much of $1,500 in cash found in Dickenson's wallet, as well as what they called a "small arsenal"—three rifles, a crossbow, and a shotgun—stockpiled in the cabin. Their emphasis of these discoveries implied this was enough circumstantially to prove Dickenson was indeed involved in a nefarious dope ring. The implication carried a sneaky bottom line: Think about it, pal, if the guy was a dope merchant in the business of corrupting your children, his corpse wasn't worth shrieking about.

The shooting catalyzed Humboldt. In the weeks afterward, as investigations were demanded and proclaimed, civil libertarians (mostly at Humboldt State College in Arcata and in the Bay Area) replied to the fed innuendoes by pointing out that in the primordial part of the wilderness where Dirk Dickenson lived everyone was well armed, especially those longhairs who survived the vigilante terrorism and the house-burnings. Besides, as one attorney later said, "I don't care if the fucking hippie was a Mafia kingpin second only to Lucky Luciano's heirs. I still worry about that bullet in his back."

Civil libertarians were troubled by unanswered and nagging questions:

Since he knew a raid on the Dickenson property was imminent, knew there was a warrant for Dickenson's arrest, why didn't dog catcher Bushnell arrest Dickenson? At least turn him over to a sheriff's deputy when Dickenson sauntered into the Garberville substation wanting to buy the burl tree?

What happened to the infallible "hard intelligence" that was the basis for the search warrant? That said the property housed a leviathan lab? Why didn't the agents conduct a land survey before nineteen men hit the cabin with their trigger fingers ready?

Why didn't agents identify themselves when they came hurtling out of the sky to the cabin door? Why didn't they state their warrant and demand entry instead of savaging the door from its hinges?

Why did the reporters along on the hunt permit the agents to view their films before those agents made their statements about the shooting (a question made critical by the fact that Filben claimed he fell at the exact moment the two films blurred)?

Why did it take three days after the shooting—and after the agents had viewed the films—for Filben to reveal his fall and for Bollmann, Krusco, and Clifton to say they saw it happen?

Why did only three men out of a nineteen-man party—the killer, his superior, and a raid organizer—see Filben's fall?

Why, if Filben did indeed fall, didn't Krusco and Clifton check him? Make sure he had been hit? Lean down and check the wound before one of them shot an unarmed man in the back?

Why, if gunplay was thought probable, was no provision made for the aid and evacuation of wounded men?

Why were the three reporters and their cameras suddenly ordered off the property after the raid? After it was clear there would be no more shooting and the reporters' lives wouldn't be endangered? Was there something to hide?

And those three lily-livered reporters? What about their sense of professionalism? How could they have agreed to an arrangement not to ask questions of anyone but Bollmann and Krusco? How could they honor that agreement once they realized they had witnessed a killing? How could they, as Ron Rose admitted, still be concerned with the lab after two of them helped hold a dying man's head? Why didn't they even ask Krusco who had done the shooting or why shooting was necessary?

Local police officials tried to explain away the shooting by blathering on about the Uptight Society. By this convoluted rationale, Dirk Dickenson was killed because of the policemen who'd been killed in America in the past. "You can't blame officers for being uptight," said Undersheriff Bollmann. "They're aware of the situation today. Officers don't go out on duty thinking they're going to shoot someone, but many times they may wonder if they're going to return home that night. 'Is today my day?' they ask themselves."

The local head of the highway patrol, Captain William O. Roberts, added: "There has been an increasing trend toward violence aimed at law officers, and as a result the normal work atmosphere becomes a little grimmer for peace officers on duty. We've stressed for years that

173

you can never get into the habit of being too cautious about the job. You've got to be alert at all times."

Agents who participated in the raid said very little, except for Ed McReedy's comment that "the idea of shooting to wound is bush league. You just get more people killed that way." Lloyd Clifton became very unavailable and was transferred from door-stomping duty to the anonymous seclusion of the BNDD chemical lab.

His fate rested with two agencies: the U.S. Department of Justice and the Humboldt County district attorney's office. Both announced high-priced investigations; no taxpayer dollars would be spared in the pursuit of "the facts." The feds could technically indict Clifton on charges of violating Dirk Dickenson's constitutional rights, of "summarily executing" him. District Attorney Ferroggiaro could seek charges ranging from involuntary manslaughter to first-degree murder. Or both agencies could do nothing, find the shooting regrettable and tragic, shed public crocodile tears, and conclude that Lloyd Clifton's muted gunshot was "justifiable homicide."

Thirty-seven-year-old Bill Ferroggiaro, looking paler each day, his horn-rimmed glasses sliding in sweat off his spoon-shaped nose, was on the hot grille again. He was a man whose once grandiose roseate political ambitions—the U.S. House of Representatives, the Senate—were being sandbagged by twists of violent circumstance. He announced, with a fine sense of politics, that he would do nothing . . . until the feds concluded their own investigation. Clifton, after all, was a federal agent, and the Humboldt County D.A. said, "We're waiting for the Department of Justice to act, and then we'll make our decisions."

In San Francisco U.S. Attorney James K. Browning, Jr., flashily told the press that the government's investigation would be far-reaching and fair. The fact that no federal narcotics agent anywhere in America had ever been charged by the government with violating a suspect's constitutional rights was coincidental and irrelevant. Browning admitted a rather brain-scalding conflict of interest: As the U.S. attorney, he was responsible for determining whether Dickenson's constitutional rights had been violated. And as the U.S. attorney, he was dutybound to act as defense counsel for all government personnel—including Lloyd Clifton.

A few weeks after the shooting, as the federal investigation got under way, U.S. Attorney Browning said: "We are attempting to be as impartial as possible. We've got an open mind."

In the next sentence, long before the government's probe was even halfway complete, he demonstrated his impartiality. "Nevertheless, on the basis of incomplete reports received by this office, I suspect it will fall into the category of justifiable homicide."

It didn't look as if either Lloyd Clifton, who pulled the trigger, or Kenny Krusco, his boss and chief corroborative witness, had much to worry about.

Meanwhile, not long after the shooting, five lonely freaks stood in bereavement outside the Eureka courthouse with a sign reading: "Oh, no, Dickenson, goodbye."

The sourdoughs of Humboldt were also sharing their feelings about the dead hippie who'd kept marijuana in his home and lived in belly-to-belly sin with his sweet-faced girl friend. The *Times-Standard*, which called vehemently for an investigation, was receiving fat sackfuls of letters to the editor:

"Why all the sympathy for a dope pusher escaping arrest? It's because of bleeding hearts like you that our valued lawmen are hampered by over-lenient courts and laws.... It's about time that we started thanking the federal agencies instead of criticizing them. *So hang in there, guys, you're all doing a great job.*"

✝

WILLIAM SMITH
1934–1972

Three weeks after Dirk Dickenson's death....

On the evening of April 25, 1972, eighteen miles north of Eureka, in Arcata, the home of Humboldt State University, an adrenalized SRO crowd jammed into a college auditorium to hear America's most renowned Marxist. Herbert Marcuse, the grand old ideologist of the American Left, mentor to Angela Davis and hero to millions of Third World peoples, drove a lot of sourdoughs raving gaga with his visit. A celebrated Red was in their hometown, brainwashing their kids with sin, sedition, and the Good Lord knows what else. Teams of police cruised the campus, ready for action—in case the genial old man's polysyllabic words inspired sudden anarchism and revolution.

At 8:30 that night, while Marcuse stood at a speaker's stand less than 500 yards away, a forty-three-year-old California highway patrolman named Robert Hahn, with thirteen years' service on the force, noticed a scruffy motorcyclist driving south on Highway 101 near the university gates.

The patrolman watched the cyclist ditch his machine on the side of the road and run through the brush. He thought the cyclist's actions suspicious and gave chase, gun in hand. The patrolman caught up with him on the embankment of the highway and yelled to the man to stop. The cyclist stopped and turned.

As he did so, Patrolman Hahn shot him between the eyes with his Colt officer's model .38 special revolver.

Patrolman Hahn walked back to his squad car and drove away; the cyclist's body was found later that night by a passing motorist. The motorist called the highway patrol. The dead man was identified as William Smith, thirty-eight years old, a Win-Ton Indian, the father of five, an employee of the Simpson Lumber Company.

The first patrolman on the scene, Edward Radelich, listed the death as a hit-and-run accident until the coroner washed the corpse's face and disclosed the bullet hole in the middle of the dead man's forehead. Radelich called another highway patrolman to help him with the investigation. He was Robert Hahn.

For three days Patrolman Hahn investigated the killing with his colleagues. On the morning of the fourth day he confessed to having killed the Indian. He said he was confessing because "I couldn't sleep." He confessed, too, to having falsified his log, placing himself twenty miles away in McKinleyville at the time of the shooting. Why did he kill the Indian? "I don't know why I shot him," he said in a statement, "whether it was the heat of the chase or what."

District Attorney Ferroggiaro had a unique case: the cop who killed an innocent man, walked away from the bleeding body, made up an alibi, and then began investigating his victim's murder.

Yet the district attorney referred to the killing only as an "accident" and called Hahn "negligent." In light of those statements, some thought it not very surprising that Hahn was charged only with involuntary manslaughter—merely a legal slap on the wrist in an instance of homicide.

American Indian activists said: "The indictment is a joke. Hahn killed Bill Smith in cold blood. Smith's body actually landed at Hahn's feet. It was a senseless murder."

Hahn was dismissed from the highway patrol, and there was a trial. His counsel was James McKittrick, in his mid-thirties, an icepick-thin, vitriolic, and flamboyant man who liked to run the table at George's Pool Hall on Third Street, drove a jewel-like Lincoln Continental, wore showy suspenders like a Roaring Twenties gambler, retained a private eye on his staff, and was an unabashed cop-lover.

Hahn testified that, when he asked Smith to stop and Smith turned, he felt an "object" strike his leg. The object, a stone, caused his gun to "discharge." He admitted the Colt was cocked and that his finger was on the trigger when Smith turned. He did not say why he was chasing a man who had violated no law nor why he had his gun cocked . . . if he didn't intend to fire. (A highway patrol official testified: "It is extremely dangerous for an officer to cock a pistol unless he intends to fire it.")

The gun discharged, the hatchet-faced McKittrick maintained, because of a "faulty trigger mechanism." More exactly, the gun had been honed so that it could be fired "with less than standard trigger pressure." It had, in short, been hair-triggered . . . souped up the way Billy the Kid and Wyatt Earp and their gunslinging Wild West sidekicks doctored their Colts . . . and a Eureka gunsmith testified that honing guns was "a common practice among law enforcement person-nel." No one knew, it turned out, who had hair-triggered Hahn's gun, though it developed the patrolman had failed to turn in his weapon for its annual highway patrol inspection.

And Hahn?—the district attorney questioned—Was he asked during his confession whether he shot Smith intentionally or whether the gun accidentally discharged? Both witnesses to the confession, another highway patrolman and an Arcata policeman, said they "couldn't remember" whether Hahn had been asked that seemingly routine and all-important question.

In his summation, defense attorney McKittrick dwelled on "the hundreds of policemen slain in America in the line of duty." He did not, understandably, tell the jury there had never been a copkilling in the history of Humboldt County.

He concluded: "The fact that people have been killed by officers is too bad, but I would say by and large they have brought their unhappy fates upon themselves."

The jury's verdict: deadlocked ten to two . . . *for acquittal*.

District Attorney Ferroggiaro announced he would not ask for a new trial; Robert Hahn filed suit to regain his job with the highway patrol; Bill Smith's widow wondered how she'd feed her five children.

Pool-playing Jim McKittrick, blessed with a smooth and soft touch,

177

scored the biggest victory of his courtroom career, a victory that would go a long way . . . all the way to the Justice Department in Washington and the bullet hole in Dirk Dickenson's body.

Two federal narcotics agents slept in Dirk Dickenson's cabin the night he was killed. They stayed on his land the next day, searching (with what must have been some desperation) for the million-dollar PCP lab their intelligence promised. They found nothing. A few days later Undersheriff Bollmann announced the property had been sealed off.

Almost a full month after the shooting, on May 2, District Attorney Ferroggiaro made his own investigative outing to the cabin site. He wanted to diagram the shooting. As the D.A. wandered around, making his precise drawings, he stumbled onto a long black hose 200 feet from the cabin. He wondered where it would lead, and—sweet creeping Jesus!—it led to the million-dollar PCP lab . . . at least a part of it. The D.A. tracked the wondrous hose 200 yards into the woods and found a wooden tent platform, two cans of a chemical component of PCP, a shattered measuring flask, and jagged bits and pieces of laboratory bottles.

Now this miraculous development was devilishly strange. The entire nineteen-man nark posse somehow had overlooked the hose on the day of the shooting, as did the two agents who scoured the ground the next day—even though the hose was right at their toes, only 200 feet from the cabin! Unless, of course, the hose, the tent platform, and the whole suspicious jimbang hadn't been there that day. Unless someone had sneaked back onto the property and conveniently planted these incriminating little items . . . ready and waiting for the headlines when the D.A. came out to make his drawings.

According to courthouse insiders, District Attorney Ferroggiaro was apoplectic that he might have blundered onto the ruins of that alleged lab. He felt he'd been set up, suckered into making a highly dubious discovery. Publicly the D.A. said, "There's a certain taint to the discovery [and] the possibility must be considered that the materials were planted on the Dickenson property subsequent to the initial search."

When he heard the D.A. had found the lab, a lawyer on Fillmore Street in San Francisco laughed. He had no doubt the evidence was planted; no doubt that the U.S. government would "obviously try every dirty sleazoid trick" to get one of its hired guns off the hook. The lawyer was Phil Ryan, one of the Bay Area's least conventional criminal attorneys, a man who once compared narcotics agents' methods and attitudes to those held by Hitler and Goebbels. Phil Ryan was representing Judy Arnold, charged after the raid on the lean-to with possession of marijuana and of LSD, but the way Ryan saw it, his real client was the dead man, Dirk Dickenson. Ryan swore to himself he would not see a man get shot in the back without his making every effort to bring the killer to justice.

Ryan examined the details of the Dickenson case, guessed at the extent to which the government would go to defend one of its own, and decided he needed some help. He turned to attorney Michael Metzger, victim of one of the most tainted busts in BNDD history, busted in that perverse raid led by BNDD agent Kenny Krusco, who led the raid on Dirk Dickenson's cabin and was now agent Lloyd Clifton's superior and his chief substantiating witness.

The stage was set for a classic confrontation. Ryan, investigated by narks, and Metzger, victimized by them, working together to protect the rights of a man killed by a nark, pitted against Clifton, Krusco, and the full power, influence, and resources of the Department of Justice of the United States.

The two men made their own investigation of the case and reached very personal conclusions. They charged that the raid on the Dickenson cabin was a zany Keystone Kops affair: Kenny Krusco had been a miserable quarterback; no one knew exactly what was going on. They alleged that Lloyd Clifton lost his head and shot Dickenson because he got carried away by the thrill and expectation of battle. They alleged that neither Clifton nor Krusco believed agent Filben had been shot . . . but that they had worked out their alibis afterward. They alleged Clifton was lying to save his skin and Krusco was lying to save one of his men and his own reputation. They alleged the "tainted evidence" had been planted for District Attorney Ferroggiaro because the government itself didn't want to "find" a lab a month late and because the feds badly wanted to soften the impact of the killing by sullying Dickenson's reputation at all costs.

Ryan shifted into high gear. He discovered a few words that seemed to weigh heavily against Lloyd Clifton, words contained in the BNDD's own manual to its agents.

A paragraph of the manual (Subsection 42–23) said: "The agent should not shoot at any persons except to protect his own life or that of some other person. The agent will not fire at fleeing automobiles, suspects, or defendants."

Lloyd Clifton had killed Dirk Dickenson, Phil Ryan underlined, in violation of his own agency's regulations. He had fired at a "fleeing suspect."

Defending Judy Arnold, Ryan and Metzger were able to prove that Clifton smashed the cabin door down without identifying himself or stating his warrant. The charges against Judy Arnold were dismissed, and District Court Judge William T. Sweigert reprimanded Clifton for his tactics. Clifton's forced entry, the judge said, "suggests the importance of better instruction, training, and discipline for narcotics agents in the proper manner of serving arrest and seizure warrants at private residences."

In addition, Ryan filed a $2-million wrongful-death suit against the federal government on behalf of Dickenson's family.

But the case seemed a bottomless pit and still needed a herculean investigative job. Ryan turned for further help to another man who'd had dealings with narcotics agents. He was Michael Murphy, twenty-eight years old, retired private detective, graduate of the Haight-Ashbury, a goblinesque, rail-thin longhair who had once convinced one of the California Bureau of Narcotics Enforcement's star informers to testify against her own superiors.

The informer was once asked by a reporter how many times she'd heard Murphy's name mentioned in the narcotics squad.

"At least twenty, maybe fifty," she said.

"How many times were threats leveled against him?"

"Every time," she said.

Murphy's constant companions were Terror and Paranoia. He kept checking his rearview mirror every time he went somewhere, and he was convinced his phone was tapped. The job devoured him, and his personal life was in ruins. His wife, who complained she hardly saw him anymore, walked out. So in the spring of 1972 Michael Murphy dropped out of the gumshoe business, stopped investigating narks, stopped investigating anything, and lay back doing odd jobs.

When Phil Ryan asked him to help with the Dickenson investigation, Murphy refused.

"I don't want all that shit fucking up my life again," he said.

Ryan outlined the case to him, describing the gruesome way the bullet had ripped into Dickenson's back and exploded his insides, and Murphy changed his mind.

On a muggy summer day in 1972 he sat with a reporter, who was also a friend—the two had helped derail one particularly sinister narcotics agent's high-speed career—and Murphy said he was happy to be investigating again. He had pulled himself together; he had patched fences with his wife; he believed in what he was doing. He'd take the risks and try to cope with the anxieties.

The reporter asked to buy him a drink, and Murphy refused. He was on the wagon, he said—no booze. Besides, he was busy, he had to run, no time to screw off. He wanted to devote as many hours as he could to this particular job.

He was investigating a man of mystery—BNDD agent Lloyd Clifton.

For five long months, working twelve hours a day, Michael Murphy delved into Lloyd Clifton's police background. When he began his digging, Clifton's image appeared snow-white: the hard-working Brigham Young sociology grad who had devoted his life to upholding the law. But as Murphy turned his reports in to Phil Ryan, agent Clifton didn't look so immaculate anymore.

This is what Murphy found:

In the winter of 1968, while he was a Berkeley policeman, Lloyd Clifton stopped a man named James Baird for a traffic violation. He found a bottle of gas in Baird's car.

On February 21, 1969, Clifton was questioned about the arrest by Baird's attorney, James Giller, in the Superior Court of the state of California. A court transcript reveals this dialogue:

Giller: Did you ask him [Baird] a question?
Clifton: Yes.
Q: And what question did you ask him?
Clifton: I asked him what was in the bottle.
Q: Did he reply?
Clifton: Yes.
Q: What did he say?
Clifton: He said, "Gas."
Q: Did you call him a name at that point?

Clifton: I referred to him as a "murderer."

Q: After you referred to him as a murderer, what did you do?

Clifton: He smirked at me, and I hit him.

Q: Where did you hit him?

Clifton: In the stomach.

Q: With what?

Clifton: My baton.

Q: Prior to beating him in the stomach with your baton, at any time did you choke him with your baton?

Clifton: No.

Q: When you hit him in the stomach, he had made no gestures or any attempt to do anything to you, did he?

Clifton: No.

Q: You just did that on your own?

Clifton: Yes.

Q: You had never seen the man before?

Clifton: No.

Q: Yet you called him a murderer?

Clifton: Yes.

Q: What else did you do to him? How many times did you hit him after that? You hit him more than that one time, didn't you?

Clifton: Not that I recall.

Giller: You don't recall that, huh?

A few months after Lloyd Clifton admitted under oath that he had beaten a man with his billyclub because "he smirked at me," a long-haired young man named Steven Wilson was arrested by the California Highway Patrol. He was arrested for ignoring some traffic warrants.

Wilson was taken to the Berkeley police station. He told the patrolmen the car in question wasn't his any more and asked their permission to make a phone call. He said he could establish the identity of the new owner. The arresting officers said fine, he could make the call.

He used the phone at the booking desk. He was going back to the patrolmen when policeman Lloyd Clifton walked into the room.

Steven Wilson alleged that Lloyd Clifton:

Grabbed him by the shirt and said: "What the fuck are you walking around here for?" Threw him into an open elevator and smashed his head against the side of it. Took him upstairs and continued beating and slapping him on the way up.

When they got off the elevator, Steven Wilson said, several Berkeley policemen saw Clifton beating him. They grabbed Clifton and told him to "let the guy go."

The policemen told Lloyd Clifton to let him go because his victim was the son of Superior Court Judge Lionel J. Wilson.

(Judge Lionel Wilson, ironically, had been sitting on the bench when Clifton admitted hitting James Baird because "he smirked at me.")

Steven Wilson filed a formal complaint with the Berkeley police department; Lloyd Clifton was officially reprimanded for his conduct.

On March 24, 1970, a young black man named Jemeral Young was being released on bond at the Berkeley city jail. Present were Mrs. Edna Young, his mother, a bail bondsman, and Lloyd Clifton.

Mrs. Young alleged that, as they were getting ready to leave, Lloyd Clifton began beating her son with his fists. When she tried to stop him and screamed she'd bring charges, Clifton said that her son was under arrest. The bail bondsman, streetwise and shrewd, talked him out of taking that tack.

Questioned by his superiors, Clifton did not deny the beating. He said he beat Young "because he called me a motherfucker."

As he read Murphy's reports, Phil Ryan was appalled. The bullet in Dickenson's back was not an isolated incident. Ryan saw a "pattern of conduct." Dirk Dickenson's killer was a man who had assaulted one suspect for a smirk, another for an obscenity, and a third for no discernible reason at all.

The Department of Justice, meanwhile, seemed in no hurry to conclude its investigation of Dirk Dickenson's death. A flurry of press releases in the spring and summer of 1972 announced the feds were coordinating a task force of bigwigs to sift facts: a department attorney from San Diego was assigned exclusively to the case; a BNDD Division of Inspection agent flew from Los Angeles to Garberville; all government investigators, the department said, were "fully cooperating" with District Attorney Ferroggiaro.

In June an assistant U.S. attorney in San Francisco said a decision whether Clifton would be indicted would be reached within three weeks. At the end of September there still was no decision and a public relations assistant to Attorney General Richard Kleindienst in Washington hinted at an even lengthier delay: "We've had recent cases in which indictments have been obtained on one-year-old cases."

At the same time, also in Washington, BNDD Chief Counsel

William Lench said the bureau had made no formal decision whether Clifton had violated its internal regulations, "but on the basis of reports we've reached a preliminary conclusion Clifton was justified in shooting." The chief counsel obviously did not attach much significance to BNDD manual Subsection 42-23, which forbids agents to shoot "fleeing suspects."

On November 15 attorneys Phil Ryan and Michael Metzger wrote Attorney General Kleindienst, demanding that the government conclude its investigation "without further delay."

The letter also detailed the fruits of hard-working Michael Murphy's labors. "Our investigation," the letter to Kleindienst concluded, "has established that the violence which agent Clifton perpetrated on April 4 was part of a pattern of behavior in which he has engaged for some time and about which his superiors at the Bureau of Narcotics and Dangerous Drugs should be familiar."

Ten days later in San Francisco the bespectacled U.S. Attorney for Northern California, Nixon-appointee James L. Browning, made the announcement that Ryan and Metzger feared and expected: In the government's eyes Lloyd Clifton had done nothing wrong. He was cleared. The fatal bullet in his back had not violated Dirk Dickenson's constitutional rights.

While federal civil rights statutes prohibited an officer from acting "with the specific intent of depriving another of a federal constitutional right," Browning explained, Lloyd Clifton did not act with an intent purposely to inflict "punishment without trial."

Browning went to great pains to describe the scope of the Justice Department probe (if they put so much effort into it, they couldn't have been wrong): "Extensive independent investigation" by his office and the BNDD over a six-month period; interviews with more than twenty-five witnesses and the collection of scores of exhibits; the results of all this digging reviewed by Browning's office as well as by the Department of Justice in Washington.

Which all meant that, if Lloyd Clifton was going to be prosecuted for firing his snubnosed .38, the man preferring charges would have to be the hapless Bill Ferroggiaro ... who was at that moment losing ingloriously to manic Jim McKittrick in the involuntary manslaughter trial of Highway Patrolman Robert Hahn. Lloyd Clifton was off scot-free, ready to boot down doors once again, unless the shell-shocked Humboldt County D.A. took some action.

Ferroggiaro said, not surprisingly, that again he would do nothing . . . for the time being, until he concluded (lost) the Hahn case.

Ryan and Metzger watched this legal tapdance with some alarm; they were being kept directly out of the case by their real client's fate (dead men can't testify), and they were thus powerless to go after Clifton in a criminal courtroom. That, if he chose, would be the task of the rather vague and muddling Mr. Ferroggiaro, who could seemingly do nothing right; branded a gutless vote-seeker by those decrying the premature deaths of Pat Berti, Bunky Ferris, and Bill Smith; considered soft on law and order by Undersheriff Bollmann and most of the sheriff's staff.

As the district attorney pondered his decision—sure to cause him further grief from either sourdoughs or creep-lovers—the routine of life in the Humboldt wilderness continued its unvarying rhythm:

Another highway patrolman stopped a Wyot Indian for drunk driving. This Indian, flashing on the bullet in the forehead the other Indian got, asked the patrolman whether "I'm going to get shot, too." The drunken Wyot was not shot but allegedly was beaten to the ground.

In the Eureka jail a policeman was questioning an Indian named Merrifield. Merrifield wasn't very cooperative. The policeman kicked the Indian black and blue and was subsequently charged with assault.

And then there was the newest caper pulled by Sheriff's Investigator Mel Ames, who had watched that marijuana plant for a whole week . . . who had been Undersheriff Bollmann's liaison with Kenny Krusco and Lloyd Clifton . . . who had conducted the airborne surveillance of the "million-dollar lab."

One night Mel Ames and another sheriff's detective named George Gatto collared a kid they heard was dealing grass. They asked him to score for them. The kid was no dummy. "You kidding?" he said. "You guys smell like cops."

At which point Mel Ames and his partner threw the kid up against the car, put guns to his head, and said they were "Mafia gunrunners from Portland." Unless the kid scored, they said, "we'll blow your brains out."

The kid scored; naturally, they arrested him. They offered him a deal. If he turned informer, they'd let him off. The kid turned informer, serving them well in a dozen cases, so well that Mel Ames lent him out to other agencies.

When the kid was burned out and everyone in Humboldt County

knew he was a nark (of no further use to any agency), Mel Ames arrested him again. The kid was charged with dealing grass.

An incredulous judge listened to these surreal details in court with eyes popping out of his skull, heard how Mel Ames had identified himself as a "Mafia gunrunner from Portland," shook his head, and threw the case out of court. "Entrapment," said Superior Court Judge William Watson.

The next day Mel Ames was heard mumbling that the judge was one of those limp-wristed, cowbrained liberals and he could prove it. Proof: The judge sent two of his children to a Free School and wasted much of his time raising goats.

✝

MICHAEL MURPHY
1944–1972

Michael Murphy, the gangly-shanked private eye, relentlessly continued his investigation of Lloyd Clifton. He was certain the narks were aware that he was mining Clifton's past, and he warned his wife, Pam, to remember all the old safeguards: Never let anyone into the house; always assume the phone is tapped; keep a close eye on *schleppy*, salamanderlike door-to-door salesmen. It was the same tired, energy-draining game, but, mindful of the threats agents had leveled against him in the past, he knew the game was high-staked. He knew, too, that the allegations impugning Lloyd Clifton's professional competence that he had unearthed . . . allegations that Phil Ryan publicized in a press conference . . . had given the BNDD a black eye at a time it was most interested in sanctifying its public image.

Murphy believed in his job, kept working at it, and was content. Doing investigative work for a cause he felt to be righteous gave him a deep sense of satisfaction; his work on the Clifton case even convinced him to apply for a California detective's license, the kind Lew Archer carried, which would enable him to work as a full-fledged private investigator. He enjoyed Christmas with his wife and two-year-old son, told friends he spent too much but, what the fuck, playing Santa Claus was a small way of making up for a stormy year.

He took his state investigator's exam four days after Christmas. He didn't study hard, because he assumed the test, designed mostly for Popeye-bicepsed yoyos, would be a mickey mouse exercise. He put in more than 4,000 manhours of grueling investigative work, and he figured if he didn't know the basics after all that sweat and worry, he never would. He got up a few minutes after 7 A.M. on the 29th, a ridiculous hour for all good Irishmen, and left his home in Berkeley just after eight o'clock.

The test began at nine o'clock. He had two and a half hours to finish it. The bozos sat at the desks around him and fidgeted. Murphy was through in an hour. He called Phil Ryan and suggested they meet for lunch to celebrate. "The test was a crock of shit," he said.

They met at Perry's, on Union Street, a block from Ryan's office, and Ryan was more than an hour late. Murphy was sitting at the bar, sipping a beer. The bartender, a professional Irishman named Shamus, leaned over to Phil Ryan and cracked: "What the hell kind of Irishman is this guy? He's been here two hours and he drinks two beers."

Perry's was filled with junior execs and hustling salesmen; so they walked a block to Thomas Lord's. Murphy drank a glass of mountain red Burgundy wine with lunch and a single Irish coffee. They talked about the Dickenson case.

Murphy was chagrined that Clifton had been cleared by the government, and, cynical and bitter, he said: "No one really cares. That's the trouble with nark cases. People say yeah yeah yeah it's terrible, but there's no movement against their excesses. People shake their heads but don't get involved, and the narks move on to slap up the next guy."

Ryan complimented him for his painstaking research. Murphy said he "hoped it would help."

Around 2:30 Phil Ryan went back to his office, and Murphy said he was headed for a music store to price guitars. "I can't work twenty-four hours a day," he laughed. "When he left," Phil Ryan was to remember, "he was stone sober."

He was back home in Berkeley at six, talking to a friend on the telephone. He was supposed to meet his friend that afternoon but didn't make it. "I'm dead tired," Murphy told him; "I had to get up at seven o'clock for that stupid test, and I ran into all kinds of traffic this afternoon." He told his friend he was going to take Pam to a movie that night and they could get together the next day.

Around 6:30 Pam, who was visiting a girl friend, called him at home. They spoke for a few minutes, and Murphy told her he'd take her to a movie.

Then he said, "Listen, something came up. I've got to go out for a little while to meet a guy. I'll be back by seven:thirty, and we can go to the show."

Pam didn't ask who the "guy" was and didn't ask what "came up." She remembered his fears about the phone being tapped and assumed from his tone it was "business."

"Watch yourself," she said.

"I always do," Murphy laughed.

No one knows who the "guy" was he met that night.

At 8:25, nineteen miles from home, Michael Murphy drove his Volvo station wagon onto the MacArthur Freeway in San Leandro. He drove it onto an exit ramp—the wrong way. He raced it at speeds up to 75 m.p.h.—the wrong way—for two and a half miles. Cars swerved out of his way; horns blared; tires screeched. Murphy drove on.

Two and a half miles down the freeway he hit a Toyota head on. He was killed instantly; so were two people in the other car.

An autopsy made by the Alameda County Coroner's Office showed he had a blood alcohol count of .29 percent when he died. A blood alcohol count of .10 is enough for a drunk-driving arrest. At .20 the function of the motor area of the brain is depressed and the individual staggers. At .30 the more primitive perceptive areas of the brain are dulled and the person is stuporous.

Phil Ryan, notified that Michael Murphy was dead, was in shock. It was, he thought, a most suspicious accident. The guy had taken his test that morning, he had gotten his loose-jointed life together, he was hardly drinking, he was cold sober when he left lunch that afternoon . . . and now Phil Ryan was told Murphy died because he got stuporously drunk.

He didn't buy it. He thought Murphy could have been lured from home by a suckering phone call and drugged. He knew Murphy had made some powerful enemies and stomped more than once on important toes.

Ryan hired a nationally respected toxicologist to examine the body. Dr. Charles Hines's tests showed no traceable drugs in the blood or internal organs—except the booze.

Pam Murphy went to the newspapers and asked the "guy" who met her husband that night to come forward. She got no response.

Michael Murphy's death was ruled "accidental."

The week after Michael Murphy was buried, the Humboldt County Grand Jury indicted Lloyd Clifton for the murder of Dirk Dickenson. The charge was second-degree murder—an involuntary manslaughter charge was tacked on later—and Clifton became the first agent in the five-year history of the government's Bureau of Narcotics and Dangerous Drugs to face homicide charges.

District Attorney Ferroggiaro further charged that the Department of Justice had very definitely *not* cooperated with his investigation; that the department "sat on its hands for a day and a half" after the shooting; that the BNDD purposely withheld its internal regulations manual from him; that "there was a delay" before the department allowed him to interview federal agents who had participated in the raid.

The government expressed surprise: "It's a classical case of justifiable homicide under state law," said James Browning, the federal attorney for Northern California. "I've seen almost the same exact facts considered by almost every other district attorney in the state, and it's been held to be justifiable homicide."

"That," said the mild-mannered Ferroggiaro, "is bullshit."

The district attorney told Phil Ryan he sought the murder charge on the basis of Michael Murphy's research. Clifton's record of past brutality, he thought, was most relevant to the single shot on Pratt Mountain.

The district attorney, courthouse observers noted, was not in good humor. He felt he'd been tricked into finding the lab; he felt the government was treating him like a smalltown briar; he felt he'd done his best in the trial of Highway Patrolman Hahn; yet he had been made to look foolish. The high-pitched Jim McKittrick, rocking back and forth on his heels like legendary San Francisco cop-lawyer Jake Erlich, had run dizzying legal circles around him. According to some courthouse analysts, the D.A. would not have pushed on the Clifton case if he had won a conviction on Hahn. Embarrassment, this logic held, put a blowtorch to the seat of his ego.

On January 16 agent Lloyd Clifton, looking paunchier, with a new haircut but the same overdose of hair spray, was arraigned at the

Humboldt County Courthouse in Eureka. He was released on bond, on his own recognizance, and was never even booked at the county jail. The courtesies he received had been afforded no other alleged murderer in Humboldt County's history.

At Clifton's side were a nondescript government attorney and the man who would be in charge of his defense. This was James McKittrick, who had concluded his summation in the Hahn case by saying: "The fact that people have been killed by officers is too bad, but I would say, by and large, they have brought their unhappy fates upon themselves."

Why was Humboldt County's hotshot mouthpiece defending Lloyd Clifton if the government was responsible for the agent's defense? The U.S. attorney quickly answered that intriguing question. Jim McKittrick was now a part of the government (he had been deputized as a special U.S. attorney). He had been whisked to Washington, where he took the oath and met with Attorney General Kleindienst. The government was paying all costs.

The district attorney's case, *The People v. Lloyd Clifton*, was based on these arguments:

Lloyd Clifton had violated his own department's regulations—first by breaking down the Dickenson cabin door, then by firing at the fleeing Dirk Dickenson even though BNDD regulations specifically prohibited "firing at a fleeing suspect."

In shooting Dirk Dickenson, Lloyd Clifton demonstrated an "abandoned and malignant heart," as the district attorney later explained, "that he had a coldness or cast of heart by which he didn't exhibit care—the brutality record plays an awful lot in this area." This coldness was the basis of the second-degree murder charge. The other charge, involuntary manslaughter, was based on viewing Clifton's action as "without due caution and circumspection, a criminal-negligence type situation."

The government, and Jim McKittrick, answered with a variety of arguments, some of them perverse, and with a few low blows. Low blow number one: Jim McKittrick had written a letter to the editor of the *Times-Standard*: "I should like to point out . . . that all of our institutions in this country are under fire today and that the police perhaps more than any other are called in question by *radical elements* in our society, who for reasons of their own desire *to bring our country down*. I do not include Mr. Ferroggiaro in this category, but I must say that his efforts during the past year must have been viewed with satisfaction by such persons." In other words, the D.A. wasn't an out-and-out Red, but he was behaving like a parlor pink or like a fellow traveler.

The government argued that the district attorney had not presented *all the facts* to the grand jury. He had not asked Lloyd Clifton to testify. The D.A. replied: "It is poor practice to request or require prospective defendants to be subject to grand jury questions, because they cannot be represented by an attorney at the hearing."

At the same time the government argued that the D.A. had given the grand jury *too many facts*—specifically, the BNDD internal regulations manual that forbade the shooting of "fleeing suspects." To support this argument, McKittrick presented two letters.

The first was from Attorney General Kleindienst, which said BNDD regulations were "internal guidelines ... not intended to negate any common-law rights or defenses." (The regulations make nice reading, Kleindienst seemed to be saying, but should not be taken too literally.)

The other letter was even more remarkable. It was from Andrew Tartaglino, acting national head of the BNDD. Notwithstanding Sub-section 42-23, Tartaglino wrote, Clifton "properly and necessarily discharged his weapon ... in accordance with BNDD regulations."

The usually low-key district attorney seemed to bristle a bit because of all that and said, "The statements are beyond belief, a brazen attempt to bootstrap an employee out of a situation created by that agency and that employee." The letters were "self-serving," the D.A. said, because Dickenson's family had sued the BNDD for $2 million. Ferroggiaro shook his head and said, "I expect next we'll have a letter from [President] Nixon himself explaining how this whole thing falls under the jurisdiction of his heroin hotline."

The government argued that the prosecution of Lloyd Clifton was interfering with the process of justice. To wit: Lloyd Clifton's reputation was being impeached in other cases involving other busts he had participated in. Attorneys representing those clients were moving to impeach Clifton's testimony by revealing that the man who had busted their client was an alleged murderer. The government expressed fear that, if the murder / manslaughter charges weren't dismissed, it would lose a whole year's worth of narcotics cases.

But the government's main argument was a black humorist's dream: The charges against Lloyd Clifton had to be dismissed because of the ... *Civil Rights Movement*!

191

It worked this way: Lloyd Clifton was acting as a federal agent, a man in the employ of the U.S. government, when he fired his revolver. The government's investigation absolved him of any wrongdoing. The county of Humboldt and the state of California had no right to institute proceedings . . . because Lloyd Clifton was a federal employee.

What would have happened, McKittrick asked, if civil rights registrars and federal marshals in the Deep South would have been arrested for "spitting on sidewalks" by redneck deputies and badge-wearing Klansmen in Selma, in Montgomery, and in Neshoba County, Mississippi? As McKittrick put it: "The Department of Justice is extremely concerned with Mr. Clifton's case. The Attorney General feels he has as great an obligation to protect Lloyd Clifton from prosecution here in Humboldt as he does in protecting federal voting rights officials . . . ."

McKittrick added: "If we are not to permit the southern states to prosecute such federal officers, are we in a position to say, 'Well, our motives are more pure than theirs, and therefore we can do it while they can't'?"

In reply to that, a member of the D.A.'s staff posed this question: Say, just as illustration, that a government agency, like the FBI for instance, is taken over by evil, ruthless, and corrupt men. Say that the FBI decides to even the score with its liberal critics and forms its agents into execution squads. Say that these FBI assassins spread out around the country and kill ten men in ten different states. The FBI director announces an extensive impartial investigation, which subsequently finds the agents innocent of wrongdoing.

Assume now that the government's argument in the Clifton case has been upheld: States cannot prosecute federal employees for alleged crimes committed in the performance of duty. What happens then? According to the government's argument, nothing. The murderous FBI men go on to their next hit.

Almost as afterthought, in reply to McKittrick's civil rights analogy, District Attorney Ferroggiaro pointed out the charges against Lloyd Clifton were not charges of "spitting on the sidewalk."

At the same time the government reiterated U.S. Attorney Browning's claim that the shooting of Dirk Dickenson was not in violation of state law and should have been ruled justifiable homicide. At issue were State Penal Codes 196 and 197, which said:

"Justifiable homicide by public officers is . . . .

' . . when necessarily committed in arresting persons charged with felony, and who are fleeing from justice or resisting such arrest . . . when necessarily committed in attempting, by lawful ways and means, to apprehend any person for a felony committed . . . or in lawfully keeping and preserving the peace."

The district attorney said the key word was "necessarily" and asked: How did Lloyd Clifton know the man fleeing toward the woodline was Dirk Dickenson, accused felon? How did he know the running man fifty yards from him wasn't a visitor to the cabin terrified by the roaring helicopter and the gunmen who never identified themselves?

Ferroggiaro referred, too, to the regulations of other police agencies. The Highway Patrol Enforcement Tactics Manual said to justify shooting "There must be actual fear for one's own life or of serious bodily injury . . . ." The Humboldt County Sheriff's Firearm Regulations said: "Members must exhaust every other means of apprehension before resorting to the use of firearms. . . . Firearms may be discharged in the defense of one's own life when all other reasonable means have failed." Was Lloyd Clifton's life threatened? the D.A. asked. Why didn't agents use a bullhorn to order Dickenson to stop when they admitted the helicopter was so loud they "couldn't hear each other"? Why wasn't Dickenson chased by the nineteen-man posse instead of being shot in the back?

The district attorney argued that his interest was to pose these questions to a jury and to let them decide. Why did the government want heavy-handedly to quash the charges before the case ever got to a jury?

The government's first formal step in trying to have the charges dismissed was to ask for the disqualification of a Superior Court judge "for prejudice." He was William Watson, the man who had tossed Mel Ames's "Mafia gunrunner" drug case far out of court, who raised his goats and was sometimes seen at a place called The Keg in Arcata, eating spaghetti and listening to a rock band. Watson didn't want the hassle and agreed to a disqualification.

That put the case before Superior Court Judge Thomas Montgomery, who had just returned from a New Zealand vacation and who said, the first time he heard the D.A. and McKittrick hammer away at each other, "I hope I don't have a Pentagon Papers trial on my hands." In mid-March Montgomery denied the government's motion to dismiss the charges, which was not unexpected. The denial made it possible for the government to appeal and seek dismissal in more friendly territory—in federal court. In mid-February Federal Attorney Browning had said: "We don't want to give the appearance of being heavy-handed by asking a federal judge to take the play away from the state courts, but we don't want to rule that possibility out."

At the same time Phil Ryan was informed that the government's file contained the transcript of a taped conversation between Judy Arnold and Dirk Dickenson's parents. Their dialogue was taped at Undersheriff Bollmann's direction three days after the shooting, as Chester and Mittie Dickenson waited to post bond for Judy at the Humboldt County jail. It was the first time they had seen one another since Dirk's death. They spoke over a telephone, separated by a pane of glass.

Judy: Hello. [*sobbing*]

Mittie: Hi, honey. We're going to take you home . . . Cry . . . I know.

Judy: I have to get out of here. I'm going crazy.

Mittie: What, dear?

Judy: I said, I have to get out of here. I'm going crazy.

Mittie: I know you are.

Judy: All I can think about is Dirk.

Mittie: It's a nightmare. I'm so sorry, Judy, so terribly sorry. [*crying*] Let Daddy talk.

Chester: Hi, hon. We'll have you out of here in a little bit. We're going home as soon as we can get the papers taken care of.

Judy: How long will it be?

Mittie: It shouldn't take very long. I'm going to check.

Chester: Just a little while, sweetheart.

Judy: It wouldn't be so bad if they just . . . They have the radio on and it seems like the news about it comes on every thirty minutes.

Mittie: I don't know why they had to kill him.

Judy: There was no reason.

Mittie: [*crying*] No.

Judy: No reason, no reason.

Mittie: Have you eaten?

Judy: No, I haven't eaten in three days. I can't.

Mittie: You've got to have something to eat, honey. We haven't eaten either. Drank coffee, and that's about it.

Judy: I don't think I even want to go to the funeral. I can't.

Mittie: I'm thinking of having a closed casket. I don't think I want it open.

Judy: I don't think I want to see him. [*softly*] I feel terrible saying that, but I just don't.

Mittie: No, honey, I know what you mean. I understand. I understand, darling.

Judy: We had everything worked out. It was all going to be all right. And then it had to happen. It's horrible.

Chester: Ask her about his dogs and everything.

Judy: Uh, we have a friend taking care of the dogs.

Mittie: Oh, God, I'm so shocked, Judy.

Judy: Yeah. It was quite a shock. It happened so fast. And they wouldn't even tell me. I didn't know he was dead till about seven o'clock. And they knew when they brought me here that he was. And they wouldn't even tell me.

Mittie: Did you have to identify him?

Judy: [*crying*] No.

Mittie: Well . . . .

Judy: But there were so many of them; I couldn't believe it.

Mittie: Senseless. It was just a senseless killing.

Judy: I know. That's what I told them. That's what they kept asking me—Why did he run? I go—What would you do if twenty men come bursting in your front door with shotguns? What would you do? And they go—Well, he didn't have to run. I go—Well, just what would you do if you were in his place? It was horrible. It was just no need for it to happen at all.

Mittie: What will we do?

Judy: I didn't get to make a phone call until yesterday. Last night was the first one I got to make. My lawyer just really flew apart at that. He raised a big stink about that and told them they had no right not letting me call. Because I asked as soon as I got here if I could make a phone call and they wouldn't let me.

Mittie: God.

Judy: It's been awful in this place. People were taking pictures and stuff. It was like a bunch of vultures. They acted like I committed murder or something.

Mittie: Are you warm enough?

Judy: Yeah, I have one blanket. It stays pretty warm in there. It's just an Army blanket.

Mittie: What clothes do you have?

Judy: Just what I had on me. I couldn't even—they wouldn't even let me bring my purse or nothing.

Mittie: Would you like a Coke or something? My mouth tastes like—I've smoked so many cigarettes my mouth tastes like a . . . .

Judy: I've had sips of coffee, and that was it. The coffee tastes so bad . . . We just didn't know what was happening. I couldn't believe it. You know, Dirk didn't run until they were inside the house, till they busted the door in, and then, you know, he jumped off the back porch. Then they were trying to do me, you know, like—Oh, did Dirk have a gun with him? They were just trying to get me all confused and everything.

Mittie: Dirk never carried any gun.

Judy: No, he never had no gun with him. We were getting the house fixed up. We were going to put the bathroom in. It was awful.

Mittie: Oh, God.

Judy: I wonder if they are going to do anything about what happened to Dirk.

Mittie: Somebody else told us too that it was just out-and-out murder.

Judy: Yeah, that's it.

Mittie: Cold-blooded murder. Some gung-ho jerk.

Judy: I can hardly talk about it.

Mittie: Where's Dirk's clothes?

Judy: A lot of his clothes are in Garberville.

Mittie: Well, he's got quite a few clothes at home, too. I've cried when I didn't think I could. I'm just numb.

Judy: [*crying*] Just think of how happy we were.

Mittie: I know it. Daddy and I were talking about that. You were just so happy.

Judy: It's going to be so hard.

Mittie: Yes, Judy, it's going to be awfully hard on you, honey.

Judy: I just can't make it without him. [*crying*]

Mittie: I'll be so glad when you get out of here so I can just love you.

In May of 1973, more than a year after the shooting, the U.S. government's motion to dismiss the case of *The People v. Lloyd Clifton*

is pending in Federal District Court. All sides agree it could take as long as two years for a final decision.

Asked whether he is optimistic, the weary District Attorney Ferroggiaro, his political ambitions a memory, answers with a wry "No comment."

"I'm optimistic," McKittrick bubbles, "we'll win."

Says Phil Ryan: "The real victory of the people in this case was actually the indictment itself. To expect that Clifton is really going to be put on trial is to entertain illusions about how the system operates. I am saddened but hardly surprised."

The sun shines on Humboldt in the spring; rivulets of spunkwater dot the meadows; herds of deer lope through the sequoias, searching for lily pods; sheep wander the bleakscapes of stumps; canyons echo the chain saws' screams.

In the spring of 1973, at a meeting of the county Planning Commission, a logger named Pete Johnson gets up to speak his piece. "Sometimes I get in trouble because of talking too much," the logger says, "but I call it like I see it. It is those hippies against us straights, and the rednecks around here better wise up. Those hippies don't contribute one thing to the area except dope."

In Whitethorn Ms. Elaine Lester, a veteran of New York and Berkeley, a grade-school teacher at an alternative school, is asked about life in the wilderness. She doesn't want to talk about it. "Things are hard enough for people just to survive," she says, "without media intervention—even the hip media."

On the nearby Samoa Peninsula the coroner recovers another body—one with a broken nose, broken hands, battered ears, startlingly blue eyes, and Indian features. The body waits for an identification. Weeks pass, and it is assumed the dead Indian will never be identified, just like the murdered Indian found near Kneeland four years ago.

A militant Indian named Russ Redner says: "We don't want to tear the whole damned thing apart. We aren't revolutionaries. But we will if that's the only way we can reach our goals. I wouldn't feel bad at all if we marched on the Humboldt Courthouse again and this time burned down the damned thing to the ground."

In early March 1973 Mrs. Mittie Dickenson writes Phil Ryan a letter. Attached to it is a news clipping, a letter to the editor of the *Times-Standard* from a Eureka housewife:

"Lloyd Clifton has been charged by our DA Ferroggiaro with the unnecessary killing of Dirk Dickenson.... I have been under the impression that we elect a DA for our protection and the grand jury is chosen to make our decisions.... From my point of view, Clifton was justified and did the public a big favor.... The past few years' record proves that it takes a lot of guts to enforce the law. So let's back 'em up and now mow 'em down."

Mittie Dickenson writes:

"I want so much to answer that letter. Lord, it's almost a year and it all still seems like a nightmare. Dirk had a right to a trial by jury, not death. I wonder if I'll ever accept his passing. The tears seem to flow more often instead of less."

In a cemetery in Lincoln, California, Judy Arnold stands in front of a gravestone, looking at the ground. She has lost weight; her eyes are sunken and hollow. She lives in Berkeley, taking the days "one by one, slowly." She is thinking about Dirk's dream. *They were coming for him. It was an execution squad. They shouldered the cabin door. Their faces were blank and waxy. He heard the gunshots and saw the glop of his own blood....* Judy Arnold stands by his grave and remembers how she comforted him: *You aren't going to die, babe, it's just a dream, a lousy, rotten, silly dream.*

In mid-March a helicopter hovers over the eastern slope of Pratt Mountain between Garberville and Alderpoint. It is headed for a cabin. It is a long green Huey borrowed from the Presidio of San Francisco. The chopper touches down in a clearing, and armed men leap from it and run for the cabin door. Leading the charge is BNDD agent Lloyd Clifton. Behind him are Undersheriff Bollmann and agent Kenny Krusco. Suddenly Lloyd Clifton is on the back porch, and there is a shot.

It is a carefully orchestrated replay of the shooting. Watching everything is attorney James McKittrick. It ends when the Huey takes off again. There is a man inside play-acting Dirk Dickenson's death. The government wants no loose ends.

May 1, 1973

[AUTHOR'S NOTE]

Almost two years after the death of Dirk Dickenson, the case against federal agent Lloyd Clifton is still pending. In June of 1973 Congressman Charles Rangel of Harlem demanded renewed federal investigation and received a reply from then Attorney General Elliot Richardson that the Justice Department was "looking into it." He has heard nothing from the Justice Department since then.

Federal attorneys, meanwhile, continue to insist that the state charges should be dropped and that Clifton violated no federal statute.

Clifton is still a paid federal narcotics agent, though a bureau spokesman refuses to say whether Clifton is authorized to carry a gun.

Judy Arnold lives in Berkeley and is trying to forget: "I'd like to think that it all happened a long time ago, but it's just like yesterday. Sometimes I find myself trying to figure out why. Why did he have to die? But then I stop because there can't ever be an answer for that."

"It should be the most controversial case of its kind," says Phil Ryan, "yet somehow there hasn't been a public uproar. A man was killed. When those agents busted those nice middle-class people in Illinois for nothing, there was a hurricane of protest. But here a man dies, and somehow that goes by the public consciousness. 'Yeah,' they say, 'too bad. So what?'"

In the winter of 1973 in Humboldt County, the loggers armed themselves with shotguns. Ecology-crazed Indians, they heard, were plotting to stop them from cutting down the big trees.

Designed by Jon Goodchild
Production: Linda Gunnarson, Robert Boylan, Maxine Nunes,
Rosemary Nightingale, Bill Cruz,
Wendy Werris & Alan Rinzler